The Lord and Giver of Life

Perspectives on Constructive Pneumatology

David H. Jensen, Editor

Westminster John Knox Press
LOUISVILLE • LONDON

Book design by Drew Stevens
Cover design by Night & Day Design

First edition
Published by Westminster John Knox Press
Louisville, Kentucky

This book is printed on acid-free paper that meets the American National Standards Institute Z39.48 standard. ⊗

PRINTED IN THE UNITED STATES OF AMERICA

08 09 10 11 12 13 14 15 16—10 9 8 7 6 5 4 3 2 1

Library of Congress Cataloging-in-Publication Data

The Lord and giver of life : perspectives on constructive pneumatology / David H. Jensen, editor.
        p. cm.
    Includes index.
    ISBN 978-0-664-23167-5 (alk. paper)
    1. Holy Spirit. I. Jensen, David Hadley, 1968–
    BT121.3.L67 2008
    231'.3—dc22
                                                                    2007045715

For Peter C. Hodgson
Teacher, mentor, friend

Contents

Acknowledgments

To the book's contributing authors, for their commitment to ongoing, vital discussions of the Spirit.

To Emily Summerfield, for expert help in readying the manuscript for publication.

To colleagues at Austin Presbyterian Theological Seminary, for their spirit of collegiality in education for service to church and world.

To members of the Workgroup in Constructive Theology, for memorable and stimulating gatherings each spring.

To Don McKim and the editorial staff at Westminster John Knox, for their enthusiasm for this project.

To Peter Hodgson, for encouragement and wisdom as my teacher and mentor.

To Molly, Grace, and Finn, for the laughter, conversation, and joy of an inspired life shared together.

Contributors

John B. Cobb Jr., Professor of Theology Emeritus, Claremont School of Theology

Roger Haight, Professor of Theology, Union Theological Seminary, New York

Barbara A. Holmes, Academic Dean and Professor of Ethics and African American Religious Studies, Memphis Theological Seminary

David H. Jensen, Associate Professor of Constructive Theology, Austin Presbyterian Theological Seminary

Molly T. Marshall, President and Professor of Theology and Spiritual Formation, Central Baptist Theological Seminary

Sallie McFague, Distinguished Theologian in Residence, Vancouver School of Theology

Amy Plantinga Pauw, Henry P. Mobley Jr. Professor of Doctrinal Theology, Louisville Presbyterian Theological Seminary

Joerg Rieger, Professor of Systematic Theology, Perkins School of Theology, Southern Methodist University

Eugene F. Rogers Jr., Professor of Religious Studies, University of North Carolina at Greensboro

Amos Yong, Professor of Theology and Director of PhD Program in Renewal Studies, Regent University School of Divinity

Introduction

The Nicene Creed, the most ecumenical of Christian confessions, describes the Holy Spirit as "the Lord and Giver of Life." Perhaps these words concerning the Spirit have been recited by more Christians than any others in the history of the church: words proclaimed in worship, memorized in catechism, interpreted by generations of theologians. What do they mean? What is the life that the Spirit bequeaths to us? How can Spirit be claimed as "Lord" of that life? At times the church has veered toward silence in matters of the Spirit. This elusive person of the Trinity, because she blows where she will, resists the categories and impositions of our words. Yet this indispensable recognition—that the Spirit cannot be confined by our language—has sometimes led to the church's avoidance of the Spirit. In the broad sweep of the church's theology, the Spirit seems to get short shrift; even the Nicene Creed devotes comparatively little space to the Spirit in comparison with the Father and the Son. At other times, the church has been quite voluble on matters of the Spirit, often mistaking some other spirit for the person of the Holy Spirit. When it has made this mistake, the guidance and inspiration of the Holy Spirit serves as a mask for the church's own greed, patriarchy, or self-interest. Amid these ambiguities and within this conflicted history, winds of the Spirit continue to move, blowing where they will. A first step in affirming the continued presence of the Spirit in the world is to recognize that the Spirit is not ours. It is God's Spirit let loose in the world, gracing and gifting the world with life.

This book, which assembles contributions from some of the most significant theologians in North America, presents the doctrine of the Spirit in a distinct way: by exploring doctrine as it informs and is shaped by issues that face life in the churches and, more broadly, the life of the world. The places where life is contested, where the struggles for life are most visible—the ecological crisis, the growth of consumerism and empire, how we read Scripture, and how we interact with persons of differing religious traditions—offer one entrée for interpreting the Spirit as Lord and Giver of life. Wrestling with these pressing issues and the earth's life-and-death struggles can offer fresh perspectives on life in the Spirit. We offer this book both as a corrective to disembodied discussions of the Spirit that ignore the nitty-gritty details of planetary life and as an example of how the church, living from the Spirit, engages its heritage in light of current challenges. The volume, moreover, is self-consciously ecumenical: Each of us writes from a particular denominational tradition, but also writes as a person informed by wider currents of the church catholic and in light of other religious, philosophical, economic, and scientific strains of thought. The result is not a series of narrowly confessional essays, but a powerful example of a multivocal approach to theological reflection: to interpret the winds of the Spirit, to discern where they are moving, one begins by listening to others.

Holy Spirit animates the body of Christ, our human bodies, and the body of the world as God graces creation; we live *from* and *into* God's Spirit. The contestability of the church's life, therefore, is a sign of the Spirit blowing where it will, enlivening the body of Christ. Likewise, the struggles for life on a threatened planet—environmental devastation, the reach of empire, the acceleration of market forces—can be illuminated by a recovery and re-crafting of church traditions on Spirit. Precisely because Holy Spirit does not belong to the church, but is set loose in the world, the gift of life and the struggle for life are sustained by Spirit's power.

This book does not attempt to provide *the* spiritual answer for the contentious issues that face church and world as much as it probes contemporary issues *and* classical resources on Spirit in order that we might encounter life in the Spirit afresh. Holy Spirit takes shape in bodies, sustaining our questions as well as the struggle for life itself. The authors of this volume, however, also assume that theological reflection is not a one-way street. We severely delimit the life of the Spirit if we assume that only classic doctrines of the Spirit must be applied to contemporary questions in a didactic fashion. Though ancient doctrines often transform our understanding of contemporary issues, sustained attention to contemporary struggles can result in the renewal and reframing of doctrine. As Spirit takes shape in bodies, the body of the church is continually transformed. The book, therefore, is neither wholly revisionist in the sense that the issues of our age fix doctrine nor wholly conservative in the sense that doctrine solely determines one's engagement of context. The book's approach is best described as multifaceted and dialectical: Life in the Spirit shakes up context *and* tradition as the Lord and Giver of life makes us God's own.

The collection begins with my own historical introduction to multiple strands within the church's articulation of the Spirit as the Giver of life. Interpreting the Nicene affirmation has not resulted in a monotone refrain over the centuries, but in polyphonic riches, as our forebears attempted to discern the Spirit in the midst of life. This brief survey of biblical, patristic, medieval, and modern voices argues that Spirit seeks bodies in the struggle for life. The questions of how life is best lived—with other species, in contact with other cultures and religious traditions, as goods and resources are hoarded or shared—therefore, are not ancillary to winds of the Spirit, because they concern the lives of bodies. Indeed, the pressing questions of our age—whether they concern ecology, empire, sexuality, or religious pluralism—help us discern the areas of life that Holy Spirit has long sustained.

Chapters 2 and 3 center on one of the more contested issues facing the churches in North America: the interpretation and abuse of Scripture. Amy Plantinga Pauw reflects on the dangerous witness of Scripture, claiming that "without the Spirit, the Word can do demonic things." In discerning the Spirit as it breathes through the Word, she points to three distinct movements: the Spirit as bond of love, giver of all life, and exorcist. Attuned to these movements, we recognize that each reading of Scripture is always provisional, guiding us to the "still unfolding grace of God to which Scripture bears witness." Molly T. Marshall, using images of the breathing, bearing, beseeching, and building Spirit, offers sorely needed words on how Scripture functions in the life of faith. We read Scripture with others—both within and outside the church—by the grace of a divine Spirit that animates our own activity and agency as people of the book.

The next two chapters shed light on another divisive issue in many churches: religious pluralism and how Christians understand other religious traditions. Roger Haight surveys recent christological approaches to the challenge of religious pluralism and points to a need for these approaches to be informed by a Spirit Christology, which yields a genuinely Christian understanding of God at work in other religions. The Spirit who creates anew draws us toward our religious neighbors. Using a different set of pneumatological resources—the practice of hospitality in Luke-Acts and the contemporary church—Amos Yong offers an approach to engaging religious diversity that moves beyond the impasse created by seeing exclusivism, inclusivism, and pluralism as mutually incompatible. The Spirit who gives life is evident in hospitality shown toward strangers.

Essays by Eugene Rogers and Barbara Holmes situate our understanding of Holy Spirit squarely on the physical. Holy Spirit does not hover above the body, but descends on persons, giving life to the body. Rogers invokes the language of paraphysicality to point to the Spirit's work alongside, in addition to, and in excess of the physical. In the divine economy of abundance, the Spirit gives life excessively, exceeding nature, making "room for God in human nature." This Spirit transgresses boundaries, effecting salvation that invokes desire, physicality, and sexuality. Holmes reiterates this theme of the Spirit's physicality by focusing on various forms of folk piety: a holiness sect in Texas, conversation in a Memphis fast-food restaurant, and the blessing of a gang member wracked by violence. In her eyes, Spirit is a "mystery that unfolds before us," embracing the priesthood of all believers and displaying an improvisational character that shakes up comfortable and commodified versions of spirituality.

Each of the book's final three chapters contends with themes particularly resonant with the reality of globalization. Sallie McFague focuses on the global environmental crisis, offering a thoroughly ecological vision of Holy Spirit and a deeply sacramental model of the universe, where we live in God through the world. There is hope amid the scourge of environmental destruction, "not because of human beings or even of nature, but because the power of life and love that was at the beginning of creation is with us still as our source and our savior." Her portrayal of Spirit reorients our understanding of God's relationship to creation, as well as it reframes our own action and contemplation on a suffering planet.

Joerg Rieger grapples with the specter of empire, "that which seeks to control all aspects of life and all of reality." His essay demonstrates how understandings of Holy Spirit have been shaped by the various empires of human history, while it also suggests a "pneumatological surplus" that resists empire's reach. Spirit's resistance to control is one of the more salient themes of Rieger's piece, offering hope amid his trenchant observations on the nature of power in a postcolonial age.

John Cobb's concluding chapter traces the movement of a Spirit that "seeks so to transform us that our minds will be made new and we will work for a society in which the quest for wealth is subordinated to the quest for the kingdom of God." By attending to biblical imagery for Spirit and the contemporary spirits of the age, Cobb offers a spirituality of resistance and hope, even if it leads to physical death.

No single contributor to the volume would necessarily agree with everything said in this book. But uniformity of theological details is not our aim. We agree, however, in one bedrock conviction: as the Spirit gives life, we are to seek life amid the forces and spirits that threaten life in our day. In the struggle for life, we encounter the Spirit at work, disrupting our comfortable theologies, surprising us in horizons yet to be unveiled.

We also offer these reflections as a tribute to the continued work of Peter C. Hodgson, an American theologian whose writings on the Spirit have been path-breaking. There are many ways to describe Hodgson's labors: as historical theologian whose translation and interpretation of G. W. F. Hegel have helped inaugurate a renaissance of Hegel studies in the academy; as Anglo liberation theologian who offered one of the first critical engagements of black theology; as constructive theologian concerned with the re-visioning of Christian doctrine in light of challenges of ecology, religious pluralism, and the quest for human liberation; as literary scholar who introduced George Eliot to a new generation. Underlying each of these dimensions of Hodgson's work, however, one can discern a theologian of the Spirit; perhaps his most significant legacy is that his theology calls our attention to the breath of Holy Spirit, especially in places that systematic theology has traditionally overlooked. Some of us writing essays in this volume have been students of Hodgson's, others have taught with him, engaged in writing projects with him, or admired his work from near or afar. All of us, in some way, have gained impetus for our own work from him, and we offer this book as one small token of thanks for his ongoing commitment to articulating a theology of the Spirit for our time. May the Spirit blow where she will.

1

Discerning the Spirit

A Historical Introduction

David H. Jensen

Holy Spirit seeks bodies. Despite its frequent disembodied diversions, the Christian faith has recognized that the incarnation means Word embraces flesh. Christian confessions about Jesus Christ, the church, and the Lord's Supper, moreover, are embodied claims: God's Son comes in the flesh; God's people are the body of Christ in the world; the Eucharist remembers and celebrates Christ's body broken for the world. Word embraces body; people assemble as a body; holy meals nourish bodies. To claim that Holy Spirit seeks bodies, however, rings strange in many Christian ears. In popular parlance Spirit implies distance from bodies and opposition to the flesh. God, as Spirit, is wholly other than our embodied selves. Hovering above the waters of creation, but not resting on them, Spirit animates the life of bodies but does not become a body. Spirit shuns the body out of holiness—a holiness reserved for spiritual matters removed from the mundane affairs of ordinary life. Confuse spirit with body too much and she vanishes in a mound of flesh.[1]

The tendency to divorce spirit from body invariably elevates the former and denigrates the latter. Such separation, no matter how subtle, also runs counter to Spirit's descent on bodies in Scripture. A disembodied Spirit does not exist in biblical narratives, only a Spirit who descends on bodies in creation. Christian theology, in appropriating this biblical heritage, has often veered from this recognition, though muffled and submerged voices within the church have insisted on Spirit's embrace of the

1

body in every age. The history of the church's reception of the Spirit, therefore, is conflicted and contested. So elusive are the winds of the Spirit, moreover, we often have not known what to say. But if Holy Spirit seeks bodies and gives life to our bodies, then we ought to have much to say. The Spirit that blows where it will is also the Spirit that draws near, closer to us than our very breath. God's Spirit, the Lord and Giver of life, gives shape to bodies, sustains bodies, and graces them with life eternal.

What do we mean when we affirm, with the Nicene Creed, that Holy Spirit is "the Lord and Giver of life"? One consequence of this affirmation is that our lives matter to the One who gives life. Another is that the struggle for planetary life indicates the movement of Holy Spirit in the world. The procession of Holy Spirit does not fly off into speculative space, but embeds itself as the pulse of the world. The struggles for the life of bodies—the fecundity of the planet, the body politic, the health of infants and elderly, the sexual expression of women and men— are dimensions of Spirit's movement. One approach to studying the Holy Spirit, therefore, is to explore the dynamic of those struggles. This book, therefore, anchors its discussion of Holy Spirit along two axes: a critical engagement with biblical and theological foundations *and* a close examination of contested questions and life-and-death issues facing church and world today. To explore topics of ecology, empire, scriptural interpretation, and sexuality is not to avert our gaze from Holy Spirit's movement, but to recognize that life is sustained by the Lord and Giver of life in the midst of struggle.

To better understand these struggles today, I turn first to a brief survey of Spirit's struggle in the life of the church. The point of this introduction is not to offer a comprehensive history of the doctrine of the Holy Spirit; rather, I will paint rather broadly some of the most salient themes that have both contributed to and detracted from Spirit's reception in the Christian church. Beginning with a brief survey of selected biblical themes, the chapter proceeds to prominent and neglected figures in the church's conflicted understanding of Spirit. Even when its articulations of Spirit avoided the body, the struggle for the body's life could not be suppressed.

BIBLICAL WINDS

The phrase "holy spirit" occurs in only two passages in the Hebrew Bible, Psalm 51 and Isaiah 63. Contemporary attempts to discern Holy Spirit's shape in Scripture need to remember the comparative rarity of an expression assumed to be commonplace. What one finds in a survey of Old Testament literature, moreover, is a fluidity of reference: often spirit refers to God's activity in the world; at other times, spirit expresses the dynamism of the human creature; in still others, spirit implies an interaction of divine spirit with the spirit of God's creatures. The nuances of the Hebrew word most often translated as spirit, *ruach*, also suggest breath and wind, indicating that spirit's movement cannot be enclosed. From the very outset, Spirit is not ensconced in heaven, but seeks others on earth, in the flesh.

Spirit whispers at the beginning of this story, wafting across the waters of chaos, exhaling God's creative and covenantal love. This primal *ruach*, the breath or wind from God (Gen. 1:2), hovers and descends: stirring up what is inert, endowing all things with life. Spirit first moves in this story in order that the *oikos* might flourish: Ecology is thus not a latter-day concern, but found in the story's first chapter. This ecological Spirit infuses flesh in the second creation narrative, where God forms Adam out of dust and the fecundity of God's breath (2:7). In prose that draws on imagery from pottery and childbirth, human life begins in the cadence of moist breath. As Adam takes his first gasp of air, he is sustained by the One who gives life: his breath is given by the breath of another. Dry places now become fertile: without the breath, they wither and die.

God's *ruach* also animates the spirit of bodily creativity. The prophets, for example, are routinely described as drawing their life and work from the spirit. Resting on Ezekiel, Micah, and Zechariah (Ezek. 2:2; Mic. 3:8; Zech. 4:6), Spirit summons people—often against their will—to be messengers of justice and repentance. In Ezekiel, the spirit "enters" the body, indicating intimacy between giver and receiver. God's *ruach* provides more than inspiration; she is embedded into the breath, blood, and body of the prophet. More ordinary labors and trades may also be objects of Spirit's descent. God fills Bezalel, the chief artisan for the tabernacle, with divine spirit for the work of metallurgy, stonecutting, wood carving, and design (Exod. 31:3–5). Spirit seeks aesthetic expression; where she is moving we behold beauty in human labor. The Spirit is no stranger to ordinary work: prophecy, masonry, and woodwork are equally recipients of inspiration. God's *ruach* breathes at the beginning of creation's story, gracing us with life, but also sustains ordinary labor throughout the course of life. As she blows, Spirit embraces the life of the people.

In subsequent stories that document Israel's migration to the promised land, Spirit expresses herself in campaigns of conquest, a spirit that enables Israel to snatch victory from the jaws of defeat. In the story of Othniel, for example, "The spirit of the LORD came upon him, so that he became Israel's judge and went to war" (Judg. 3:10 NIV). As spirit rests on judges, battles rage and blood spills. These narratives are not easy to read, as they can be twisted rather easily into justifications for war on the basis of divine favor, sounding hauntingly similar to current arguments that seek divine blessing of the American empire for its military campaigns. In one difficult text, when the Spirit of God takes possession of Gideon, he sounds a trumpet, rallies the troops to victory, and returns home with trophies of severed Midianite heads (Judg. 6:34–7:25). Such narratives may lead interpreters to conclude that God's *ruach* is a spirit of war and vengeance. Yet a closer examination of these terrifying texts yields different results. Michael Welker suggests that these texts attest to "the action of God's Spirit [in] situations of danger in which no escape could be seen. . . . And they report wholly unexpected deliverance."[2] To a distressed and desperate people, God's Spirit brings hope of freedom, not vengeance. Nonetheless, the terrifying aspects of these narratives remain, reminding us of Spirit's involvement and resistance to the powers of war, conquest, and empire.

In the face of death-dealing struggles for power and conquest, Spirit brings new life out of slaughter. In Ezekiel's vision of Israel's return from exile in Babylon, where God plants a new spirit within the people, excising a heart of stone and inserting a heart of flesh, God's *ruach* resuscitates the body (Ezek. 11:19). In this macabre scene of death, the breath of God binds bone, tendon, and flesh together, as living beings emerge from a charnel house. In the face of an empire that exiles God's people, the spirit of God exhales life and welcomes a people home.

This breath of new birth inaugurates the story of Jesus in the New Testament. Matthew describes Mary, the teenage mother, as being with child from the Holy Spirit (Matt.1:18, 20). Though the church has typically interpreted these phrases as the Madonna's escape from human sexuality, the pregnancy of Mary by the Spirit and Jesus' subsequent birth suggests that Spirit embraces sexuality. The Christ child comes to the world like every other infant, amid the blood, mucus, and anguish of physical birth. Holy Spirit does not avoid the body, but enters the body of a young woman who bears within her womb the life of the world. Sexuality is not avoided here, but is claimed and blessed by God. Because the language is so delicate on the Savior's conception, the church has typically assumed a virginal conception, that Jesus was conceived without sexual intercourse. But the language of virginity to describe Mary is ambiguous, as many have noted, and may refer simply to Mary's youth. The Gospel narratives neither exclude nor affirm the possibility that Jesus' birth was the result of coitus; they simply affirm that Mary's pregnancy and the life she bears are granted uniquely by the Holy Spirit. In the incarnation, and in Mary, Spirit rests on sexual bodies.

This Spirit who claims a teenage mother and an infant as her own also descends on Jesus in baptism at the beginning of his public ministry. By submitting himself to baptism by John, Jesus indicates his submission to the reign of God, becoming sin for the sake of sinful humanity. As Jesus is submerged in the water, he undergoes death and resurrection *for our sake*, entering into full solidarity with the sinful world. At baptism, Holy Spirit descends on Jesus "in bodily form like a dove" while the Father expresses pleasure and love for the Son (Luke 3:22). This rare instance of Trinitarian interaction in the New Testament invokes basic elements of creation: water, dove, word.[3] Holy Spirit comes as a bird, alighting on a body that will be broken on a cross. Spirit seeks the body of nature (dove and water) and a broken human body so that the *oikos* can be made whole. The well-being of creation is manifest as bird alights on body in water: a portrait of ecological wholeness as well as Trinitarian self-giving.

As Jesus seeks bodies to heal, the Spirit of his baptism sends him into the wilderness and thereafter into encounter with unclean spirits that afflict the suffering. Jesus, filled with the Spirit, commands the unclean to leave and touches those whom respectable society deems untouchable (Mark 1:23–26; 5:2–8). Jesus heals persons wracked by physical illness, mental disease, social ostracism, and bodily discharges alike, making bodies whole again. The health of the body is the path of Spirit's descent. Wherever Jesus heals, there we glimpse the Lord and Giver of life.

Jesus' public ministry is also marked by a confrontation with powers that enslave and marginalize the poor. Holy Spirit takes shape in economic life, descending on a poor Jew, a man who worked with his hands and lived and died under the yoke of the Roman Empire. As Luke records the beginning of Jesus' public ministry, a new economic vision unfurls: "The Spirit of the Lord is upon me, because he has anointed me to bring good news to the poor. He has sent me to proclaim release to the captives and recovery of sight to the blind, to let the oppressed go free, to proclaim the year of the Lord's favor" (Luke 4:18–19). Holy Spirit claims the lives of the poor as her own, enmeshing herself in economic dimensions of human life: consumption, distribution, sharing, and giving.

In John's Gospel, Spirit is an advocate for humanity and a comforter in loss. At the Last Supper, Jesus promises that the Paraclete will abide once he has departed. "It is to your advantage that I go away, for if I do not go away, the Advocate will not come to you; but if I go, I will send him to you" (John 16:7). The Spirit represents God to the disciples (as Christ did), represents humanity to God, and assures the disciples of God's presence in the experience of abandonment in the wake of a rabbi's crucifixion. Here the interweaving of divine and human spirit is prominent: the One who has departed is present in the Advocate who remains, comforting and sustaining the spirits of those mourning.

In Luke's Gospel, Jesus' crucifixion offers a preeminent glimpse of the fellowship among Father, Son, and Holy Spirit. As Jesus gasps for his last breath, he cries, "Father, into your hands I commend my spirit" (Luke 23:46). The final moments of the Savior's life are bordered by a breath that ascends to the heavens. Father, Son, and Spirit are not locked in a dance of death, but break forth in an embrace of life, a foreshadowing of resurrection: The Spirit released to the Father is given to the world. Jesus' last gasp is the Spirit that animates creation; the one who dies on the cross will be raised in the Spirit, breathing new life into the world.

John records this interweaving of Spirit and the risen Christ in vivid detail. In an appearance to the disciples, Jesus breathes on their bodies, "Receive the Holy Spirit" (John 20:22). Jesus' last gasp thus returns to creation, in the moist breath of peace and forgiveness. The Christian church begins with a breath from the risen One and is sustained as it lives from Christ's Spirit.

As the church continues to take shape in Jerusalem, wild winds of Spirit unleash themselves on those gathered in Christ's name. The Spirit of peace also comes in tongues of flame, resting on the heads of disciples, cavorting in a howling rush. Here Spirit expresses nature in its wildest form: a violent wind beyond our control, fire that burns but does not consume. Human bodies cannot contain Holy Spirit; the wild spaces and bodies of nature display her movements. Spirit does not tame these elemental forces of wind and flame, but breathes within them. The *oikos* flourishes, according to this Spirit, not when nature is subject to our control, but when the wind blows where it will. As this wind blows, those gathered in Christ's name, filled with wild Spirit, begin "to speak in other languages, as the Spirit gave them ability" (Acts

2:4). Spirit's power cannot be expressed in one language, but breaks forth in tongues that sound at first like Babel. But unlike Babel, those gathered from all corners of the earth hear *their own* language; understanding rather than confusion results from this profusion of speech. This manifestation of Spirit's wild power is inherently pluralistic: Spirit requires many languages and people to express herself. To domesticate Spirit by restricting her to certain peoples, places, and religions is to claim that she is the Lord of some lives but not all. Issues of cultural and religious pluralism are not recent phenomena, but are bound up in the Pentecost experience, an experience of the Spirit that breaks the stranglehold of any one language.

This movement of Spirit that fails to conform to the comfortable and familiar is evident in the first Gentile convert from the book of Acts. Here, the Spirit leads Philip to join the chariot of an Ethiopian eunuch, a cultural outsider whose very body is an icon of gender subversion. Spirit manifests a queer presence here, blessing a body that does not conform to conventional sexual expectations. Spirit here proves boundary-breaker, impelling Philip to encounter this cultural other, to teach one who is already reading the Scriptures (Acts 8:28–29). Spirit moves through this outsider's words: The eunuch invites Philip to sit with him, teach him, and eventually to baptize him. "When they came up out of the water, the Spirit of the Lord snatched Philip away; the eunuch saw him no more, and went on his way rejoicing" (Acts 8:39). In the strange movement of Spirit's grace, even Gentiles and eunuchs are welcome.

Paul, missionary to the Gentiles, often describes the Spirit as inhabiting human bodies: "You are in the Spirit, since the Spirit of God dwells in you" (Rom. 8:9). The presence of the risen Lord is a presence in the Spirit, which enlivens the body not to conform to the flesh, but to the living will of God. Paul talks rather fluidly about God's Spirit intermingling with ours: "it is that very Spirit bearing witness with our spirit that we are children of God" (Rom. 8:16). The life of Christ's body, the church, is sustained by a Spirit that enters our bodies not as a stranger, but as the source of all gifts. Paul's oft-invoked exposition of love is coupled with sustained attention to spiritual gifts. Granted by the Spirit, the gifts of healing, teaching, prophecy, leadership, and tongues all animate the life of the body (1 Cor. 12–13).

At the close of the Bible's pages, we encounter a wild and welcoming Spirit that stirs up prophecy and vindicates the righteous. Amid the blood and violence that saturate these pages, the Bible ends with a promise and a welcome from Spirit: "The Spirit and the bride say, 'Come.'

And let everyone who hears say, 'Come.' And let everyone who is thirsty come. Let anyone who wishes take the water of life as a gift" (Rev. 22:17). After seals are broken, empires clash, horsemen gallop, and beasts are overthrown, a promise abides: to drink the water of life, bright as crystal, to inhabit a city where people bring the glory and honor of the nations, and to eat from a tree that provides healing for the nations. Here nature and civilization are both at home: the well-being of the *oikos* rests in the Spirit's invitation to live abundantly with others.

As the Bible depicts the movement of Holy Spirit, bodies, nature, empire, health, and religious pluralism are no strangers, but are sustained in the life Spirit gives to the world. Given by the Spirit, these ordinary matters of creation matter to God. Blowing where it will, Spirit's breadth in the biblical witness is staggering. The history of the church's interpretation of Spirit at times gives voice to this breadth, but at others constrains it. In this conflicted history, Spirit continues to rest on bodies, no matter how much theology attempts to disembody Christian spirituality.

IRENAEUS: THE BODY OF SALVATION

Second-century theologian Irenaeus (ca. 135–ca. 200) offers the first extensive treatment of the Spirit for the Gentile church. His exposition, though not Trinitarian in the strictest sense, explicitly identifies the Spirit's divinity. For him, Holy Spirit is the Spirit of the Father[4] who is personified in bodily images, seeking bodies in the world. One of his favored metaphors for Spirit and Son is the "two hands of the Father," an image that portrays the unity of divine purpose. Son and Spirit carry out the Father's work in shaping, sustaining, and gracing creation. Though Irenaeus does not claim that God *has* a body, his metaphor points to the communion of creation with God. God's activity is accomplished in the touch of two hands. Spirit does not shun bodies but draws near to them in a divine body: hands that represent God's expression of Godself for the life of the world.

Central to Irenaeus's account of the Spirit's handiwork is his understanding of human embodiment. We are a union of flesh and spirit, who become spiritual creatures by receiving God's Spirit or slaves of the flesh when we reject Spirit's counsel.[5] God's Spirit animates our spirit, granting life without remainder. We become ourselves as we participate in Spirit's life for the world. Without this Spirit, humanity is dead: "The flesh, therefore, when destitute of the Spirit of God, is dead, not having life, and cannot possess the Kingdom of God. . . . But where the Spirit of the Father is, there is a living man."[6]

As human persons receive the Spirit, they are formed for salvation. This transformation, however, does not destine human persons for a life beyond the body: Spirit does not vaporize bodies in an ascent to the heavens. Spirit's sanctifying grace results in the "salvation of the flesh."[7] Bodies occupy central stage in Irenaeus's understanding of salvation: as Christ recapitulates, embodies, and redeems the history of the world—saving in and through his body—Spirit gives life to bodies meant for communion with God. The resurrection of Jesus Christ affirms the resurrection of our bodies.[8]

God's hands are not restricted to the life of human bodies. For Irenaeus, Spirit descends to earth as dove and as water that gives life, saturating the ground with divine presence: "As dry earth does not first bring forth unless it receives moisture, in like manner we also, being originally a dry tree, could never have brought forth fruit unto life without the voluntary rain from above."[9] Irenaeus's understanding of salvation in the Spirit is ecological, stressing that all creation—flora, fauna, and minerals—are blessed, renewed, and sustained for the sake of relationship.[10] For Irenaeus, the Spirit, as the hand of the Father, brings healing and living water to bodies broken by sin. Spirit's grace is for the life of bodies, expressed in the unity of God's life for the world.

ORIGEN: RESTRICTIVE SPIRIT, UNBOUNDED SPIRIT

Third-century theologian Origen (ca. 185–254) is more skeptical of bodily images for Holy Spirit than Irenaeus. His pneumatology, particularly in *First Principles*, signifies a subtle distaste for the body and a gradual restriction of Spirit's reach so that not all bodies in creation are sanctified. At the same time that he limits those who receive the grace of Holy Spirit, he expands the work of the Spirit in biblical interpretation, discerning the spirit of a text from its mere letter.

In contrast to Irenaeus's warm embrace of the body, Origen writes that the Spirit is not corporeal, but "a sanctifying power."[11] Though Spirit moves, sustains, and affects bodies, she cannot be depicted *as* a body. Origen's ambivalence about corporeal representations of Spirit is no doubt tied to his ambiguous regard for human bodies: his account of a twofold fall, whereby disembodied rational souls fall first into embodiment and then secondarily into sin. Materiality and embodiment are thus secondary and not part of God's original creation. Origen's biography, moreover, bears the marks of this struggle with embodiment on his own body. Interpreting Matthew 19:12 in a bizarre manner, Origen understood the reference to making oneself a eunuch for the kingdom of heaven to warrant his own castration; maiming the body became for him a physical mark of his journey into God's reign.

Origen's restraint on the body is mirrored in his further specification of the Spirit's activity in the world. Though he affirms Spirit as Lord and Giver of life, Origen denies that all creation partakes fully in the life Spirit gives: "Every one who walks on earth . . . is a partaker also of the Holy Spirit . . . but the operation of the Holy Spirit does not take place at all in those things which are without life, or in those which, although living, are yet dumb."[12] If the Spirit gives life indiscriminately, the sanctification of life, or a "share in the Holy Spirit," is distributed only among human saints.[13]

This restriction of Spirit's effect, however, is tempered by a liberal regard for Spirit as the guide to biblical interpretation in discerning divine mystery. For Origen, the Spirit alone "searcheth even the deep things of God."[14] The first step in discerning God's mystery, then, is to acknowledge that mystery is not a possession of the saints, but expresses intimacy solely shared between Father and Son, sustained by the Spirit. In expressing this intimacy, all words fall short. The Holy Spirit teaches us "truths which cannot be uttered in words . . . [or] indicated by human language."[15] Scripture, then, is not a written template through which we capture God's mystery, but God's Word, which, read under the inspiration of the Spirit, leads to truths beyond words. Origen developed a threefold typology of biblical interpretation that guided Christians in their understanding of the witness of Scripture. Holy Spirit enables Christians to grow in truth in their reading of the Bible, as they move from *literal* interpretation to a fuller appreciation of its *moral* and *spiritual* dimensions: "Our contention with regard to the whole of divine Scripture is, that all has a spiritual meaning, but not all a bodily meaning."[16] Sticking to the letter of text, indeed, may lead to false assertions about divine mystery. Interpretation of Scripture can never be reduced to words alone, since life in the Spirit encompasses more than words, even if—for Origen—those words tend to avoid the body.

GREGORY OF NAZIANZUS:
TRIUNE LIFE GIVEN FOR THE WORLD

Gregory of Nazianzus (ca. 325–389), referred to as "the theologian" in the Eastern church, draws on earlier references to Holy Spirit's divinity and makes the first explicit identification of the Spirit *as God*. His legacy, along with his Cappadocian contemporaries, Gregory of Nyssa and Basil of Caesarea, is the foundation of Eastern Trinitarianism, a fully fledged account of God's relational life for the world. For Gregory, the difference in Triune names is the result of different mutual relations: the Father is unbegotten, the Son is begotten, and the Spirit processes.[17] The persons of the Trinity are what they are within and because of their relationships: relating and giving to each other for the life of the world. Holy Spirit, for Gregory, claims and blesses human life, destining us for God's life. When Christians worship, he maintains, "it is the Spirit in whom we worship and in whom we pray."[18] Spirit claims our bodies and our prayers and makes them participants in the life given for the world.

One of the most intriguing aspects of Gregory's theology is his division of time into different epochs symbolized by distinct persons of the Trinity. The empires, people, and cultures that define history appear in a grand scheme of salvation, culminating in an age of the Spirit. For Gregory, "The Old Testament proclaimed the Father openly, and the Son more obscurely. The New manifested the Son and suggested the deity of the Spirit. Now the Spirit himself dwells among us, and supplies us with a clearer demonstration of himself."[19] Spirit manifests herself within time, within history: the letter of Scripture is fulfilled in a life granted by the Spirit. For Gregory, the Triune life does not enclose Holy Spirit, but shares itself with the world.

AUGUSTINE: INTERIORITY AND EMPIRE

If Gregory of Nazianzus and the Cappadocians proved most influential in formulating Trinitarianism in the Christian East, Augustine (354–430) occupies that position in the West. His legacy on the Spirit, however, is more difficult to determine, especially given his vast literary corpus. Though he was influential in discerning Spirit's role in the process of biblical interpretation,[20] two areas of his pneumatology

proved novel: relating the life of Spirit to the interior life, and identifying Spirit's presence with the City of God. These turns to psyche
(instead of body) and empire set the stage for further developments in
the West.

In *The Trinity* Augustine offers the analogy of memory, understanding, and will for understanding the Triune God's relationship with the
world. This work is in many respects a spiritual quest that invites us
into fuller participation in God's life. Psychological imagery is significant for Augustine because it points to the image of God in humanity: a life lived not merely in the flesh, but as the person journeys
deeper into God. Many critics have accused Augustine of psychologizing the Trinity, as if an understanding of God's life can be gained
through introspection. But Augustine begins his discussion of Holy
Spirit by talking about the mission (sending) of the Holy Spirit to a
broken world, not with the image of God in the human psyche. Only
after speaking about the mission of Holy Spirit to the earth's body, sustaining and sanctifying that world, does Augustine turn to the procession of the Holy Spirit and the eternal relationship within God that is
mirrored in human memory, understanding, and will. As much as
Augustine avoids "psychologizing," however, his use of mental
imagery proved enormously influential in subsequent theological
reflection. The life of the mind rather than the life of bodies together
became the chief analogy for God's life, and as a result the body often
seemed distant from Spirit's life.

Augustine's understanding of Triune life avoids disembodiment
through his emphasis on the love shared among the persons. Here Holy
Spirit occupies an indispensable position: In the eternal dance of giving,
Holy Spirit is the "gift of God . . . a kind of inexpressible communion
or fellowship of Father and Son."[21] As love is carried out in human life,
under the grace of the Spirit, it unites bodies to one another.[22]

In *City of God*, Augustine identifies the upbuilding of God's reign
with the work of the Spirit. In the face of the worldly city, the empire
of his time (Rome), the godly city is emerging by God's grace. The life
of the Spirit does not shun worldly concerns such as power, order, and
civilization, but reorients them to be reflections of divine glory. In this
grand vision, empires of death crumble while the one empire that gives
life makes itself known within the world and not beyond it. For Augustine, bodies, world, and empire matter in the life of Spirit. Even if his
Trinitarian theology stresses interiority, Augustine's Spirit also seeks
expression in the midst of struggles that affect bodies in history.

WILLIAM OF ST. THIERRY: THE SPIRIT AND THE FLESH

For medieval monasticism, reflection on Holy Spirit displayed two movements that appear, at first, contradictory: a disparagement and celebration of human sexuality. On the one hand, Holy Spirit animated human persons in a special way. As the objects of sanctification by the Spirit, human persons are distinct from the rest of creation because they move beyond animal nature. Some persons, moreover, grow in the Spirit more than others; monasticism represents the pinnacle of spiritual life.[23] Distinctions of the working of the Spirit appear in many guides to monastic life, separating our higher, spiritual nature from the lower, carnal self. At the same time, however, monastic reflection on the life of the Spirit evinced a highly charged eroticism and celebration of sexuality as a dimension of new life in the Spirit. Sex, which connects the human race to the other animals, thus was both disparaged as a husk of animal nature *and* celebrated as it offers an intimation of beatific union with Christ through the Spirit.

William of St. Thierry (ca. 1085–1148), a Cistercian abbot, offers one example of this seemingly contradictory attitude toward sex in Spirit's life. His *Golden Epistle* can be read cover to cover as an exhortation that guides the novice away from animal nature and its attendant carnal desires, toward the rational nature, where the mind is occupied with contemplation, into fulfillment of a spiritual kind, where the whole of human life is suffused by Holy Spirit. The itinerary is long and slow, requiring discipline, supervision, and a community of fellow travelers. Little by little, however, Spirit tames flesh. The misdirected loves of our animal nature, which hunger for another flesh, are redirected by Holy Spirit, so that we are brought into conformity with God's love.[24] In the blessed life, it seems, all real sex is left behind.

However it was tamed by monastic guidebooks, sexual desire found new expression in many depictions of beatific union. During the heyday of medieval monasticism, more commentaries were written on the Song of Songs than on any other biblical text.[25] William is no stranger to this tendency. The love of the Triune life becomes the pattern by which human relationships are transformed and sanctified. Heavenly love bears the imprint of flesh upon flesh, as Holy Spirit is the kiss and embrace that unites Father and Son in mutual love.[26] The sharing of breath and touch points to the indwelling of each person for and with the other. Father, Son, and Holy Spirit exist in eternal interpenetration of love, a love whose analogue takes decidedly fleshy expression. To be sure, *The Golden Epistle* does not claim that Trinitarian eroticism gives warrant to our sexual expression; quite the contrary, our desires are taken up and sublimated in God's life. As monks avoid sensual pleasures, divine love plays in eternity. Eroticism abides, albeit in a transformed mode. This imagery climaxes in William's beatific vision, where the spiritual life reaches consummation in an unadulterated relationship with God and the giving over of one's life—by grace—to Triune love.[27]

Though William contrasts a life in the Spirit with life in the flesh, his understanding of Trinitarian love and the goal of religious pilgrimage takes a decidedly erotic turn. Beatific vision is expressed through erotic imagery: kissing, sweetness, jubilation. As much as William avoids the flesh, Spirit seeks expression in the mutual touch and indwelling of bodies, even if these bodies are transposed in heavenly places. For William, the longing of our bodies culminates in the Spirit who transforms them.

THOMAS MÜNTZER: THE AGE OF PEOPLE'S SPIRIT?

Spirit's power has often inflamed the passion of radical prophets. In every age, self-appointed persons have claimed the mantle of Holy Spirit for programs to inaugurate a new age. Frequently these prophets shun the established channels of church and institutional power: for them, Spirit blows violently, shaking up the status quo and breaking down walls that divide person from person. Set loose from the constraints of ecclesial hierarchy, Holy Spirit reveals herself as the people's spirit. It is not surprising, then, that institutional Christianity has been highly suspicious of such movements. The radical writings and practice of Thomas Müntzer (ca. 1489–1525) offer a case in point.

Müntzer argued for a people's spirit in opposition to the tyranny of scholars and clerics. The work of the Spirit, he claims, is more visible to the disempowered than to those with academic credentials. The "spirit is given only to the poor in spirit,"[28] the lowly who have suffered under the yoke of economic and ecclesial oppression. One of the consequences of Müntzer's pneumatology is that it makes scriptural interpretation the work of the people, not the work of scholars and priests. In a foreshadowing of liberation theology's emphasis on base communities, Müntzer claims that the plain sense of Scripture is more readily available to the poor gathered in Christ's name. Guided by the Spirit in interpreting Scripture, the people may discover new truths beyond the literal text. Here, Müntzer is blunt: the leading of the Spirit is more important than the letter of Scripture: "If someone had never had sight or sound of the Bible at any time in his life he could still hold the one true Christian faith because of the true teaching of the spirit, just like all those who composed the holy Scripture without any books at all."[29] The Spirit, indeed, is a more secure testimony than Scripture, which can be stolen by thieves.[30] For Müntzer, the testimony of Holy Spirit does not require the authorization of an established church, but is accessible to all. In Müntzer's eyes, Spirit takes a life of its own, flying free from the text; those who discern her movement best are generally ignored by the powerful who want to co-opt the text as an instrument to preserve their own power.

This struggle to discern the Spirit rightly takes a decidedly apocalyptic turn. In a sermon in Allstedt, Müntzer exhorts his audience to "seize the very roots of government, following the command of Christ . . . kill the godless rulers, and especially the monks and priests who denounce the holy gospel as heresy."[31] Nothing less than truth and life in the Spirit were at stake. This exhortation to take up the sword, smite, and kill by the power of the Holy Spirit and Müntzer's glib claims to be acting in the name of the Spirit are glaring examples of how easily one might confuse spirits, substituting a bellicose spirit for the Spirit of peace. Despite this obvious inadequacy, Müntzer's articulation of Spirit stresses the abandon and profuse giving of Spirit. In his vision, Spirit is no discerner of nobility or pauper, but gives herself to the oppressed, empowering people long silenced to claim their voice.

JOHN CALVIN: NOT EVERY SPIRIT

Surrounded by the whirling dust of Reformation-era chaos, John Calvin (1509–1564) attempted not to constrain the life of Spirit, but to discern its seemingly small voice amid the din of competing winds. His articulation of Holy Spirit seeks grounding in Scripture as the surest testimony of Spirit's life. Spirit rests on the body of the church, inspiring the biblical witness as well as its contemporary readers.

The Bible, for Calvin, provides the "spectacles" through which we discern God's presence and purpose in the world. What is dimly perceived without the aid of glasses—general revelation—comes into sharp relief under biblical lenses. As we read Scripture, under the illumination of the Holy Spirit, we recognize that the text is not subject to our control: Scripture *reads us*. Holy Spirit rests on the body of a people, the

Christian church, who read the Word of God together. As the church reads and interprets that text, it is fashioned by Holy Spirit into God's people. Text, body, Spirit, and church therefore intertwine with one another. The Holy Spirit "is the Author of Scripture: he cannot vary and differ from himself. Hence he must ever remain just as he once revealed himself there."[32] Spirit is never untethered to text or church: if the Spirit leads us into new truth, contra Müntzer, it will not overturn the plain sense of Scripture, that which is gathered from reading the biblical text as a whole. This plain sense of Scripture, however, is only discerned in the life of the body, a life that is animated by Holy Spirit. For Calvin, Spirit does not take precedence over church or text, but reveals herself beneath, behind, and within the body of Christ as it reads—and is read by—God's Word in Jesus Christ. The interpretation of Scripture, in this sense, is endless. The life of the Spirit manifests itself as the people of the book live under the inspiration of God's Word.

JOHN WESLEY: THE SPIRIT OF GIFT

The father of Methodism, John Wesley (1703–1791), offers a powerful theology of the Spirit that emerges from sermons and occasional writings. Though hardly systematic, Wesley's writings display traces of a Spirit concerned with economic life and the bearing of fruit in Christian life. His doctrine of Spirit, moreover, takes shape at the dawn of the modern industrial economy, just as capitalism is being theorized and practiced in his native Britain. The life of Spirit rests on the body economic, presenting alternatives to a spirit of consumption and acquisition in an economy of gift.

In many of Wesley's sermons, he laments the spirit of consumption that pervades economic life. Capitalism is blind to the fact that much of its so-called progress is built on waste: acquiring things so that one can have more, hoarding them from others, and throwing away baubles once they have been used up. Where capitalism encourages the stockpiling of capital, so that wealth will increase, Wesley employs an economy of gift, empowered by life in the Spirit. The Christian life, he claims, is characterized by industriousness that results in gain not for its own sake, but for saving and profligate giving. One "has," through gaining and saving, only in order to give away.[33] Hoarding treasure on earth proves deathly in the end, because wealth that is not shared gathers rust. Life in the Spirit, by contrast, is shared in ways that seem reckless to economies of scarcity. We earn and save, Wesley claims, not to have more, but in order to give out of the abundance of God's life. Giving, thus construed, results not in the depletion of resources, but in the increase of shared bounty.[34] As Holy Spirit is gift, giving from the Spirit keeps on giving. For Wesley, life in the Spirit always includes economics: Spirit rests on backs broken by the spirit of consumption and scarcity, pointing to new ways of living into divine abundance.

G. W. F. HEGEL: SPIRIT AND THE RELIGIONS

G. W. F. Hegel (1770–1831) has been dubbed a "theologian of the Spirit."[35] In many respects this designation is apt, since Hegel's work is suffused with God, the Spirit who offers Godself to the world. The grand story of the world's creation, fall, redemption, and consummation is also the story of the divine life: positing an other for relationship, experiencing estrangement and division in that relationship, and fulfilling that relationship in the union of what had formerly been estranged. Fully Trinitarian, Hegel's vision is one where Spirit expresses itself in world history. Because the infinite God reveals Godself in the finite, Hegel is able to overcome many of the dualisms that have plagued Christian thought: of spirit over matter, subject over object. Spirit is realized not in a flight from matter, but within it. In Hegel's scheme of salvation history, *all* of creation is caught up in the grand movement of the one subject Spirit, who makes us all subjects to one another, and summons our matter and bodies as components of the divine life.

One of the most striking aspects of Hegel's pneumatology is his recognition of Spirit's movements throughout the world's religions. He is one of the first Christian thinkers to offer a fully theological account of religions other than Christianity. Rather than relating the religions to Christianity as falsehood to truth, Hegel listens to the wisdom present in other traditions. Spirit, he claims, takes shape in particular cultures and rests on bodies embedded within those cultures. The life of Spirit does not require an ascension from cultural particularity, but a full engagement of those cultural contexts. The different religions of the world, then, are expressions of the life Spirit gives to the world. Though he argues for Christianity as the "consummate religion," this designation is not on the basis of cultural superiority, but because in Christianity religion "is for itself, that is objective to itself."[36] Spirit expresses itself to the world in stages, beginning with nature religion, progressing to the consummate religion. At each step along the way, however, Christians can learn from other religions as they attend to their own vision of life in the Spirit. For Hegel, Spirit does not conquer human life with one monolithic vision, but opens life to hearing other voices and seeing with new eyes. Though Spirit is one, its children are many.

AFRICAN AMERICAN TRADITIONS:
SPIRIT OF PEOPLE, SPIRIT OF FREEDOM

Some of the most powerful articulations of Spirit in the United States have occurred on the fringes of the ecclesial establishment. The story of the black churches documents a continual movement of Spirit seeking freedom, descending on people regardless of status, breathing fresh air into Scriptures that had been twisted into instruments of oppression. For slaves and their descendants, Spirit let loose in the world disrupts structures that divide persons from one another, making all children of freedom.

Sister Kelly, an ex-slave and washerwoman, echoes earlier strains in the tradition that correlate Spirit with the life of the body. Speaking of a secret gathering of the slave church, she told of sensing the presence of God in every extremity: "I tell you it's a wonderful feeling when you feel the spirit of the Lord God Almighty in the tips of your fingers, and the bottom of yo' heart."[37] Christian spirituality, in Kelly's account, does not merely animate the body, but penetrates the body so that our lives are open to the divine embrace. The Spirit is as palpable as breath on skin, tingle in toes, lips upon lips. Living from the Spirit, we taste her presence every moment.

This experience of being laid low by the Spirit, or enlivened by the Spirit—both of which are tangible to bodies—stood in direct opposition to the institution of slavery that attempted to break bodies. Chattel slavery, whereby some owned the bodies of others, was built on the assumption that some bodies are more worthy than others and that therefore some could extract the blood and use the muscles and sweat of others for their own benefit. Institutional slavery, moreover, fed on religious rhetoric, with Scripture the instrument to beat slaves into further submission: "From about 1772 until 1850 the Bible was the primary source of authority and legitimation for the enslavement of Africans."[38] In this atmosphere, slaves discovered in the Bible not the bad news that the white slaveholders proclaimed, but the good news of liberation for God's people. The letter of the text, according to Jarena

Lee (b. 1783), one of the first female preachers in the black church, had to be read in light of the witness of the Spirit. The restless movement of Spirit, in other words, expressed freedom in an otherwise oppressive text. Life in the Spirit enabled African slaves to access the full range of biblical witness rather than the distorted form that slaveholders imposed on them.

The Spirit of freedom, in the words of Lee, hears us into speech: "My tongue was cut loose, the stammerer spoke freely."[39] Where tongues have been stopped, Spirit cuts loose in words; where voices are ignored or deemed irrelevant, Spirit claims that all are created in God's image and have a voice. Spirit descends on bodies and takes flight in multiple tongues; in gaining speech, the slaves refused to let other voices—the voices of those who "owned" them—determine their fate. By hearing them into speech, the Spirit pointed to their freedom in being owned by God, not by the master.

This cutting loose of tongues in racist society offers a window on the birth of Pentecostalism. William Seymour (1870–1922), a black man who was denied the opportunity to attend an all-white theology class in Houston, listens from the hall in 1905 as white preacher Charles Parham (1873–1929) speaks of being gripped by the Spirit. Captivated by this message, Seymour moves to Los Angeles and sets up a makeshift church in an old warehouse on Azusa Street. His preaching initially attracts little attention, but in 1906 a spontaneous outpouring of tongues is unleashed. In one of the largest cities of segregated America, blacks, whites, Latinos, and Asians unite to participate in a fresh movement of Spirit. Men and women, young and old from diverse corners of the globe, are heard into speech. One observer noted on that day that "the 'color line' was washed away in blood."[40] The so-called mainline churches have yet to come to grips with this polyglot baptism by the Spirit, a movement that continues to grow in nearly every corner of the world. But the movement of this restless spirit is stunning in its capacity to hear the marginalized into speech. The Spirit of Azusa Street is a spirit that takes shape in the people, expressing freedom, claiming and shaking bodies as Spirit's own.

KARL BARTH: THE SPIRIT OF AWAKENING POWER

Arguably the most influential theologian of the twentieth century, Karl Barth (1886–1968) has often been accused of having a minimal doctrine of the Spirit. On some reads, his theology epitomizes a Protestant avoidance of pneumatology. Yet this portrait is overstated, since a strong doctrine of the Spirit emerges on the edges of his dogmatic work. For Barth, Holy Spirit is the "awakening power in which Jesus Christ has formed and continually renews his body,"[41] the church. This sustaining and awaking power takes shape not merely in individual lives, but in the body of Christ. We discover Holy Spirit not when we look at our own religious experience; rather, Spirit molds us as we hear the Word proclaimed and take life from that Word. Holy Spirit is not the spirit of the church, not the spirit of the Christian, but the Spirit of God.[42] "The Holy Spirit is God the Lord in the fullness of Deity, in the total sovereignty and condescension, in the complete hiddenness and revealedness of God."[43] Holy Spirit reveals herself to creation in otherness, condemning our justification of self through works, drawing us into the obedience of faith.

The same Spirit who exposes our disobedience and self-justification, however, is the Spirit who reconciles and redeems. The Christian life, lived in the Spirit, is one of preeminent hope. By the grace of Holy Spirit, we become who we are, living in gratitude wherever two or three are gathered in Christ's name. "In the realm of creation we are servants, in the realm of reconciliation we are subdued enemies: in the realm of redemption, however, we are—yet again—children of God."[44] The Spirit is the expression of God's eternity intersecting with our bodies, our histories, who makes us children of God once again. Spirit is not ours, but we are hers, body and soul.

ELIZABETH JOHNSON AND PETER HODGSON: SPIRIT OF WISDOM, SPIRIT OF LIFE

Two voices from the United States—one Roman Catholic, the other Protestant—capture some of the renaissance in contemporary understandings of the Holy Spirit. Elizabeth Johnson (b. 1941) and Peter Hodgson (b. 1934) attend to the centrality of human experience in articulating Spirit as the Giver of life and the work of the Spirit on behalf of justice and wholeness in a fragmented and violent world. Johnson's work is self-consciously feminist while it draws on submerged resources within Catholic traditions. She agrees with early feminist assessment that decried the over-spiritualization of Christianity and its denigration of the body. The culprit, in this view, was not Holy Spirit as much as dualism that identified the spiritual and rational with maleness and the material and natural with femaleness. Because Spirit was often interpreted as a disembodied presence that shook itself free of the body, few early feminist theologians developed full-fledged pneumatologies. Recovering the sacredness of women's bodies and experiences and developing alternative depictions of God's power and agency were far more urgent tasks. Johnson's work gathers together these tasks with an eye toward revised pneumatology, cognizant of the body's life and wisdom.

Johnson grounds her rearticulation of Trinitarian theology by beginning with a theology of Spirit that attends to our experience of God. Spirit-Sophia is the expression of God's wisdom, shaping and transforming our experience as a window of God's activity for the world. For Johnson, Spirit-Sophia is "the creative and freeing power of God let loose in the world,"[45] or "the active presence of God in this ambiguous world."[46] Spirit, in her vision, rests on the bodies ignored and broken by tradition: women, nature, children. The glory of God is creation, fully alive in the Spirit. The irony of "malestream" theology is that it has proclaimed the Spirit as Lord and Giver of life, but has ignored the life-experiences of women, who number more than half the human race. Spirit-Sophia, in her words, "is the source of transforming energy among all creatures. She initiates novelty, instigates change, transforms what is dead into new stretches of life."[47]

As Johnson articulates Trinitarian theology she reverses the traditional order of loci, beginning not with the Father, but with Spirit. Spirit, in her vision, is not simply described by its procession from Mother-Sophia and Jesus-Sophia, but is viewed as divine life given for the other persons and the life of the world. Spirit as a result is not subordinated to the other persons in the Trinity, but is glimpsed as a fountain of divine life given to the world. Spirit-Sophia seeks others with whom to share the divine love, vivifying, renewing, and gracing creation. Her account, then, offers more than a linguistic shift, or the heaping of stereotypically feminine attributes on the Godhead. Rather, in exploring traditional theological claims in light of feminist wisdom, we are opened up to a deeper participation—in our bodies—in Spirit's life. "We are loved in order to love; gifted, in order to gift; and befriended in order to turn to the world as sisters and brothers in redeeming, liberating friendship."[48] For Johnson, Spirit continually seeks expression in the world, as we are conformed more deeply in the divine image. Spirit graces the bodies and experiences that patriarchy ignores, affirming each creature as fully alive.

Like Johnson, Hodgson laments the covert suppression of Spirit in many church traditions, connecting its de-emphasis with grave injustices: "Subordination of the Spirit, marginalization of women, and exploitation of nature have gone hand in hand in the history of the church."[49] Hodgson's systematic work, which offers more than a corrective to this collective neglect, represents a thoroughly Trinitarian theology that centers on the life of Spirit. In an age that is threatened with planetary extinction, "the Spirit is the final and most encompassing figure of the divine life. God *is* Spirit in a way that God is not simply Father or Son."[50]

Hodgson's pneumatology avoids some of the conundrums of traditional Trinitarianism. Instead of focusing on the single- or double-procession of Spirit or depictions of intra-Trinitarian life, he speaks about the Spirit in terms of its continual arrival to the world and the energy of relationship within that world. The Spirit is not simply "sent" to the world to give life so that we may describe its presence "here," but is continually arriving, approaching, infusing, and luring. Hypotheses about the Spirit's eternal preexistence can mislead Christians to think that the Spirit dwells as a person within God apart from concrete relations with creation: "There are no such preexisting persons in God but rather potentials for relations that become actual when God creates the world as other than God."[51] Without relations, Spirit-language becomes vague and disembodied; God's Spirit, however, takes shape in relationships within creation, in the struggle to breathe and live in the face of historical ambiguity and threats against life.

This connection of Spirit with the pulse of life leads Hodgson to revise traditional formulations of the Trinity and accounts of the Spirit's procession. "The appropriate Trinitarian formula is God-World-Spirit, or God-in-Christ-in-the-world-as-Spirit. The Spirit proceeds from the emerging love between God and the world, and the Spirit then becomes the power of reconciling freedom in this differentiated love."[52] Again, Hodgson's account privileges the interrelation of God and creation. The Trinity is not some a priori account of God's aseity, but a portrayal of a divine life passionately involved with the world in all relationships. Hodgson affirms the double procession of the Spirit, but in a different vein—proceeding from God and the world: the life of God in the Spirit is given and shared with the world so that it, too, becomes the life of the world. The "work" of this Spirit, then, is nothing short of the liberation of the world from all that holds it in bondage, injustice, and ecological travail, *and* the consummation of the world in God: a pneumatology of radical hope.

CONCLUSION

Holy Spirit gives life to bodies. No matter how distant theological reflection becomes from the life of the body—the body of Christ, the body of the earth, the bodies of people—Spirit remains the Lord and Giver of life. As this survey of biblical and theological resources has shown, the flourishing of those bodies is one object of Spirit's movement. Spirit blows where she will, carrying us to new places, breathing fresh insights into dusty corners of supposed comfort, reminding us that our bodies are never alone in God's world. As Christian faith is carried out in that world, as the life of Spirit takes shape in bodies of people and the body of the church, the everyday concerns of embodiment are never far behind. Ecology, empire, economics, health, sexuality, scriptural interpretation, and religious pluralism are not ancillary currents as God's *ruach* blows through creation. Rather, these contested issues offer a window to Spirit's dynamism in a world that God longs to redeem. As Spirit gives life to bodies, the life of the church and the world are continually renewed. A critical recovery of the church's traditions on the doctrine of the Spirit, therefore, is necessary for contemporary confession of the Spirit as Lord and Giver of life. Engagement of the contested, life-and-death issues that face the planet, moreover, can assist the church as it professes a faith that lives in and through the Spirit. This book offers one attempt to explore contested issues as sites for Spirit's movement. Our conviction is that theologies of the Spirit *matter* for the life of the world.

2

The Holy Spirit and Scripture

Amy Plantinga Pauw

In 1849 a public debate was held at Zion Church in New York City over a campaign to solicit funds to provide contraband Bibles for slaves in the American South. Arguing in favor of the campaign was Henry Highland Garnet, a learned Presbyterian minister. Arguing against it was the famous orator and religious leader Frederick Douglass. Both men were African Americans who had escaped slavery in Maryland. Both were fervent abolitionists, rooted in the stories and cadences of Scripture.[1] As a young man, Douglass had so thirsted for "a thorough acquaintance with the contents of the Bible" that he "gathered scattered pages of the Bible from the filthy street-gutters, and washed and dried them, that in moments of leisure [he] might get a word or two of wisdom from them."[2] Despite their common allegiance to Scripture, the two men found themselves on opposite sides of the debate. Garnet thought that the biblical message of justice and freedom was irrepressible, and that the presence of Bibles in the cruelly oppressive context of southern slavery would be a liberating force, fueling slaves' moral and physical resistance to their bondage. Douglass, by contrast, feared that putting the Bible in the hands of slaves would fuel reckless insurrections that would leave many of them dead. He also thought the presence of Bibles would be exploited by the forces of proslavery propaganda. "I have met many religious colored people, at the south," wrote Douglass, "who are under the delusion that God requires them to submit to slavery and to wear their chains

with meekness and humility."[3] That delusion, he insisted, was incul-
cated through biblical teaching.

Douglass's ambivalence reflects the paradoxes of the African American encounter with Scripture. Generations of mostly enslaved African
Americans had "created a circle of social solidarity" around the biblical
stories of Israel's bondage in Egypt and their miraculous deliverance, the
prophets' thunderings against social injustice, and the compassion, suffering, and triumphant resurrection of Jesus. "Faith became identification with the heroes and heroines of the Hebrew Bible and with the
long-suffering but ultimately victorious Jesus."[4] Yet, as Allen Dwight
Callahan remarks, the Bible spoke to African Americans "with a voice
that sometimes echoed their oppressors. The words of life could deal
death, and its text could become noxious. The Talking Book was also a
poison book."[5]

How can the same Scripture function in such contradictory ways?
Theological reflections on the relationship between Scripture and the
Holy Spirit suggest a way into this conundrum. Frederick Douglass,
though not a Calvinist like Henry Highland Garnet, saw clearly the
truth of John Calvin's insistence that "without the Spirit, the Word can
do nothing."[6] Or rather, without the Spirit, the Word can do demonic
things: the Gospel stories depict the devil himself twisting Scripture to
his purposes (Matt. 4:5–6; Luke 4:9–12). The Bible becomes a "Talking Book" as life is breathed into it. When the breath that enlivens
Scripture is the Holy Spirit, the results are life-giving. However, when
other spirits breathe through Scripture, the Bible can become a "poison book."

These other spirits are referred to in the New Testament as *powers
and principalities* (Rom. 8:38; 1 Cor. 10:20; Col. 1:16; 2:15). Christians
disagree over whether these are best understood as autonomous spirit-
beings. In any case it is theologically important to assert their multivalent impingement on human life as a spiritual dimension of material
institutions, structures, and systems. William Stringfellow insisted that
principalities and powers are indeed *legion*, and include "all institutions,
all ideologies, all images, all movements, all causes, all corporations, all
bureaucracies, all traditions, all methods and routines, all conglomer-
ates, all races, all nations, all idols."[7] Each of these "spirits" has been willing at times to usurp the place of the Holy Spirit and to demand
idolatrous service and loyalty from Scripture. Frederick Douglass recognized a demonic spirit in the institution of American slavery. American
slaveholders had commandeered the Pauline instructions to slaves

regarding their place in a well-ordered household for their own death-dealing purposes. As a result, those texts had become so poisoned that Douglass argued in favor of keeping Bibles out of the hands of southern Christians, and Howard Thurman's grandmother, and many others like her, simply stopped reading those parts of Scripture.[8]

Because the Talking Book can become a poison book, it is vitally important to "test the spirits to see whether they are from God" (1 John 4:1) when reading Scripture. The role of the Spirit is not to furnish readers with a fail-safe list of exegetical rules or to guide them to some self-enclosed, already accomplished totality of meaning within Scripture. Frank Macchia notes that "there is a certain 'present-tenseness' to the Pentecostal reading of Scripture"[9] that other Christian traditions would do well to emulate. With the Spirit we hear the word of Scripture in expectant anticipation of how the living God will act among us now, and we respond accordingly. Scripture is an interactive text, in conversation both with its contemporaneous neighbors and with centuries of readers. The Spirit's work is not to convict us of a single authoritative interpretation, but to guide us to the still-unfolding grace of God to which Scripture bears witness. Thus testing the spirits of our readings is an ongoing task.

The phrase "reading Scripture" may suggest a private intellectual or devotional activity. Certainly, personal prayer and intellectual reflection have a role to play in testing the spirits. However for most Christians in most times and places, Scripture has been primarily an oral word, not a written one: Scripture is the word sung in worship, received in testimony, and enacted in mission. *Readers of Scripture* should thus be construed broadly as those who speak and hear and perform the scriptural word in community. The stories and commands of Scripture are open-ended, always demanding from us a fresh hearing and response. Texts that are dormant in one cultural setting spring to life in another. Texts that are ensconced in particular theological traditions take on fresh meaning in new social contexts. Testing the spirits is best understood as a task of ethical discernment, aimed at the faithful communal embodiment of Scripture.

Testing the spirits is ambiguous work because both the writers and the readers of Scripture share in the finitude and sinfulness of the human condition. The Spirit's inspiration of the writers of Scripture does not result in a docetic Scripture—one that only *seems* human. Nor does the Spirit's work in illuminating the readers of Scripture erase human limitations and fallibility. All our engagements with Scripture are interested and partial, and none can claim complete righteousness before God. Yet the hermeneutical context of Scripture "is always more than the social-ideological matrix," according to Rowan Williams. Both the writers and the readers are, in Williams's words, "responding to a gift, an address or a summons not derived from the totality of the empirical environment," and neither the writers nor the readers of Scripture control or confine that divine gift.[10] To discern the Spirit as we read Scripture is to put ourselves at the disposal of that gifting presence.

There is an inevitable circularity in Christian understandings of the Spirit and Scripture: readings of Scripture guide Christian perceptions of the character and activities of the Spirit, and the Spirit, in turn, is understood to guide Christian readings of Scripture. Both as theological doctrines and as central elements of the Christian life, Scripture and Spirit belong together: they are not rightly understood in isolation from each other, but are experienced in their dynamic engagement. The Scripture is not merely a calcified record of other people's religious experience, but, through the work of the Holy Spirit, an ongoing source of contemporary religious experience. In Martin Luther's words, "The Bible is alive, it speaks to me; it has feet, it runs after me; it has hands, it lays hold of me."[11] Yet this reciprocity between the Spirit and Scripture also contains a profound asymmetry. While life-giving readings of Scripture are bound to the presence of the Holy Spirit, the Spirit is not bound to Scripture: according to Christian understanding, God's Spirit is richly poured out over the whole creation. No area or dimension of created life is utterly bereft of the Spirit's presence, and no one community or tradition can claim a monopoly on the Spirit.

This essay will reflect this asymmetry in tracing a threefold movement of discerning the Spirit, a dynamic that moves both inside and outside communities of Scripture readers. Three pneumatological images will guide this exploration of the relationship between the Holy Spirit and Scripture: the Spirit as bond of love, the Spirit as giver of all life, and the Spirit as exorcist.

BOND OF LOVE

Ephesians 4:3 exhorts Christians to seek "the unity of the Spirit in the bond of peace." A central role of the Spirit in Christian community is to bind believers to God and to each other in loving union. In Western Trinitarianism this economic role is seen as consonant with the Spirit's eternal role in the Godhead as the bond of love between the Father and Son. However, human beings, unlike God, are material beings, and the Spirit's work of binding them to God and each other in love employs material means. Christian traditions have emphasized various means of the Spirit's work: Scripture, sacraments, ecstatic gifts. But the end of them all is to bind us more closely to God and to deepen our union with our brothers and sisters. Thus we should expect that reading Scripture according to the Spirit's leading will result in tangible manifestations of love to God and neighbor.

"Teach me," implores the psalmist again and again. The Christian understanding is that human beings stand in desperate need of ongoing instruction, correction, and reminders of God's promises. Christian existence is a life-long tutorial in the gracious ways of God with us and in the paths we are to follow toward God and neighbor. Scripture is a primary resource for this tutorial. Whatever progress Christians may make in trusting God and loving neighbor, they never outgrow their need for the promises and guidance contained in Scripture. Left to their own devices and desires, human beings are frequently self-deceived, both as individuals and as communities. They proclaim peace when there is no peace (Jer. 6:14). They become captive to human traditions and "the elemental spirits of the universe" (Col. 2:8). Preoccupied with their own concerns, they tune out the cries of the needy and the oppressed. They fall into despair over their own failings and afflictions. Alienated and confused people need a word that comes from beyond themselves to remind them of God's promises and to set them on a right path toward God and neighbor. Scripture offers that word—a treasure trove of moral and ethical instruction, the laments and rejoicings of God's people, and stories of God's persistent and surprising grace toward the creation, stories culminating for Christians in the witness to the life, death, and resurrection of Jesus Christ. Scripture is a primary means of the Spirit's work in the Christian community as the bond of love.

In one of his charming theological speculations, Augustine suggests that although God could have taught all persons individually and immediately by means of angels, learning from other humans was part of God's good plan because it makes a "way for love, which ties people together in the bonds of unity, to make souls overflow and as it were intermingle with each other."[12] To be a reader of Scripture is to be bound in love by the Spirit to the ancient writers and redactors of Scripture and to an enormous community of fellow readers, both past and present.[13] Our identities have been profoundly shaped by our dependence on a host of witnesses we have never met, most of whom remain nameless. Even today, as Scripture is enacted in gesture and speech, at the baptismal font and at the protest rally, the Spirit binds the community of readers together with the ligatures of love.

Receiving instruction and correction from fellow human beings through Scripture can also be a lesson in humility, as John Calvin notes: "when a puny man risen from the dust speaks in God's name, at this point we best evidence our piety and obedience toward God if we show ourselves teachable toward his minister, although he excels us in nothing."[14] While Calvin was referring to preachers of Scripture, his point also applies to the writers of Scripture. In accepting the authority of Scripture for their community, Christians bind themselves to those voices that they might otherwise be tempted to disregard out of a misguided sense of chronological or cultural superiority. The Spirit binds Christians to God and neighbor in love through the particular writings of Scripture, with all their disturbing angularities and baffling silences. In granting authority to precisely this canon of voices, Christians confess that these writings are "*sufficient* for the ends to which they ought to be used in the church."[15] The promise of the Spirit is neither that Scripture has been infallibly written nor that it will be infallibly read, but that these writings are sufficient to nurture and shape our love to God and neighbor.

It is appropriate, then, for Christians to seek the help of the Spirit in making Scripture, in Ellen Davis's words, "the functional center of our life, so that in all our conversations, deliberations, arguments, and programs, we are continually reoriented" to its demands and promises.[16] Orienting ourselves to Scripture's demands and promises is more than a noetic exercise. As Wayne Meeks notes, the scholar's historical and textual tools are not in themselves sufficient for figuring out "what the text meant," because a degree of "empathy with the kind of communal life which 'fits' the text is necessary for full understanding." Being immersed in the larger practices of the faith creates this kind of empathy in a way that more abstracted scholarly attention to texts does not. Likewise, "what the text means" entails, in Meeks's words, "the competence to act, to use, to embody, and this capacity is also realized only in some particular social setting."[17] Both the context and the aim of reading Scripture are fundamentally tied up with communal ethos and practice. Discerning the Spirit when reading Scripture must always culminate in asking about the form of its social embodiment.

The Christian aim in the communal reading of Scripture, as James Alison has said, is to give glory to God and to create "merciful meaning for our sisters and brothers as we come to be possessed by the Spirit" of the crucified and risen Jesus. Faithful readings of Scripture will aim at "undoing our violent and evil ways of relating to each other," and show us "how together to enter into the way of penitence and peace."[18] When our readings seem to *perpetuate* our violent and evil ways of relating to each other, we must once again test the spirits pervading our readings to see if they are of God. As Christians continue to test the spirits in their readings of Scripture on controverted issues, a central guide must be the rule of love. Does a given reading create "merciful meaning" for others? Does it bind us closer to God and neighbor?

GIVER OF ALL LIFE

There is a peculiar double-edgedness in the Christian liturgical and theological tradition concerning the Holy Spirit. The Spirit has always had an institutional affiliation, as the one who indwells the church and functions through the church's means of grace as a bond of love. But there has always been another side as well—the mysterious and free Spirit who blows where it chooses (John 3:8), transcending church structures and even the boundaries of human society to renew the whole creation. The particular edge of the Spirit's work is blunted by attempts to construct a "universal" theory of religious experience, in which the Spirit masquerades as a generic term of human religiosity or world process. The Spirit is understood by Christians according to the particular witness of Scripture and within the pattern provided by the life, death, and resurrection of Jesus Christ. Yet the Spirit is not found only among those who read Scripture and confess Christ. This universal edge of the Spirit's work cuts against the church's perennial attempts to cage the Spirit, restricting its role to granting a seal of divine approval to the church's established structures and teachings. As Hildegard of Bingen proclaims in one of her antiphons for the Holy Spirit:

> The Holy Spirit is life that gives life,
> Moving all things.
> It is the root in every creature
> And purifies all things,
> Wiping away sins,

anointing wounds.
It is radiant life, worthy of praise,
Awakening and enlivening
All things.[19]

Christian pneumatology, while rooted in the particularities of Christian belief and practice, asserts the universal scope of the Spirit's activity in the world.

Affirming the Spirit as the giver of all life helps Christians avoid certain misunderstandings about Scripture. To claim that the Spirit inspires Scripture is not to view it as a divine word in contrast to all other, merely human, expressions of religiosity. The writers and redactors of Scripture did not exist in political, religious, or intellectual isolation from their geographical neighbors. Instead, they freely borrowed and adapted materials close at hand for their own purposes. For example, teachings in the biblical book of Proverbs closely resemble the instruction literature that has survived from ancient Egypt. For better and for worse, New Testament household codes look very similar to those of other Greco-Roman communities. Christians should not be surprised or embarrassed by these commonalities. The sacred texts of Christians have no monopoly on the Spirit's presence, and are not exempt from common human limitations. Christians confess Scripture to be God's inspired word to us because through it we can reliably expect to be brought into God's presence and to have our faith nourished and our hope sustained.

Readers of Scripture, like its writers, are also imaginative and inveterate borrowers and scavengers. Scripture readers do not inhabit a self-contained world. The story of Christianity is one of repeated creative interactions with "new cultures, with different systems of thought and different patterns of tradition."[20] Christians interpret Scripture with the conceptual tools they have at hand. As Karl Barth notes, "Everyone has some sort of philosophy, i.e., a personal view of the fundamental nature and relationship of things. . . . In attempting to reflect on what is said to us in the biblical text, we must first make use of the system of thought we bring with us, that is, of some philosophy or other." Just as it was both unavoidable and legitimate for the prodigal son to rise and go to his father just as he was, in his poverty and rags, so, Barth insists, it is both unavoidable and legitimate for us to approach Scripture with our own interpretive tools.[21] As the giver of all life, the Spirit may also be at work in the other philosophies and systems of thought we bring to the reading of Scripture. The revelation of God in Scripture "is addressed not so much to a will called upon to submit as to an imagination called upon to 'open itself.'"[22]

To be sure, these interpretive systems are part of the powers and principalities surrounding and impinging on us. Like us, these "spirits" are fallen creatures and thus they deserve at best our partial and provisional loyalty. But our entanglement with them is unavoidable, and sometimes the Spirit uses these spirits to guide us as we read Scripture. For example, when Presbyterian abolitionist Albert Barnes prophesied the end of slavery in the United States, he boldly appealed to the spirits of his time:

> The church will be free. The time will come when in all this land every church shall be wholly and forever *detached* from all connection with slavery. Nothing can be more certain than this. The spirit of the age demands it; the religion which is professed in this land will ultimately secure it; the spirit of our civil institutions will make this certain in the church; the onward progress of liberty among the nations will compel the churches, if they will save the world from infidelity, to detach themselves altogether from slavery.[23]

In response to Christian defenders of slavery who were reading Scripture according to the letter, Barnes sensed the larger movement of the Spirit in the political and cultural winds of his time. Given the frequency with which the church functions as the taillights rather than the headlights of culture,[24] this sort of overt appeal to the spirits of the age should not be peremptorily dismissed.

Appeals to the spirits are at least implicit in every reading of Scripture. The spirits guiding each reading are the spirits of a particular age or location, and so each reading of Scripture is culturally inflected and therefore incomplete. Yet in established Christian communities, interpretive traditions that were once the result of daring cultural translations and assimilations become so normalized that they come to be seen as "common sense." It then becomes easy to confuse the parochial or time-bound spirits of particular interpretive traditions with the Holy Spirit, the giver of all life. Established churches in both the West and the East are especially prone to this confusion. In their eagerness to rediscover or maintain their theological heritage, it is tempting for them to assume that all that is needed for interpreting Scripture faithfully can be found in their own cultural backyard. The burgeoning churches of the global South provide a needed reminder that the Spirit is the giver of all life. As they bring different cultures and systems of thought into interaction with Scripture, Christians in the southern hemisphere enlarge Scripture, revealing new, previously undiscovered dimensions of it. Portions of Scripture rendered mute in the life of the older churches take on new authority. Familiar texts take on new cultural resonances. As Kwame Bediako notes, "the conditions of Africa are taking Christian theology into new areas of life, where Western theology has no answers, because it has no questions."[25] Through these new questions, the Spirit works to challenge and transform the whole church, calling the church to recognize the provisionality of all its readings of Scripture. In interpreting Scripture, no part of Christ's body, past or present, can say to another, "I have no need of you" (1 Cor. 12:21).

This essay has so far concerned itself with the relation of the Holy Spirit to Christian Scripture. But other religious communities also claim sacred texts, and most Christians today do not live in the predominantly monoscriptural context that Western Christians once took for granted. If the Spirit is the giver of all life, how should the Spirit's presence be understood in a world of multiple scriptures? On the one hand, Christians should avoid an easy relativism that sees all scriptures as simply particular religious on-ramps to the highway of generic spiritual enlightenment. Denying genuine and irreducible religious plurality is not a road to interreligious honesty and respect. On the other hand, Christians should guard against a cramped reading of Scripture that assumes that other religious communities and their sacred writings are bereft of the Spirit's presence. As Stanley Samartha asks, "Is the limited and narrow experience of Israel with its surrounding nations or one sermon by Paul to the Athenians sufficient grounds to pass heavily negative theological judgments on neighbors of other faiths in Asia today?" Confident that the Spirit blows where it chooses, Christians should approach other communities' scriptures with respect, and with the expectation that they will be enriched by them. "Different scriptures," Samartha insists, "should not be regarded as passport documents that divide different nationalities but as signposts that point to a more promising future."[26]

In recent years, Christian, Jewish, and Muslim scholars and believers have formed trialogue groups that gather to read each other's scriptures together. According to David Ford, a leader in these efforts at "Scriptural Reasoning," the goal is "to read our scriptures together in mutual hospitality and attentiveness." Friendships can flourish among people of different faiths, even when their scriptures do not lead them to theological consensus. Through intense focus on each other's scriptures, participants learn "to recognize the strength of our bonds in the family of Abraham and the call to live patiently with our deep differences; and throughout to conduct our reading according to an ethics, and even politics, of justice, love and forgiveness."[27] As the giver of all life, the Spirit can use a variety of scriptures to bind people together in love.

More work still lies ahead in incorporating readers of scripture beyond the Abrahamic traditions. Stanley Samartha notes that "the major religions in the world today, the Semitic and the Indian, originated in isolation from each other. The formation of particular scriptures and the development of the canon took place without reference to what was happening in other places and at other times among other people."[28] As these internally diverse scriptural communities interact with each other, Samartha urges Christians to adopt a hermeneutic of generosity toward our religious other, and to acknowledge that the mission of the Spirit in the world is broader and deeper than the mission of the church. This is not to advocate a bland religiosity that seeks above all not to appear foolish or give offense. But it is to insist that in interreligious contexts, a forthright accounting of the hope that is within us is not incompatible with "gentleness and reverence" toward the religious other (1 Pet. 3:15, 16), confident that the Spirit is already at work in them and in their scriptures.

"The Bible is an important element in the operation of the Spirit in the community," insists Mar Gregorios. "But we will certainly need to know more about the larger operation of the Spirit not only in the community of faith, but also in humanity as a whole, and in fact in the whole universe, before we can understand in perspective what the Spirit is saying to the churches."[29] Christians believe that Scripture's particular demands and promises somehow reflect the purpose and reality of God, but they also trust that the same Spirit who illumines Scripture also brings them into a fundamental interrelatedness with the entirety of God's creation. Listening to this larger voice of the Spirit may involve joining with people of other faiths to address common problems too big for any single religious community to handle. Whether it is confronting the ecological crisis, global violence, the HIV/AIDS epidemic, or the crushing problems of world poverty, Christian commitment to the demands of their own Scripture can be manifested in banding together and standing in solidarity with readers of other scriptures. As Christians continue to test the spirits in their readings of Scripture, a central guide, in addition to the rule of love, must be the freedom and beneficence of the Spirit as the giver of all life.

Does a given reading reflect a confident hope in the Spirit's generous and surprising presence? Is it open to perceiving the "new thing" God is doing in the world (Isa. 43:19)?

EXORCIST

Hyun Kyung Chung declares, "I want to put a warning sign on a Bible just like tobacco companies put them on their cigarette packs. The label should say that without guidance, this book can lead to various side effects, such as mental illness, cancer, rape, genocide, murder and a slavery system."[30] Her sharp comment signals the need for a third dimension in the relationship of the Holy Spirit to Scripture. So far, this essay has pursued two complementary avenues for discerning the Holy Spirit's presence in reading Scripture: (1) the Spirit works through Scripture to bind us to God and to neighbor in love, and (2) the Spirit guiding our readings of Scripture is the giver of all life, blowing through institutions, worldviews, and other scriptures. Both of these images suggest paths to testing the spirits in our readings of Scripture. If our readings feed our alienation from each other or deny the Spirit's presence in the world God loves, something has gone wrong. But these guides are not fail-safe, even when followed with the best intentions. Bonds of love can become parochial and suffocating; openness to the spirits of the age can become idolatry. Because Christians have sometimes read Scripture in ways that produce deep and long-lasting harm, the Spirit must also function as exorcist, freeing us from the interpretive demons that possess us personally and communally.

But there is a prior question. Does Scripture itself need exorcism? There is no shortage of troubling texts in Scripture. What are Christians to say, for example, about claims for divinely sanctioned genocide in Joshua 10:40, the charge to slaves to endure unjust suffering in 1 Peter 2:18–21, or the vengeful fantasies of Revelation 19:17–21? Some of the writings of Scripture seemed touched by the same demons of ideological self-interest that haunt our own readings of Scripture. Are some texts in Scripture *predisposed* to harmful misreadings, and would we be better off without them?

Just as the heroes of the biblical narratives are deeply flawed people of faith, so are the writers of those narratives. But the fallibility of the biblical writers does not authorize the various attempts across Christian history to purge the canon of Scripture of elements deemed offensive, dangerous, or outmoded. We should eschew a false spiritual evolution-ism that would presume the right to exorcise particular texts of Scrip-ture. As Kevin Vanhoozer asserts, the canon in its entirety "both recounts the history of God's covenantal dealings with humanity and regulates God's ongoing covenantal relationship with his people."[31] The account rendered by the canon shows both God's gracious words of promise and hope, and the human struggle, not always successful, to respond in faithful ways. In respecting the integrity of the canon, we heed the Spirit's call to stand in solidarity with the whole people of God, recognizing in their weakness our own temptations. The Spirit's work of exorcism is aided by keeping troubling texts before the church, rather than excising them from lectionaries and Sunday school curricula, as a reminder that the roots of demonic readings lie finally not in particular texts but in the human heart.

In a striking image, Vanhoozer likens Scripture to "a canonical *atlas*: a collection of maps that variously render the way, the truth, and the life." The diversity of maps that make up this atlas "provide different types of orientation to the whole. Certain biblical maps are useful in some contexts, while different maps are useful in others."[32] Not all texts should be received as if they demanded our unquestioning obedience and directly represented the mind of God; some of these canonical maps may be useful in revealing to us our own predilections to misappropri-ate God's word by passing it through the filter of our own hatred and prejudice.[33] But we can still insist with 2 Timothy 3:16 that all of Scrip-ture "is useful for teaching, for reproof, for correction, and for training in righteousness, so that everyone who belongs to God may be profi-cient, equipped for every good work."

"Women are created inferior to men." "The Jews killed Christ." "Slavery is in accordance with God's will." As much as we may be ashamed of these readings of Scripture, we can give thanks that the faith of the larger church was deep enough to dare to put these interpreta-tions into question. The exorcist Spirit was at work, untangling us from the net of ignorance and malice that fostered and perpetuated these toxic readings. If the Spirit does not exorcise harmful entrenched read-ings of Scripture, whole communities can be driven to cease reading Scripture altogether. In 1992 indigenous peoples in the Americas com-memorated "five hundred years of conquest" by handing a letter to Pope John Paul that read in part, "We, Indians of the Andes and America, decided to take advantage of John Paul II's visit to return to him his Bible because in five centuries it has given us neither love, nor peace, nor justice. Please, take your Bible and give it back to our oppressors, because they need its moral precepts more than we."[34] That the Bible can become a poison book for a whole group of people impels us to look critically at our collective history of readings of Scripture to see which must be cast out.

Exorcising the false spirits of our readings is a long-term proposition. The Spirit's confrontation with the powers and principalities takes place within Christian hearts and Christian communities, in the midst of chronic human disorder and imperfection. Exorcism tends to be associated with sudden and dramatic public acts, but the Spirit's work of exorcism is often quiet and gradual. The release from the bondage of widely shared communal readings can take hundreds of years. This exorcism is usually brought about through the web of communal practices, rather than individual feats of exegetical brilliance. It happens through prophetic words, repentance, efforts at reconciliation, and large-hearted attention to the spiritual gifts and discernments of others. The Spirit's work of exorcism is so agonizingly difficult and slow because it aims at nothing less than opening heaven and converting earth, bringing all creatures into joyful, eternal fellowship with the triune God. The Spirit triumphs over evil powers not by annihilating evildoers, but by winning sinners over to the good.

It is not only inherited readings of Scripture that need exorcism. The Spirit also works to nurture a hermeneutic of suspicion toward our contemporary readings of Scripture. As Ellen Davis notes, "whenever we pick up the Bible, read it, put it down, and say, 'That's just what I thought,' we are probably in trouble."[35] One of the most spiritually dangerous questions we can ask in this connection is: "What does Scripture say about *them*?" Whether it is Christians asking that question about Muslims, or Pentecostals asking that question about Catholics, or straight people asking that question about gay people, when we as readers ask that question—what does Scripture say about *them*—we often hear a self-justifying answer. It is all too easy to read Scripture in ways that reinforce rather than challenge our comfortable perceptions of ourselves and others. Without the guidance of the exorcist Spirit we are in danger of turning aside from the hard truth offered us through Scripture, subscribing instead to "a lying vision, worthless divination, and the deceit of [our] own minds" (Jer. 14:14). As much as the Christians who went before us, we too need the exorcising power of the Spirit to release us from the spiritual captivity of our readings.

"Come, Creator Spirit," the church has prayed for many centuries. As we consider the relationship of the Holy Spirit to Scripture we too join in that prayer: "Come, Creator Spirit, exorcise our demonic readings. Come, Creator Spirit, open us up to the wide world in which you move. Come, Creator Spirit, bind us to God and each other in love."

3
Breathing, Bearing, Beseeching, and Building
Reading Scripture with the Spirit

Molly T. Marshall

Holy Scripture and Holy Spirit go together. The forming of the Bible and the forming of the people of God through Scripture are expressions of the Spirit's midwifery, a praxis that does not eviscerate human participation. My early years of teaching in theological education were freighted with responding to a blunt fundamentalist challenge—if you did not believe in the inerrancy and infallibility of Scripture, you "do not believe in the Bible."[1] The divine origin of Scripture was sustained only by diminishing human instrumentality in all the process of the text's production, preservation, and interpretation. The biblical view of the Spirit as divine breathing that generates language, bearing prophets and apostles to speak God's word, beseeching the people of God in all times to build consensus in congregational life, was subordinated to a modernist vision of propositional truth.[2]

In this essay, I want to focus more on the function of Scripture than its origin, although I will briefly address the key texts of the Bible's own witness to its nature. What is the role of the Spirit in assisting readers of Scripture, especially when individuals and congregations face daunting questions about suffering and evil, human sexuality, political perspectives that war against peace and justice, and nonbiblical forms of faith and spirituality? Practices of discernment are critical for decision making; however, the role of the Holy Spirit in them seems indeterminate, at best. Hence, this constructive exercise will address the aligning of pneumatology and spiritual practice.

41

As background for this pursuit, I find John Webster's description of Scripture as "fields of the Spirit's activity in the publication of the knowledge of God"[3] compelling; it allows a constructive human and divine interface throughout the process of inscripturation, canonization, and interpretation. The activity of the Spirit in assisting the church in faithful reading of Scripture is not unlike the Spirit's activity in bringing the canon into being and granting its recognition as divine "self-presentation of the triune God."[4] Pneumatological activity can only be rightly articulated within a Trinitarian context; hence, the parameters for this construction are a fully Trinitarian doctrine of Scripture.[5]

BREATHING THE WORD

Creation issues forth from breath and word. Jürgen Moltmann uses the lyrical imagery of music in describing the combining of word and breath to evoke creation. Breath makes word possible; word gives intelligibility to breath. Son and Spirit, begotten and proceeding, are God's own self-communication. Breath sustains the word; word allows breath to find hearing. As Moltmann writes of the unity of breath and voice, "all things are called to life through God's Spirit and his Word."[6] The Psalter picks up this weaving of Spirit and Word as ingredient to creation. Psalm 33:6 offers an explicit link: "By the word of the LORD the heavens were made, and all their host by the breath of his mouth." *Ruach* and *dabar* thread their way throughout the Hebrew Scriptures, always closely related as means of God's self-communication vivifying creation or prompting speech that illumines God's actions. Basil the Great relates these two intimately, seeing the Spirit as the *Breath of God who always accompanies the Word.*[7]

Ruach, primarily a word naming God's presence and power as Spirit, also conveys insight into human and natural entities.[8] Once again, Moltmann offers perceptive analysis.

> The *creative* power of God is communicated to the beings he has created in such a way that in talking about *ruach* we are talking about the energy of *their* life too. It is not wrong to talk about the Spirit as the "drive" and "instinct" awakened by God.[9]

This drive and instinct is seen in the leadership God provides for the Hebrew people and later for the community gathered around Christ. The Spirit breathes the word from Yahweh that communicates God's "gracious and self-bestowing turn to the creation."[10] Frequently the narratives convey this process of empowerment: Yahweh's *ruach* came upon Othniel (Judges 3:10); Yahweh's *ruach* began to stir Samson (Judg. 13:25); "The Spirit of the LORD will posess you" (1 Sam. 10:6).

The role of the Spirit in breathing the "word of the Lord" is accented more strongly in the early preexilic prophets. Fearing the ecstasies of their prophetic forebears, the later classical prophets are much more likely to speak of their calling through Yahweh's *dabar.*[11] For example, in Isaiah's testimony we read, "The word that Isaiah son of Amoz saw concerning Judah and Jerusalem" (Isa. 2:1); in like manner Jeremiah bears witness: "Now the word of the LORD came to me saying, 'Before I formed you in the womb I knew you, and before you were born I consecrated you; I appointed you a prophet to the nations'" (Jer. 1:4–5); so also Micah begins: "The word of the LORD that came to Micah of Moresheth" (Mic. 1:1).

Even though these "literary prophets" might refrain from describing their vocation in proclaiming the word as borne along by the Spirit, we can affirm that indeed this was the case as we regard their time through the lens of the Trinitarian history of God with humanity. Spirit and Word, while distinct in their participation in the triune life of God, are always united in their *ad extra* functioning with creaturely beings.[12] The Spirit as *ruach Yahweh* prompts prophetic speech; God's "Holy Breath" sustains the Word of God as it goes forth to accomplish divine intent.

Akin to the creation narrative, 2 Timothy 3:16 illuminates the role of God's breath as bearing the word in Scripture. Eschewing "inspiration" (*theopneutos*) as too limited a rendering, Thomas Hoffman argues that "the Greek, 'God-breathed,' suggests not just the breath but the pneumatic Word *breathed,* and the Father who breathes him. Its Trinitarian implications are often ignored when it is treated simply as 'inspiration.'"[13] Kilian McDonnell safeguards this inextricable relationship through what he calls the "trinitarian dynamic."

> One model of this dynamic is God reaching through the Son in the Spirit to touch and transform the world and the church to lead them in the Spirit through the Son back to God. Within this rhythm—the dynamic of life from the Father to the Father—is to be found the extension of the Trinitarian life beyond the divine self to cosmos and church in the missions of the Son and the Spirit.[14]

When describing the Spirit's relation to Scripture, several scholars have preferred the language of sanctification to inspiration, believing that inspiration has a larger generic meaning in literature and was not necessarily correlative with the Holy Spirit. Three decades ago C. F. D. Moule made a strong case for discarding inspiration when speaking of Scripture: "inspiration, while describing a profoundly important aspect of the Spirit's activities, is not a term than can be successfully used in the interests of the infallibility of canonical pronouncements or the uniqueness of Scripture."[15] Webster offers his definition of sanctification: "As the Holy Spirit's work, sanctification is a process in which, in the limitless freedom of God, the creaturely element is given its own genuine reality as it is commanded and molded to enter into the divine service."[16] Relating this work directly to Scripture, he writes:

> Sanctification is not to be restricted to the text as finished product; it may legitimately be extended to the larger field of agents and actions of which the text is part. The Spirit's relation to the text broadens out into the Spirit's activity in the life of the people of God.[17]

The Word is breathed by God, and the Spirit rests upon the body[18] of those called to proclaim and narrate the mode of God's presence in the world. In the next section, we will examine how the Spirit moves individuals and communities to speak, hear, and interpret the word as it becomes Scripture.

BEARING THE MESSENGER

Second Peter 1:21 can be rendered: "Those moved by the Holy Spirit spoke from God." The text wants to make clear the source of revelation; it comes from God and is manifested through the dynamic work of the Spirit in the messenger (*pheromenoi*). Theologians usually summon this text as a means of construing the nature of biblical authority and interpret it as relating to a textual property more than the ongoing movement of God through messengers, both textual and embodied. Pheme Perkins suggests that 2 Peter 1:20–21 is responding to a charge that "prophecy is not secure"[19] because it is based on the prophet's own interpretation; thus the emphasis of this text on God's initiative. A delicate hermeneutical balance ensues: how much freedom does the interpreter of Scripture possess? Is there a way to guarantee truthfulness in biblical interpretation?

The mode of the Spirit's work with humanity is collaborative; thus guarantees that creaturely beings will infallibly be conduits for *ipsissima verba* (the very words) from God are overreaching. Yet, the testimony of Scripture and countless faithful interpreters is that the Spirit quickens understanding in concert with God's intent.

Once again, Webster's insight is illuminative: "Being 'moved' by the Spirit is not simply being passively impelled . . . the action of the inspiring Spirit and the work of the inspired creature are concursive rather than antithetical."[20] The concept of *concursus* suggests a model for receiving and bearing the word of God that denies neither God's intentionality—that is, sovereignty—nor the receptivity and instrumentality of the human messenger. In humility, God condescends to human speech, thereby granting dignity to human participation.[21]

Granted, there is a mystery to being borne by the Spirit of God when offering proclamation, teaching, or spiritual counsel. Often we credit the level of spiritual maturity or receptivity of the messenger when observing the life-giving work of the Spirit through him or her; surely this is a part of the mystery of being "moved," yet there remains a mysterious movement of the Spirit's activity as generous grace. More than a few biblical (and contemporary) characters find themselves surprised to be as earthen vessels carrying treasure far beyond their imaginations.

Cynthia Campbell suggests that the creedal declaration "We believe in the Holy Spirit, Who has spoken through the prophets" is a living and active affirmation about the nature of Scripture. She observes, "We cannot know that God *spoke* through the scriptures unless we experience the reality that God *speaks* through the scriptures."[22] The resonance of a sermon in the hearer begins with the resonance in the interpreter who becomes proclaimer. The "answering character" of humans in whom the Spirit dwells vibrates with recognition when the word of God is perceived. As Stephen Fowl perceptively writes, "Experience of the Spirit shapes the reading of scripture, but scripture most often provides the lenses through which the Spirit's work is perceived and acted upon."[23] The circularity of this reality is inescapable, just as the arguments for biblical authority have been. We cannot help but resort to the self-authenticating nature of Scripture when speaking of its canonical status in the life of the church. The Spirit who originally moved messengers to speak and write moves persons to read and hear the voice of God today.

Nearly fifteen years ago, I had an experience in worship which could only be described as the text "reading me." It was during a time that many professors of Southern Baptist Theological Seminary in Louisville,

Kentucky, were under fire; many had departed, and many more would. We gathered at a church near the seminary and an alumnus, a gifted preacher, was invited to help us celebrate the good we had been able to accomplish, even though it was being foreshortened. He selected Psalm 126:5–6 for the message.

> May those who sow in tears
>   reap with shouts of joy.
> Those who go out weeping,
>   bearing the seed for sowing,
> shall come home with shouts of joy,
>   carrying their sheaves.

Almost before the end of the textual reading, people (including me) began to weep.[24] Written for a different people in a different time and place, this psalm gathered up the hurt and frustration of more than a decade of personal attack amid a hostile takeover of our seminary. "Sowing in tears" was the only way I had been able to exercise my vocation in the face of accusations that I was not trustworthy to form students theologically. Faithfully "bearing the seed for sowing" in the classroom was all my colleagues and I were able to do as the political machinations whirred at a different level.

The consolation of the psalm was found in the promise that weeping could turn to joy and seed would bear good harvest. In this public reading and proclamation of Scripture, this particular psalm had functioned as a "mirror to the soul," as Athanasius, the great fourth-century theologian and bishop of Alexandria, wrote.[25] Further describing the work of the Spirit in the Psalter, he wrote:

> Each Psalm is both spoken and composed by the Spirit so that in these same words . . . the stirring of our souls might be grasped, and all of them be said as concerning us, and [the psalms] issue from us as our own words.[26]

The Spirit was profoundly at work in this gathering—and long before. Prior to it, of course, was the divine moving in the life of the psalmist, the collecting and receiving of such canticles, the impress of divine movement on the proclaimer, and the vulnerable nearness of the Spirit in my heart, vibrating with the textual tuning fork. Athanasius's insight proved true; the words of Psalm 126 issued from me and others "as our own words." The Spirit used Scripture to pierce beneath the surface, to interrogate and comfort the heart.

BESEECHING THE CONGREGATION

A recent collection of essays, *The Art of Reading Scripture*,[27] is suggestive of ways in which the Spirit beseeches the congregation as faithful readers of the Bible. The Scripture Project, a colloquy composed primarily of teachers in theological schools (leavened by a couple of congregational ministers), set out to assess what denotes faithful reading of scriptural texts, an exercise that led them far beyond the usual critical methodologies privileged in theological education.

The fruit of their labor was nine theses on the interpretation of Scripture. I want to appropriate four of them to assist in this exploration of how the Spirit helps the congregation read and practice aright. The sustaining conviction of the church in its varied forms is that the Spirit continues to address the people of God through the Scripture, beseeching them to listen for the word of God. I will deal with each of the theses in turn, for there is wisdom in these distilled assessments of how Scripture functions.

1. *Faithful interpretation of Scripture invites and presupposes participation in the community brought into being by God's redemptive action— the church.*[28]

Only those who experience the salvific grace experienced in Christian community can fully appropriate Scripture's treasure. Faithful interpretation of Scripture is winsome for those coming to faith, for it promises a worldview conformed to the cruciform story of God's self-giving—good news, indeed.

Several years ago, I taught a required course in religious studies at a nearby university. As a part of the course, I asked learners to read several narratives that portrayed the expansiveness of God's love. Of course, Luke's story of the Prodigal Son was included; it mirrored the life stage of many of the class members as they were moving toward greater dimensions of autonomy. One young man without any religious training was incredulous after reading the story. "Is that really in the Bible?" he asked. "It seems too good to be true." Only later in a paper did he reveal his estrangement from his family of origin, especially his father. Several years later I received a letter from him. He had graduated,

become a middle school teacher and coach, and found his way to a community of faith. He said it was because he wanted to learn more about
such a welcoming parental figure. Scripture, breathed by the Spirit,
invited him to experience grace found in acceptance and sustained by a
community formed by faithful reading of the Bible.

My student's experience is shared by many. Hearing a word of grace
invites participation in a community that allows him to interpret his life
as one beloved and welcomed by God. The welcome of the people of
God makes believable God's own hospitality.

It is only possible to learn the redemptive story we inhabit[29] through
an ever enlarging understanding of God's story in Scripture. Most
parishioners have only a faint understanding how their life story relates
to the trinitarian history of God narrated in Scripture.[30] A pastoral col-
league observes that there is a lack of literacy about the great biblical
story of creation-redemption-consummation. Perhaps it is because neg-
ligent catechism in Sunday school and preparation for baptism has only
imparted an atomistic understanding of the meta-narrative; or perhaps
it is simply because the majority of church members attend sporadically.
The result is that too few understand how it all fits.

Regular participation in Bible study, worship, and personal *lectio
divina* contribute to an engagement with Scripture that plows the soil
of the heart,[31] making it receptive to the word of God. Reading Scripture among the faithful allows the layers of experience of the Spirit to
be shared and one's own testimony to gain hearing.

2. *The saints of the church provide guidance in how to interpret and perform Scripture.*[32] Telford Work urges the role of saints in beseeching congregations through Scripture. "Like icons of the saints, which have
become warranted through the new indwelling of the Holy Spirit in saints'
bodies, the words of old and new prophets and apostles are transformed
by the Spirit's outpouring and made into dwelling places for God."[33]

Protestants are belatedly catching up in the larger Christian family
with regard to the significance of saints. Not only is there a deepening
acquaintance with those in the common pre-Reformation heritage of
the church, there is also a new appreciation for "ordinary saints" that
grace the church both past and present. Invariably, these saints make
Scripture reading a *habitus* that forms their worldview and discipleship.

The deep acquaintance of saints with Scripture reveals a depth of
understanding that leads to transformed living. I want to mention
briefly two saints out of my own Baptist tradition, Walter Rauschenbusch and Martin Luther King Jr.

Rauschenbusch, pastor and theologian, shook the heights and depths of academia and congregational life with his convictions about the social nature of the gospel.[34] It was primarily his reading of the Synoptic Jesus' view of the "kingdom of God" that shaped his thinking. This brief observation is illustrative: "Only those church bodies which have been in opposition to organized society, and have looked to a better city with its foundations in heaven, have taken the Sermon on the Mount seriously."[35] As his writings demonstrate, Rauschenbusch was steeped in the whole of Scripture. In his little treatise on love, he writes:

> The world of the Bible . . . is a great world. I have wandered through it all, but I have never made it all my own. But some friendly hills and valleys in it are mine by right of experience. Some chapters have comforted me; some have made me homesick; some have braced me like a bugle call; and some always enlarge me within by a sense of unutterable fellowship with a great, quiet Power that pervades all things and fills me.[36]

Yet it was his constant engagement with the sayings of Jesus that evoked and sustained his vision.

Martin Luther King Jr. was most at home in the semantic landscape of Scripture. As he spoke in the cadences of an Old Testament prophet, the source of his preaching was evident. In his famous speech-sermon, "I Have a Dream," the language of Isaiah is palpable. Amos and Micah were other favorites that granted images of power and eloquence. Like Rauschenbusch, King was drawn to the words of the Sermon on the Mount. He wrote: "It was the sermon on the Mount, rather than a doctrine of passive resistance, that initially inspired the Negroes of Montgomery to dignified social action. It was Jesus of Nazareth that stirred the Negroes with the creative weapon of love."[37] When King proclaimed, "Let justice roll down like waters, and righteousness like an ever-flowing stream," he presumed, according to Gregory Jones, "that no matter how poor Christian embodiment of the Scriptures might have been in the United States, the vast majority . . . would hear those words as Amos's critique of people who worship God without practicing justice."[38]

These two Baptist saints both interpret and perform Scripture. They continue to guide communities to read the clear mandates of Jesus and live accordingly. On the significance of saintly interpreters, Jones insists, "we can see the grace and holiness of God working in and through their fallible, often conflicted lives to shed specific light on our own readings and embodiments of Scripture."[39]

3. *Christians need to read the Bible in dialogue with diverse others outside the church.*[40]

Because the Spirit is at work outside the lives of Christian believers and the church, it is helpful and necessary to listen for divine movement that comes through diverse others. Indeed, the Spirit breathes through other ways of faith—those who claim other traditions and other holy texts.[41] The challenges that come from their reading of our texts and their presentation of their own quickens new insight and respect.

Recently I participated in an interfaith dialogue sponsored by the National Council of Jewish Women. Three women were invited to reflect on dimensions of Abraham's life; we were Jewish, Muslim, and Christian. (Actually I would have preferred to talk about Sarah, Hagar, and Mary, but that is for a future program!)

In addition to focusing on the Abraham cycle in Genesis (including the horrific scene on Mount Moriah), the Muslim woman and I brought texts from the Koran and New Testament to further illumine our reading of the Torah. We wrestled with questions such as (1) What is the role of Abraham in your faith? (2) What other texts does your tradition use to increase your understanding of Abraham? (3) What message does your faith take from the event of the binding of Isaac? and (4) At the end of his life, Abraham makes provision for Isaac's future. How does your faith follow this model?

This was a fascinating exercise in interpretation, and we learned from one another. The relative authority accorded the texts was distinctive, but respectful. Of surprise to some in attendance is the substitution of Ishmael for Isaac in the Koran; some were surprised that Hebrews 11:17–19 links Isaac to the power of the resurrection, that is, keeping a promise when there is no ground for it. Frankly, I came to understand my own intertextual reading more clearly, for example, juxtaposing Genesis 22 with Romans 8:31–32:

> What then shall we say to this? If God is for us, who is against us? He who did not spare his own Son, but gave him up for us all, will he not also give us all things with him? (RSV)

The careful reading and appreciative hearing of this conference enriched all who gathered. There was a sharpening of difference, yet gratitude for the opportunity to pursue this kind of fruitful reading. God's Spirit made possible the "ground of meeting" between these sisters.[42]

BUILDING GENERATIVE CONSENSUS

One more thesis from the Scripture Project will be helpful as we think about the practice of discernment, the demonstration plot for how the Spirit assists in reading Scripture. The last of the nine theses is:

4. *We live in the tension between the "already" and the "not yet" of the kingdom of God; consequently, Scripture calls the church to ongoing discernment, to continually fresh rereadings of the text in light of the Holy Spirit's ongoing work in the world.*[43]

In this last section, we will explore how the Spirit assists in discerning the guidance of the Bible when we face critical decisions. Kilian McDonnell speaks of the Holy Spirit as "a way of knowing."[44] We trust that a richer understanding of the Spirit's function will lead the church to know and embody truth in dynamic trajectories. It is a process of winnowing which eludes easy certitude.[45] Spiritual discernment is fraught with uncertainty, even danger, for it can be either "prophetically subversive or grossly self-deceptive."[46]

In the New Testament, spiritual discernment is directly connected to faith in Jesus Christ. Paul speaks of "distinguishing" of spirits (*diakreseis*), one of the gifts of the Holy Spirit (1 Cor. 12:10). Earlier in the chapter he has insisted that no one who curses Jesus is led of the Spirit, and no one can say "Jesus is Lord!" except under the influence of the Holy Spirit (1 Cor. 12:2–3). The first letter of John advises of the need for the community to "test the spirits" (1 John 4:1). Here we are instructed not to believe that every spirit is from God. In a time when docetic impulses were threatening to undermine the received tradition, the Johannine community had to confront heresy. The test by which one can know that this is the true Spirit is this: "Every spirit that confesses that Jesus Christ has come in the flesh is from God" (1 John 4:2). Authentic christological confession is made possible by the Spirit who "guides into all truth" (John 16:13). Christopher Morse wisely perceives that faith in the Holy Spirit is a "refusal to deify human subjectivity."[47] Yet human subjectivity is always a part of the equation.

The problem faced by the Johannine church recurs; it is an ongoing struggle to discern who is really being faithful to the Jesus story. Denis Edwards concludes that what "these texts require is not simply an abstract *orthodoxy*, but a following of Jesus that expresses itself in love, a Christian life lived in *orthopraxis*."[48]

No spiritual practice is more needed in our communities of faith today than discernment. Luke Timothy Johnson names the challenge of this practice. It is a theological process that "enables humans to perceive their characteristically ambiguous experience as revelatory and to articulate such experiences in a narrative of faith."[49] While there are assorted methods—from Ignatian[50] to Quaker[51]—the problem is not really about method. In my judgment, the problem lies in five things: (1) impatience with a process that requires careful, forthright, time-consuming listening and reflection; (2) an assumption that this is the work of religious professionals; (3) lack of trust that the Holy Spirit really will guide; (4) patterns of Scripture reading shackled to deadly literalism; and (5) a persistent expectation that we will reach a perfect conclusion, unsullied by human opinion and sociocultural context. The Holy Spirit makes haste to help us in each of these dimensions of discernment.

More often than not, churches function without clear intentionality about their vision and mission, which is why the work of decision making is so difficult. What are the formative criteria that determine direction for a discrete congregation, including all-important budget allocations? Usually a congregation will simply state that "we are following the Bible." While said in good faith, it is a naive perspective on the nature of Scripture and tends to discard the crucial role of the Spirit in reading and discerning these texts. Johnson offers a nuanced perception of biblical authority.

> The issue of biblical authority, therefore, is not whether it gives a consistent blueprint for every aspect of our lives, or that our lives conform exactly to that blueprint. Given the diversity within the canon, any such claim would be specious. The issue of authority is whether the texts are taken seriously as normative, even when—as is often true—they diverge or even disagree.[52]

Scripture cannot be read in the abstract, for life experiences, tradition, and reason converge in interpretation. The Bible simply does not address every situation, and the Spirit helps us sift other resources in considering pressing issues. Here is where listening to the voice of God through the perspectives of others in the community, especially the mature, can be of signal assistance.

I belong to a Sunday school class named "Contemporary Issues Class" in which most of the members are well past retirement age. It is far from business as usual! A few weeks ago we addressed the issue of homosexuality and to what degree our church would or should be welcoming. One of our members, the widow of a pastor, now nearing eighty, gave her ringing testimony about how her mind had changed on this matter. She spoke about a concerted study of Scripture, literature (both pro and con), and her friendship with a same-sex couple. She concluded that the church of Jesus Christ should include all. Later that Sunday she telephoned me. "Was I too strong?" she asked. I assured her that Baptist polity honored such liberty of conscience and, more important, her words had great credibility because of her own faithful witness.

Recently this same American Baptist Church has been engaged in a visioning process to determine both identity and priorities in mission and ministry. Spanning nearly two years, this process of discernment has realized the sheer diversity of theological perspective in our congregation (if not much ethnic diversity) and the complexity of aligning identity and practice.[53] Primarily driven by thoughtful nonstaff members, the process has utilized, in addition to Bible reading and prayer, "Appreciative Inquiry"[54] and "Worshipful Work"[55] practices as means of attending to the Spirit. Even with the best intentions, it has been hard for us to get beyond self-protective concerns. The one thing needful, in my judgment, is a different hermeneutic in reading Scripture—one closely related to the Spirit's witness to the salvific work of Christ.

Webster argues persuasively for this kind of reading "as an instance of the fundamental pattern of all Christian existence, which is dying and rising with Jesus Christ through the purging and quickening power of the Holy Spirit."[56] Further, he notes: "Reading Scripture is thus best understood as an aspect of mortification and vivification: to read Scripture is to be slain and made alive."[57] Absent from most congregations is this kind of passionate reading, where the Spirit moves hearts to repentance and calls the community to cruciform living.[58] Richard B. Hays writes of the promise this kind of reading portends: "The Resurrection purges the death-bound illusions that previously held us captive and sets us free to perceive the real world of God's life-giving resurrection power."[59]

The witness of the Spirit to dying and rising with Christ is the center of gravity for biblical narratives. Apostolic preaching in early Christianity is a demonstration of reading the whole of Scripture in light of this surpassing event in salvation history.[60] Because Christ had endured the extremities of human suffering, yet conquered death, a new horizon had been placed before humanity. His disciples, liberated from the grasp of sin and death, could embrace his *kenōsis* and live in the freedom of resurrection power.

As long as a congregation makes self-preservation its priority, it cannot move toward generative self-giving. The Spirit is seeking to guide congregations to embody scriptural exhortations to be "crucified with Christ" and to "know the power of his resurrection." Building a consensus toward this direction will not occur apart from the convicting movement of the Spirit, conforming the body of Christ to his death and resurrection. And the Spirit invites our consent in this. Spirit-led consensus is generative, allowing members of the Christian community to decenter themselves for the sake of extending the grace of Christ. When the church can say, "it has seemed good to the Holy Spirit and to us . . ."(Acts 15:28), it has discerned the guidance of God.

FINAL THOUGHTS

The Spirit makes possible hearing and living the Scripture's pathway to righteousness. The breathing, bearing, beseeching, and building work of the Holy Spirit makes the Bible an instrument of grace concordant with the will of the triune God. A more robust theology of the Spirit will prompt congregations to lean into the divine movement that makes Scripture relevant for the living of these days. Pneumatological readings of Scripture do not cast aside the history of interpretation of varied texts, but such reading does allow the *sensus plenior*[61] (surplus of meaning) of the Bible to well up. Thus, there is both freedom and control—"liberty to reinterpret and remould the original kergyma, but also the original kerygma remains as a check and restraint."[62]

We dare not read Scripture alone—without the Spirit or without the community that calls to accountability. Personal devotion is always enlarged by the wisdom of saintly interpreters and the wider community of faith.[63] The Spirit is always beckoning the church to read with the paschal rhythms of the life of Jesus, which lead us to resurrection practices of justice and hope.

4

Holy Spirit and the Religions

Roger Haight, SJ

One of the most serious problems in Christian theology at this time concerns the status of Christianity relative to the other religions. I call it serious for several reasons. The question engages central issues such as the status of Jesus Christ, whom the tradition of Christianity and the current language of the churches consistently characterize as absolute savior of all. The question is complex and has generated a multitude of quite different answers. Since none has rallied a consensus, it remains an open question among Christian theologians. The problem also touches the sensibilities of ordinary Christians who look upon Jesus as the mediator of salvation from God. Most thinking people have raised for themselves the comparative question of the status of Jesus but do not have the resources to answer it in any technical way. How could they, when the theologians themselves are divided?

I propose to take up this issue once again and in so doing add another voice to the mix. But this is entirely fitting in a book dedicated to the doctrine of the Holy Spirit, because therein lies an approach to the problem that has proven to be quite satisfying if not conclusive for many. But before entering into the argument, I propose to lay out a few suppositions about how I conceive the problem and the way I will go about addressing it.

This discussion presumes that a good number of Christians today have moved beyond mere tolerance to some recognition and acceptance of the world's religions as having a divine source and authorization.

They may have come to this view spontaneously; they may or may not be able to justify it from an explicitly Christian standpoint. The traditional language of the church about Jesus Christ which dominates our liturgies, public prayer, and official documents presents many difficulties and, in the end, makes positive assessments appear as some sort of compromise that waters down true faith. On that supposition, the aim of this chapter is to present a reasonable analysis of traditional faith that can expand it to include a positive recognition of other religions.

One way of beginning such a process consists in phrasing the question that is being asked in a way that opens up the imagination in a constructive way and does not impose false alternatives. Edward Schillebeeckx has proposed just such a positive way of addressing the question of the status of Christianity and Jesus Christ vis-à-vis the religions in these terms: "how can Christianity maintain its own identity and uniqueness and at the same time attach a positive value to the difference of religions in a non-discriminatory sense?"[1] The response must satisfy two norms: it must remain faithful to the tradition of the church, especially its biblical foundations, and the position must reflect the increasing respect for other religions and the growing conviction that they are willed by God on their own terms.

Christology lies at the center of this discussion. Narrowly conceived, Christology concerns the person of Jesus Christ and usually includes an account of the traditional doctrine of the divinity of Jesus Christ. The main reason why Christians have had a lesser esteem for other religions does not lie in knowledge of these religions but in the superlative terms in which they relate to Jesus Christ. In straightforward language, since Jesus Christ is the incarnation of God, Christianity is God's own religion, and all other religions relate to it as "relative" to "absolute." No Christology will be acceptable to mainline Christians if it does not account for faith in Jesus' divinity. Thus an explanation of how Christians can relate to other religious people as possible "equals" must pass through Christology. This essay aims at showing that the doctrine of the Spirit and Spirit language can help us thread the narrow passage between the traditional demands of faith and a new respect for the autonomous value of other religious traditions.

This development of a response to the question, with special emphasis on the doctrine of the Holy Spirit, moves in three large steps. The first part will briefly outline three different christological approaches, each one of which has some plausibility. The review will show some examples of the plurality of approaches to the question and provide some useful insights and distinctions that may be helpful in developing a Spirit-centered answer. The second part develops the main tool for constructing the response of this essay, namely, the meaning of the symbol "Holy Spirit." The third will use the results of these first two parts in a constructive effort to portray the logic of the relation between Christ and the other religions from a Christian perspective.

THREE STRATEGIES USING TRADITIONAL LANGUAGE

This first probe into a way of speaking about the divinity of Jesus Christ that opens up space for other religions consists in surveying three somewhat different approaches to the problem. A consideration of these strategies will supply categories that will be helpful in the constructive effort of the third part of the chapter.

Trinitarian Language

A good number of theologians explicitly appeal to the Trinitarian character of God to explain the relationship between Christianity and other religions. I have chosen four examples, each one of which has a slightly distinctive emphasis.

The first is Bernard Lonergan as he is interpreted by Frederick Crowe.[2] His recommendation is that we reverse the way Christians think about how God deals with history. "Commonly we think of God first sending the Son, and the Spirit being sent in that context, to bring to completion the work of the Son. [My] thesis says that, on the contrary, God first sent the Spirit, and then sent the Son in the context of the Spirit's mission, to bring to completion . . . the work which God conceived as one work to be executed in the two steps of the twofold mission of first the Spirit and then the Son. The corollary to this thesis will define a consequent approach to the world religions from the Christian side."[3] This way of looking at things depicts the religions as not strangers but sharers together in a common Spirit. "What I am affirming, then, is our religious community with the world religions in some true and basic sense of the word, community, if not in the full sense of a common confession of faith, a common worship, and a common expression of hope in the eschaton. This community is effected by our common religious conversation, which, in Lonergan's view, is our common orientation to the mystery of love and awe through the indwelling Holy Spirit who is given to us."[4]

Karl Rahner has written extensively on the subject of the relation between Jesus Christ and the other religions in the economy of salvation. But one can discern a firm logic to his position, and I will try to digest it into a brief schematic statement.

Rahner's position rests on the doctrine of the Trinity as a presupposition. For him the doctrine of the Trinity implies that the Son and the Spirit represent dynamically two distinct but inseparable modes of God's self-communication to human existence. The Son is God's communication to the human race definitively in Jesus; the Spirit to each human being personally. Thus the Trinity implicitly contains Rahner's conceptualization of the creative origin of the cosmos and a theology of human history. Another major premise of Rahner's thinking rests on the New Testament's witness to the universal saving will of God: God wills the salvation of all (1 Tim. 2:4). The central category for speaking about *how* God saves, Rahner draws from the theology of grace where "grace" means precisely the love of God made effective in God's saving action. With these three terms Rahner constructs the following argument.

Regarding God's universal saving will, one cannot say that God wills something and at the same time think that God's will is ineffective. Confession of God's universal saving will has implications. But grace, which Rahner describes as the self-communication of God to human beings in loving, forgiving presence and active influence, represents the way God saves. Another name for this interior communication of God to human beings is Holy Spirit: grace and the Spirit of God are synonymous in his theology. It follows, then, that God as Spirit must approach all human beings from the very beginning of their existence with the personal invitation to salvation. But where, Rahner asks, is such an invitation most likely to become public if not in the religions of the world which represent ultimacy to their people? For Rahner, all human responses to the appeal of transcendent grace have to be mediated through some external and objective set of symbols. The religions are thus interpreted by him as those vehicles by which the Spirit of God becomes publicly available in history.

Jesus Christ fits in this vast picture of the dialogue between God and human beings that constitutes human history as the culminating and encompassing climax: Jesus Christ constitutes the event of the final unity toward which the whole of history moves. In Jesus Christ God fully and finally identifies with humanity, and human existence responds in complete loving fidelity. In sum, the world's religions have a relative autonomy and validity of their own due to God's Spirit at work in them, but they relate to Christianity as their definitively realized goal.

Two other theologians who are inspired by Rahner and do not really transcend his position are Jacques Dupuis and Gavin D'Costa. But whereas the language of the Trinity remains in the background of much of Rahner's writing, these theologians emphasize the Trinitarian character of their thinking.

The point of emphasis in Dupuis' thinking can be located in an expansive view of God's dealing with human beings that the doctrine of the Trinity releases to the Christian imagination. He strongly asserts the identity of the Word of God with Jesus of Nazareth, and the sending of the Spirit by the risen Christ. But he does not want the particularity of Jesus and the boundaries of the church to limit appreciation of the range of God's action as Word and Spirit. While it is true that God acted in Jesus definitively and for all, "it remains also true that this event does not by itself exhaust—nor can it exhaust—the revelatory and salvific power of the Word of God."[5] He makes a parallel argument relative to the Spirit of God. "It should be added that the trinitarian perspective prompts observations about a universal presence of the Holy Spirit, similar to those about the ongoing action of the Word as such. A Spirit christology helps make it clear that the Spirit of God is universally present and active, before and after the Christ event."[6] The doctrine of the Trinity thus provides a way for Dupuis to view the religions as having a certain relative autonomy outside of the historical sphere of Christianity.

The view of Gavin D'Costa bears similarities to that of Dupuis because both are indebted to Rahner.[7] He emphasizes how the doctrine of the Trinity allows an appeal to the role of the Holy Spirit. The Spirit connects what was effected in the particular event of Jesus Christ to the universal activity of God in the whole history of humankind. In other words, the Spirit is at work abroad in the religions.[8] Therefore, dialogue with other religions can influence the church: the church can learn new things and be changed by other religions because of the Spirit. The doctrine of the Trinity provides a basis for "Christianity's openness in meeting other religions, knowing that in 'dialogue' the church must be attentive to the possibility of God's gift of himself through the prayers, practices, insights, and traditions found within other religions. Such an acknowledgement facilitates a critical and reverential openness towards other religions."[9]

In conclusion, it is important to notice that none of these Trinity-based theologians grant the religions of the world autonomy or equality of status in relation to Christianity. In all of them, Christianity represents the fullness of God's revelation and initiative toward humanity, and Christianity constitutes, ratifies, or fulfills what is going on in the other religions.

Word-Centered Incarnation Language

The Indian theologian Michael Amaladoss proposes a second approach to the divinity of Jesus Christ that opens the way to a Christian understanding of how God works in other religions. Amaladoss phrases the question he is addressing quite sharply: "We are searching to make a place for other believers in the perspective of our own faith, while respecting the identities of the others without somehow reducing them to or interpreting them in terms of our own."[10] A solution to that question requires first of all a large vision of God's relation to the world and history. God is not absent from the world after creation and before Jesus Christ; God is always close, as creator involved in the world. One must also keep in mind that God, not religion, saves. "Speaking of the primacy of God's action in salvation will also help us not to isolate God's action in Jesus, but to set it in the context of the totality of God's action in the world seeking to communicate Godself to human beings which embraces the whole process of history from creation through redemption to its ultimate consummation."[11]

Against this background, Amaladoss argues for the activity of "Christ" or the Word of God in other religions in a manner analogous to but distinct from the way God acted in Jesus. Indian (Asian) theologians, he says, "tend to use the term *cosmic Christ* to indicate the reality of the Word which transcends while englobing the humanity of Jesus." "Therefore the *cosmic Christ* must never be de-linked (separated) from the historical Jesus, though it has to be distinguished from and not be confused with it."[12] This distinction allows a conception that is both inclusivist and pluralist. "It is inclusivist insofar as it reflects in the perspective of the Christian faith in the mysteries of the Trinity and of the Incarnation and their ongoing action in history. But because of the differentiations I have made between the Word and the Spirit, between the Jesus of history and Christ, and between Christ and the church, the inclusion is only at the level of the mystery of God and Christ whose

universality we affirm in faith. It is pluralist, not merely at the historical, phenomenological level of the religions, but also at the level of the
plural manifestations of God in history, through the Word eternal and
also incarnate and through the Spirit."[13]

Spirit-Centered Empowerment Language

Another distinct approach to the divinity of Jesus Christ that does not
subtract from but enhances our understanding of the autonomous
validity of other religions centers its language on the doctrine of the
Holy Spirit. Although Rahner does not live in this house, he presents
such a thoroughgoing pneumatology that it can be taken out of his context and used to support this position. Many theologians have developed Spirit Christologies that parallel Word or Logos Christologies and
show how this conspicuous New Testament Christology can accommodate religious pluralism. I will limit myself to presenting Peter Hodgson's approach.[14]

Hodgson proceeds in three constructive steps: the first defines the
symbol of the Spirit of God from Christian sources but with expansive
intent; the second shows its relevance for Christology; and the third
applies it to a theology of religions. To begin with the first step, the
Spirit of God is the power of God. "Spirit is simply the creative and
redemptive power of God at work in the world. It is the power by which
God calls into being and dwells within all that is. It is the power of
being by which beings are. Without this power, beings would collapse
into nonbeing, the abyss of nothingness from which they are fashioned
and preserved. God is the supreme or perfect being who has this power
of being absolutely and who is thus supremely spiritual—Holy Spirit
or Absolute Spirit."[15]

The second step raises up the way God as Spirit has been used in the
Christian tradition to understand Jesus as the Christ and the church.
"The Spirit both precedes Christ and follows Christ. Spirit, in the
shape of Logos or Wisdom, is the power that indwells or 'inspirits' Jesus
of Nazareth, making him the Christ, the anointed one of Israel, who
does not triumph but is crucified, thereby becoming a different kind
of savior figure. . . . According to the Gospels, Christ sends the Spirit
into the church and the world for the purpose of taking up and completing his mission."[16]

The third step compares with the construal of the Word in the approach we just considered. The Spirit of God cannot be limited to Jesus of Nazareth and the Christian sphere. Hodgson says that "the Spirit transcends Christ and appears in a diversity of religious figures and traditions, which also contribute to the delineation and enrichment of spirituality. Thus we cannot say exhaustively what Spirit is; Spirit is both concretely configured and open to new possibilities."[17] In this way the theology of the Spirit gives the Christian imagination a way of seeing truly God at work in Jesus and looking in a noncompetitive way for manifestations of the Spirit at work in the other religions of the world.

All of these approaches to the problem have strong points that recommend them. I will borrow from all of them, especially the approach of Peter Hodgson, in bringing out the congeniality of a Spirit Christology to a positive approach to the religions.

THE SYMBOL OF THE SPIRIT OF GOD

I move therefore to the second stage of an argument in support of a Spirit Christology that will help Christians understand the traditional claims about Jesus Christ in a way that opens up an appreciation of the positive autonomous value of other religions. I begin by explaining the meaning of a religious symbol and how it cautions about understanding theological language in a literal fashion that reduces God to a human level by implying that God is open for our inspection.

The term *symbol,* when applied to religious and Christian theological language, contains a logic much like the traditional notion of a sacrament. A sacrament refers to an external action or rite or object that communicates God or in which one encounters God. Through the seen, human consciousness is drawn to the unseen, transcendent reality of God. In this sense Jesus was and is considered the sacrament of God, because in his life and ministry, in his passion and death, and especially in his resurrection he mediated God's saving approach to human beings. As a consequence, human beings are drawn to God through him. By analogy symbols and symbolic language draw the mind of the believer into the transcendent sphere of God. They point to the reality of God beyond themselves, and they represent to human consciousness meaningful expression that corresponds with God's approach to human beings. Symbols in the religious sphere should not be reckoned as weak predication because they communicate something about transcendent reality that cannot be known without them. By contrast, if language whose meaning we know from the created sphere applied to God literally, it would reduce the infinite reality of God to the level of the world. This fundamental mistake of idolatry can only be overcome by a symbolic language that allows God's presence to crack open all reductions of God's absolute mystery.

It would be appropriate at this point exegetically to draw out the meaning and experience that are latent in the Spirit language that fills the two Testaments of the Bible. What the many uses of the symbol "God's Spirit" contain and mediate in various contexts would show the deep nuances and resonances of the religious experience of God. Because of spatial constraint I have to be satisfied with a flat, discursive, and all-too-limiting definition of "Holy Spirit." The Spirit in the Jewish and Christian Scriptures refers to transcendent power at work in the world, power which ultimately goes back to God. "Spirit" is a metaphor; it stands for unseen force and energy, like that of the wind, which accounts for movement and action that requires it as an explanation. How were the prophets able to prophesy, and the leaders able to lead, if it were not the unseen Spirit of God working within them? Holy Spirit accounts for life, which ultimately comes from God, and so is able to put dry bones together, give them flesh, and make them live.

When I refer to the symbol "Holy Spirit" I mean God construed with the symbol Spirit. This deep archetypal root of the symbol lingers in the doctrinal development of the early church. It is not transcended but reconfigured. When in the first half of the fourth century the symbol "Word of God" was understood to be of the same substance as the Father, and in the second half of the same century the symbol "Spirit of God" was also declared divine, thus constituting the doctrine of the Trinity, the deep basis of these symbols in religious encounter with the Spirit was not abandoned but expanded. It is absolutely crucial to keep in mind the symbolic character of all language about God. Without this constant caution all three schemas for speaking about how God is operative in Jesus Christ and the religions for human salvation are reduced to nonsense. Christians do not believe in three Gods, and God cannot be conceived as a divine committee with tasks assigned to individuals. As Thomas Aquinas firmly insisted, when God acts outside of God's self, the whole or essential Godhead acts, not a single "person." The actions and essential attributes of God are "appropriated" to "each person" of the one triune God by a likeness or fittingness judged by human estimates.[18] In order not to foster the simple mistake of thinking of the persons of the Trinity acting independently in history I use such phrases as

"God as Word" and "God as Spirit." This usage explicitly recognizes appropriation and is fitting in theological construction. It also reinforces the symbolic character of all knowledge of God and appreciation of God's self-revelation.

With this background we are now in a position to extol the positive role of religious symbols in opening up human perception to discover signs of God's power in the world. The Christian imagination, following the Jewish imagination, attributes the order and design of reality, no matter how it came to be, to the wisdom of the creator. This symbol of God's "wisdom," in fact, was sometimes used synonymously with "Spirit." As Crowe, interpreting Lonergan, proposed, God as Wisdom and Spirit works throughout the universe, so one can expect that the effects of God's actions will be spread abroad. Genesis links the Spirit of God which swept over the deep to creation (Gen. 1:2). In Rahner's construction God as Spirit takes on special meaning as God's self-communication which becomes effective with the rise of humanity that can respond in freedom. For Rahner, the whole of human history beneath the surface consists in a dialogue between God's offer of personal intimacy and love and human response, however veiled it always seems.

Turning to the New Testament account of Jesus Christ, the symbol of the Spirit of God provides the most consistent "explanation" of the incarnation and what later was defined as the divinity of Jesus Christ. The premise for this contention presupposes that the many New Testament Christologies all confess an encounter with God's power and salvation in Jesus of Nazareth. This is why he was designated Messiah or the Christ. Luke, for example, offers a consistent account of how God as Spirit was operative in Jesus' conception and birth, the inauguration of his mission, the power of his ministry, the constitution of a new community after Jesus' death and resurrection, and the guidance of the mission into the Hellenic world. This internal divine presence and power constituted him a saving mediation of God. This witness to Christian faith encounter with Jesus Christ found expression in both of these New Testament symbols. Spirit language reflects an extensive, rudimentary, and pervasive symbolic account of Jesus' divinity.[19]

The New Testament tells in dramatic narrative how the same Spirit that was at work in Jesus was poured out on the disciples and the Jesus movement. It animated the gradual emergence of the church. What Luke depicts in narrative form Paul presents in analytical religious terms: "God's love has been poured into our hearts through the Holy

Spirit that has been given to us" (Rom. 5:5). The communities should thus let the same mind that was in Christ Jesus animate them (Phil. 2:5). The church takes up the mission of Jesus in history in the power of his Spirit.

In his theology of the mission of the church, Friedrich Schleiermacher firmly insisted that the Spirit at work in the Christian community is not the generic Spirit immanent to the world of the Old Testament, but quite specifically the Spirit of Jesus Christ.[20] I interpret this not as an ontological differentiation of the one God as Spirit but as an epistemological issue concerning what is known of God as Spirit through Jesus Christ. In other words, to be caught up in God's self-revelation as a Christian means to experience God in the light of an encounter with Jesus Christ. Christian salvation refers precisely to this internalized encounter with God mediated by the preaching and ministry, and the death and resurrection, of Jesus Christ. This mediation of God as Spirit by Jesus Christ provides a measure or criterion of the authenticity of the many manifestations or revelations of God that abound. This notion of a criterion needs further nuance than can be stated here, but what Schleiermacher insisted upon reflects the message of the New Testament itself. It is not that the Spirit is limited to the Christian sphere. The Spirit of God pervades human history. But in the Christian dispensation and from a Christian perspective, by definition, Jesus Christ becomes the open norm for discerning the Spirit truly.

A CHRISTIAN UNDERSTANDING OF GOD
AT WORK IN OTHER RELIGIONS

The second part of this chapter should help locate Spirit Christology in the doctrinal tradition: Spirit Christology has New Testament backing and offers a language that can coherently expresses Christian experience of Jesus Christ and the salvation he mediates. I now want to show how it can readily be used to open up a noncompetitive view of other religions and yet remains authentic by the same scriptural and dogmatic warrants.

I begin this all-too-schematic outline with three large conceptual frameworks for representing the economy by which God relates to the world and human history. I do this in order to show that this consideration requires an adjustment of the big picture that serves as the

background for more particular understandings or constructs. Without any attempt at being exhaustive, let me stipulate three ways of con-
ceiving the divine-human economy.

A first way reflects a pattern of creation, fall, and redemption in
chronological sequence. This picture reads the story of the relationship
of God to humankind verbatim off the pages of the Bible. Everything
began with a pristine and perfect world fresh from the hands of the creator God. This was spoiled by a first sin and then a whole history of
human infidelity and confusion. But God decided in the aftermath to
rectify the situation objectively through the intervention of the divine
Son, who effected salvation by a transaction with God that included his
death and resurrection. After this event, which constitutes a center or
dividing line of before and after in human history, humanity now lives
in a new redeemed or restored economy of history. This mythic structure can take many forms, but it has been so deeply ingrained in the
Christian imagination by traditional language that it seems always close
at hand.

A second and modern appropriation of this pattern abandons the
chronological sequence and sees creation and redemption as distinct
layers of the one relation of God to humankind and human history. In
this view redemption—or better, salvation, because the metaphor of
"redemption" already decides the issue—does not follow upon creation
as a second thought, but precedes it as the very motive for God's creation. God creates in order to save. This results in a single relation of
God to human existence that is two-layered and corresponds to the distinction between nature and grace. God wants to enter into dialogue
and communion with another in order to share God's love. Therefore
God creates a dialogue partner who, in freedom, which is the condition
for interpersonal relationship of love, does not respond mechanically or
faithfully but at best fitfully. In this view, the real distinction between
creation and grace shows that God loves human beings out of genuine
freedom; but the revelation of God in Jesus shows as well that creation
and grace are never separated. God's love is a never-failing constant.

A third picture of the divine-human relationship abandons the real
distinction between creation and salvation in God and postulates that
these are distinctions that the human mind has created. This framework
construes God's relationship to the world and humanity as simply lov-
ingly creative, a relationship of creation out of love. The distinction
between creation and grace which has been introduced here reveals the
freedom of God's love, but it is not a distinction that has an objective

correlate or reference. God does not relate to creation in two distinct ways. The single gratuity of creation and grace points to levels of being and being open and responsive to God on the part of creatures. On the one hand, God loves each creature according to its ontological character. Only humans can respond in a knowing, intentional, free, and personal way to the personal love God offers them.[21]

This third view opens up a way to envision God in relation to an evolutionary universe. The creative ontological power of the loving God underlies emergent creation. However the universe came to be concretely, and it is not for theology to discover this, the doctrine of creation affirms that the ontological power of its coming to be is named God. God's efficient creativity sustains the processes of what we call nature in the coming to be of the universe. This conception, indeed this story, must be filled out by the scientific disciplines that calculate our origins. These scientific conceptions can then be used imaginatively and religiously to translate such graphic biblical metaphors as "the Spirit hovering over the deep." The creating Spirit of God readily encourages the religious imagination to conceive God as the inner power of an emergent universe and the infinite energy that paradoxically through randomness directs evolution. But this all-powerful divine source of creative energy remains conscious, intelligent, benevolent, and solicitously loving. The Spirit that symbolizes God's awesome power also signals God's faithful and loving care for each creature. These two dimensions of God as Spirit—divine power and infinite caring love—cannot be separated because they are the very dimensions of God revealed in Jesus Christ. The power of God as Spirit is the power of emergent creation who creates new reality: novelty, complexification, augmentation of being. The love of God as Spirit points to personal presence, personal self-communication, entering into communion with those creatures who can respond. If God as Spiritual power creates new being, God's personal self-communication (Spirit) creates new religions.

The argument for this last point I draw from Karl Rahner, who, as we saw, states it straightforwardly. We must take seriously the New Testament statement that God wills the salvation of all. This is less so because it is bluntly stated in a particular verse, and more so because it describes the full burden of the event of Jesus Christ to which the New Testament as a whole gives witness. Christ came for our salvation, and all who received Jesus Christ did so on the basis of experiencing God's salvation in him. But if God wills the salvation of all, this will of God must be effective. One cannot readily affirm that when God, the creator of heaven and earth, wills something, God's will may or may not be effective. Such a conception is simply incoherent. But at the same time the universal will of God for human salvation leaves to the human theological imagination a way of deciphering how this saving will of God becomes effective so broadly. To this question Rahner says two things: first, there must be historical traces of this saving will of God. It would be too facile and ultimately implausible merely to postulate that God works the salvation of the great majority of the race privately in the interior of their consciences in a manner ultimately unknown to them. The divine agency of human salvation should be conceived as employing earthly means and leaving public traces. Second, where else would such a vehicle be than the religions of the world? These are precisely the places and the means by which human beings ask the questions of ultimacy and respond to transcendence. The religions thus provide a way in which to conceive the personal love of God reaching historically to individual people and groups and eliciting their response.

The Christian must conclude that Spirit of God is at work in other religions. The grounds for this assertion, however, do not come primarily from an empirical study of the religions. It is precisely a Christian affirmation of faith based on Christian revelation. If what is revealed about God in Jesus Christ is true, namely, that God, the creator of all, is also the lover of all God's creation and all human beings in it, and if this love is effective, its effects will appear in human history. Such a love cannot be effective and at the same time go without actual influence on creatures, without being experienced, without being shared, and without creating a community. The point that is driven home, then, is not a grudgingly tolerant view of the religions, but a vision of God's relation to history revealed in Jesus Christ that validates the autonomous saving character of other religions.

Finally, then, the key to a religiously satisfying and theologically coherent view of Christianity that opens up a place for other religions lies in a theology of the Spirit. It takes the move made by Crowe after "the Lonergan idea" seriously. But in the conception offered here the pneumatological recentering of thought does not depend on Trinitarian theology but transforms it as well in a direction that shifts the framework from christocentrism toward theocentrism. This entails a focus of the theological imagination on creation and employs the symbol of the Spirit of God at work consistently in creation, evolution, history, the world's religions, the person of Jesus, Christian community, and other religious communities.

To conclude, I return to the new question about religion and the religions today that was framed by Edward Schillebeeckx. Appropriation of the way he poses the question of the theology of religions today depends on an appreciation of the degree to which our situation and context have been permanently altered. One can no longer think in imperial terms of one absolute religion in relation to which all others appear dependent or defective. Pluralism, that is, a common humanity with different religions, sharing the same space and interacting with each other, has replaced it as a supposition. The new theological context simply demands a more expansive framework. We must live together in a non-competitive world; we cannot compete as though one part of humanity were truly enlightened and the cultures of the great majority were ignorant and religiously benighted. The Christian vision of God contradicts this view. But a new open attitude toward other religions has to be connected with traditional faith values. God as Spirit representing God at work in the world and in Jesus Christ as a God of power and might and of love and care helps to make sense of this new situation. In this vision nothing that the Christian has affirmed about God and Jesus Christ has changed. Only the way the Christian now sees the world has changed, and rightly so, because the new situation has provided new perspective. In the light of the all-pervasive Holy Spirit of God the world appears more friendly metaphysically. This does not of course make history more morally friendly; it surely is not. But Christians are no less to blame for that than any other religious group. The doctrine of the Holy Spirit thus impels rather than simply allows Christians to enter into dialogue with other religions. The long-term result of such dialogue with other religious people about their experience of ultimate reality should be not competitive theologies of the Spirit of God but comparative theologies of how God may be more fully experienced in our world today.

5

Guests, Hosts, and the Holy Ghost

Pneumatological Theology and Christian Practices in a World of Many Faiths

Amos Yong[1]

INTRODUCTION

In this essay I wish to bring together two emerging discussions—that of theology of religions and that of a pneumatological theology of hospitality—to argue the thesis that a pneumatological theology of hospitality provides one way around the current impasse in some theological circles that sees exclusivism, inclusivism, and pluralism as incompatible constructs for understanding the relationship between Christianity and other faiths. At one level, my argument assumes exclusivism, inclusivism, and pluralism are theologically distinct and irreconcilable positions.[2] So a theologically exclusive understanding of the religions would insist that there is no Christian salvation outside either confession of Jesus Christ as Lord or Christian initiation (through baptism or otherwise) into the church. But this position would be compatible neither with a theological inclusivism that may assert the possibility of salvation in other faiths, albeit predicated on person and work of Christ, nor with a theological pluralism that insists that the religions are historically and culturally shaped responses to the divine, each mediating salvation to its devotees in its own way. If these definitions are assumed, one stakes a claim on one viewpoint, and either agrees to disagree with those who hold other positions, or actively and apologetically resists those arguments.

I suggest, however, that there is another level of analysis related to but distinct from a theological or doctrinal approach that has not been given sufficient consideration in this debate: that regarding Christian practices. While exclusivism, inclusivism, and pluralism may represent contrary theological positions, they may also be derivatives of basic forms of Christian practices, all of which, I believe, remain essential for the Christian encounter with other faiths in the twenty-first century. So then perhaps we need a new formulation of Christian theology of religions, one explicitly connected with Christian practices, in order to reintegrate Christian beliefs and practices regarding the religions in our time. I propose that a pneumatological theology of hospitality might serve the purposes of such a project designed to reconnect Christian beliefs and practices vis-à-vis the many faiths of the world.

I will present the basic building blocks for such a theological reconstruction in three steps. First, I proffer what I call a pneumatological theology of hospitality through a rereading of Luke and Acts. Second, I bring this Lukan theology of hospitality into dialogue with one of the most distinguished contemporary theorists of hospitality, the late Jacques Derrida, in order to further develop the idea of hospitality as a resource for thinking about the interrelationships between Christian beliefs and practices in a pluralistic world. The last section of this essay will make explicit how such a Lukan, Derridean, and pneumatological theology of hospitality can reinvigorate Christian theology of religions precisely through interweaving Christian beliefs about other faiths with Christian interfaith practices today. What follows, however, does not present a comprehensive argument for such a theological reorientation;[3] rather, my goal is to make some preliminary suggestions about one way of rethinking Christian theology of religions today: through the lens of a pneumatological theology of hospitality.

LUKE, THE SPIRIT, AND HOSPITALITY: MANY TONGUES EQUALS MANY PRACTICES

Of all the authors of the Christian Testament, arguably Luke can be called the theologian of the Spirit.[4] In his two-volume contribution to the Christian Testament, Jesus is consistently presented as the anointed one (the Christ) who is empowered by the Holy Spirit to preach the gospel to the poor, to release the captives, to free the oppressed, and to proclaim the saving Day of the Lord (see Luke 4:18–19; cf. Acts 10:36–38). By extension, the earliest followers of Jesus were also anointed and empowered by the same Spirit so that they could do the works that Jesus did. At least in terms of his understanding of the Spirit's work as being central not only in the life of Christ but also in the lives of the early Christians, Luke might be said to be the first pneumatological theologian.

I suggest, moreover, that the Spirit's anointing and empowering work in Luke-Acts can be further developed when read through the lens of hospitality.[5] To begin, Jesus himself can be understood to represent and embody the hospitality of God. This means not only that Jesus is the paradigmatic host of God's hospitality, but that he is also the exemplary recipient of hospitality, which is equally important. From his conception in Mary's womb to his birth in a manger through his burial (in a tomb of Joseph of Arimathea), Jesus was dependent on the welcome and hospitality of others. As "the Son of Man has nowhere to lay his head" (Luke 9:58), he relied on the goodwill of many, staying in their homes and receiving whatever they served. Thus during his public ministry, he is a guest of many hosts: Simon Peter, Levi, Martha, Zacchaeus, and various Pharisees and unnamed homeowners (e.g., 5:17; 7:36; 11:37; 14:1; and 22:10–14).

But it is in his role as guest that Jesus also announces and enacts the hospitality of God. Empowered by the Spirit, he heals the sick, casts out demons, and declares the arrival of the reign of God in the midst of the downtrodden, the oppressed, and the marginalized. Throughout his public ministry, Jesus as the recipient of hospitality also heralds and personifies the redemptive hospitality of God. More to the point, he is the "journeying prophet" who eats at the tables of others but also proclaims and brings to pass the eschatological banquet of God for all who are willing to receive it. From this perspective, the meal scenes have been rightly understood as speech acts through which Jesus calls for the religious leaders to repent of their self-serving interests precisely in order to "share in the meal fellowship with repentant and forgiven sinners."[6] Hence, Jesus frequently breaks the rules of hospitality, upsets the social conventions of meal fellowship (e.g., Jesus does not wash before dinner), and even goes so far as to rebuke his hosts. Luke thus shows that it is Jesus, not the religious leaders, who is the broker of God's authority, and it is on this basis that Jesus establishes the inclusive hospitality of the kingdom.

But Jesus is not only guest and host according to conventional understandings of hospitality; the inclusive hospitality of God that he preached and embodied involves also women, children, and slaves, as well as the poor, the crippled, the blind, and the lame, who are the oppressed and marginalized of the ancient world (Luke 14:21).[7] In other words, the hospitality of God in the life and ministry of Jesus covers not only interpersonal relations between guests and hosts, but also the wider sphere of social and political relations. This grander vision of divine hospitality is most clearly seen in the parable of the Good Samaritan (10:25–37). In spite of the fact that the Samaritans had just rejected Jesus' visitation (9:51–56), Jesus nevertheless presents a Samaritan as fulfilling the law, loving his neighbor, and embodying divine hospitality. We must not miss the fact that Samaritans were the social, cultural, political, and religious "others" to Jews in the first century. Against this background, what implications does this parable hold for contemporary relationships that span socioeconomic divides and that cross cultural and religious lines? Might those who are "others" to us Christians not only be instruments through whom God's revelation comes afresh to us, but also perhaps be able to fulfill the requirements for inheriting eternal life (10:25) precisely through the hospitality that they show to us neighbors?[8]

Now the question for us is this: what does the hospitality of Jesus—that given as host, and that received as guest—mean for those who confess him as Christ and Lord? Part of Luke's answer comes in his follow-up volume, the book of Acts. Put succinctly, the hospitality of God manifest in Jesus the Christ in Luke is now extended through the early church in Acts by the power of the same Holy Spirit. On the one hand, the Spirit is the divine guest resident in the hearts and lives of all the people of God upon whom she has been poured out; on the other hand, the Spirit empowers the body of Christ to bear witness of the hospitable God to the ends of the earth. As with Jesus, then, his followers are also anointed by the Spirit to be guests and hosts, in either case representing the hospitality of God. In Acts, this divine hospitality is most clearly reenacted in the life and ministry of the apostle Paul.

As with Jesus and Peter before him, Paul is also both a recipient and conduit of God's hospitality. He was first the beneficiary of divine hospitality through those who led him by the hand, and then through Judas on Straight Street, Ananias, other believers in Jesus who helped him escape from conspiring enemies, and Barnabas. Then during his missionary journeys, he is "prevailed" upon by Lydia, a new convert, to stay in her home, and then has his wounds treated by the Philippian jailer. Like Jesus the wandering Galilean, Paul the traveling missionary is also a guest of Jason of Thessalonica, Prisca and Aquilla and Titius Justus at

Corinth, Philip the evangelist (and his daughters) at Caesarea, Mnason in Jerusalem, and unnamed disciples at Troas, Tyre, Ptolemais, and Sidon (and who knows how may other places), staying with each for varying lengths of time.

Along the way, Paul is escorted by Bereans, protected by Roman centurions at different times and places, and entertained by Felix the governor. During the storm threatening the voyage to Rome, under custody, Paul hosts the breaking of bread, which itself becomes significant as a life-giving event that foreshadows the salvation of the 276 people on the ship (27:33–37). After the shipwreck, Paul is guest of the Maltese islanders in general and of Publius the chief official in particular—and here the guest extends the hospitality of God to his sick host (Publius) "by praying and putting his hands on him" (Acts 28:8b)—and then later of some brothers on Puteoli. The book of Acts closes with Paul as host, welcoming all who were open to receiving the hospitality of God.

I suggest that Paul, following in the footsteps of Jesus, is the paradigmatic guest and host representing the practices of the earliest Christians who took the gospel to the ends of the earth by the power of the Holy Spirit. For them, the house or home "becomes a new sort of sacred space, where the reign of God produces the community of grace, the house of God, Beth-El, where God dwells."[9] If the meal scenes in Luke's Gospel anticipated the eschatological banquet of God to come, in Acts these same meal and home scenes enact and realize the fellowship of God that marks the reconciliation of Jew, Samaritan, and Gentile, male and female, young and old, slave and free (cf. Acts 2:17–18) in the life of the early church. Hence the first Christians who had received the gift of God's Holy Spirit "had all things in common" (2:44), cared for one another, and ensured a "daily distribution of food" (6:1). It is within this framework of mutuality and hospitality that "day by day the Lord added to their number those who were being saved" (2:47b).

The foregoing Lukan theology of hospitality reflects the Trinitarian character of the hospitable God. The God who invites humanity to experience his redemptive hospitality in Christ by the Holy Spirit is the same God who receives the hospitality of human beings through Christ and the Holy Spirit. In this Trinitarian framework, Jesus is the normative, decisive, and eschatological revelation of the hospitable God, the Son of God who goes into a far country, to echo the words of Karl Barth.[10] Luke's portrait of the journey of the Son of God confirms his humiliation, his taking the form of a slave in obedience to the Father by the power of the Spirit, even to the point of death. But those who were hospitable to Jesus are now empowered by the same Spirit to walk in the footsteps of his filial obedience, to journey into the far countries at the ends of the earth, and to bear witness to the redemptive hospitality of God. Hence Trinitarian hospitality as manifest through the body of Christ is not only christomorphic but also pneumatocentric: empowered by the Holy Spirit.

We can see, however, that the Spirit's empowerment to bear witness to the gospel takes the form of many practices in the lives of Christ and the early church, each related to being guests and hosts in various times and places. I suggest that these many practices of the Spirit correlate with the diversity of tongues inspired by the Spirit on the Day of Pentecost.[11] Put alternatively, the many tongues of the Spirit announce the redemptive hospitality of God, even as the many deeds of the Spirit enact God's salvation through many hospitable practices. I suggest that many tongues require many hospitable practices because the life of church includes its mission in a pluralistic world. Hence believers in Jesus are sustained by the hospitable God not only because they have been born again into a new community, but also because the Spirit drives them into the world to interact with and receive the hospitality, kindness, and gifts of strangers of all sorts, even Samaritans, public or governmental officials, and "barbarians" (from the *barbaroi* on the isle of Malta, in Acts 28:2)! In a pluralistic world, many practices of hospitality are essential for the church's mission. Insofar as the Son of God has indeed journeyed into the far country, and insofar as the people of God have also been carried into far countries by the power of the Spirit, to that same extent the lines between those who are near and those who are far off have now been through the divine economy of redemptive hospitality.

DERRIDEAN HOSPITALITY: ABSOLUTE AND CONDITIONAL EMBRACES OF THE SPIRIT

I have so far presented a brief rereading of the pneumatological theology of Luke-Acts through the lens of hospitality. In this section, I wish to bring this Lukan theology of hospitality into dialogue with recent thinking about hospitality, specifically that articulated by the late Jacques Derrida (1930–2004). I think Derrida is an important dialogue partner for at least three reasons: first, in the way he invites us to think about the wider social and political dimensions of hospitality that we have already seen at work in the early church; second, in how his logic of absolute hospitality might compare and contrast with our pneumatological logic of Trinitarian hospitality; and finally, through his helping us identify what, if any, are the limits or conditions of hospitality. All of these matters deserve careful consideration as we anticipate application of our pneumatological theology of hospitality toward the reconstruction of a viable Christian theology of religions for the twenty-first century.

From the beginning, Derrida's thinking about hospitality has been shaped by the human rights debates (involving activists) in Prague, apartheid in South America, the question of "Algerian" refugees, and controversies about immigration and amnesty in France.[12] Amid these issues, Derrida observes that the primordial or originary violence is that such people have to ask for hospitality to begin with and that in a language not their own. Yet things get worse for strangers in foreign lands since the reception of hospitality itself creates an obligation on the part of guests to repay their hosts. Hence the offering of hospitality under the conditions of the economy of exchange sets in motion a never-ending cycle of indebtedness.

This leads to Derrida's observations about the impossibility of hospitality. It is not just that we have infinite obligations to others, but that insofar as we are caught up in the economy of exchange, there can be no true hospitality that is not already tainted by debts and obligations. And if what is owed or obligated cannot be freely given, then the paradox of hospitality is that it is continually threatened if not deconstructed by what might be called the logic of indebtedness. This is because even to say "I invite you" places the guest under obligation to reciprocate the host's invitation.

Derrida hence distinguishes between absolute hospitality that is freely given and the conditional hospitality of reciprocal indebtedness. The latter is structured by the economy of exchange and the logic of gratitude, depending in many ways on the conventions of place and time. The former, however, cannot depend on the "invitation," over which "we" retain control as hosts—whom we invite, under what conditions, and so on—but must be beholden to the "visitation." The visitation implies "the arrival of someone who is not expected, who can show up at any time. If I am unconditionally hospitable I should welcome the visitation, not the invited guest, but the visitor. I must be unprepared, or prepared to be unprepared, for the unexpected arrival of *any* other."[13] With the visitation, it is the guest (rather than the host) who is in charge, to arrive whenever he, she, or even it, wishes. With the visitation, not only neighbors but also strangers, even nonhumans (such as the animals in Noah's ark), are welcomed, so that "Hospitality is the deconstruction of the at-home."[14] In fact, the guest takes the place of the host, even to the point of holding the keys to the house. Derrida thus writes of the homeowner or master

> awaiting his guest as a liberator, his emancipator. . . . This is always the situation of the foreigner, in politics too, that of coming as a leg-islator to lay down the law and liberate the people or the nation by coming from outside, by entering into the nation or the house. . . . [It is] *as if,* then, the stranger could save the master and liberate the power of his host.[15]

The Derridean reversal is now clear: the host is hostage to the guest even as the guest now hosts the host/age's salvation, redemption, liberation.

I suggest the realization of Derrida's absolute hospitality presumes if not requires a theological dimension that we might call the Trinitarian logic of abundance. Amid the conditions of finitude, the impossibility of hospitality parallels the impossibility of the gift, structured as both are under the logic of exchange, reciprocity, and scarcity. Both hospital-ity and gifts are never unconditional—witness our "much obliged!" Fur-ther, givers themselves may be self-congratulatory about their charitable deeds. Finally, once the gift is taken, it is now a possession, not a gift. Precisely here we see why works righteousness based on the economy of exchange cannot finally save. Rather the divine economy of redemption can only be efficacious through the absolute gift of God, most lavishly bestowed in the incarnation and at Pentecost.

From a Lukan perspective, I suggest that the gift of the Holy Spirit and her outpouring "upon all flesh" (Acts 2:17) signifies this radical extension of God's economy of abundant hospitality to the whole world. In the economy of redemption, the unconditional gifts of God in Christ and the Holy Spirit mean that there is never any lack of divine hospi-tality to be offered and received. Rather, the graciousness of God over-turns the world's economy of exchange and reciprocity so that there is only an endless giving and receiving that now characterizes the relational identity of the people of God. This is because what is being given and what is being received is not any *thing*, but the triune God as manifest in the body of Christ and animated by the power of the Spirit.

So if what is needed, as Derrida suggests, is the redemption of the economy of exchange, then the answer might be found in such a Trinitarian theology of gracious mutuality. Rather than an excessive giving that would be taken as squandering if conceived within an economy of scarcity, the outpouring of the divine life through the Spirit reveals instead the abundance of a God whose gifts are extravagant, inexhaustible, free, and undeserved (completely gratuitous), but yet simultaneously directed nonsuperfluously toward equality and justice on the one hand, and toward the creation of a community of mutual givers on the other.[16] The Trinitarian logic that reveals God as Giver, Given, and Giving—a truly perichoretic hospitality—initiates, sustains, and solicits, rather than requiring (by law or otherwise) our own giving. In this pneumatological and Trinitarian framework, receivers do not "pay back" any incurred indebtedness dictated by an economy of scarcity so much as allow the gifts poured out to overflow through their lives into those of others because of the boundless hospitality of an excessively gracious God.

From a theological and pneumatological point of view, I argue that the Christian condition of being aliens and strangers in this world means both that we are perpetually guests, first of God and then of others, and that we should adopt the postures appropriate to receiving hospitality—from God through others—even when we find ourselves as hosts. Hence we need to take seriously our always being both guests and hosts, albeit in different respects in different contexts and relationships. As guests and hosts, sometimes simultaneously, we are obligated only to discern the Spirit's presence and activity so that we can perform the appropriate deeds representing the hospitable God. Which tongues we speak and what practices we engage will depend on where we are, whom we are interacting with, and what the social, political, and economic structures are that give shape to our encounter with others. In a pluralistic world, no one set of practices suffices. Yet the diversity of tongues and practices is possible only because we are caught up in the excessive hospitality of God that has been revealed in his Son and poured out through his Spirit upon us, and even upon all flesh.

THE SPIRIT, THE RELIGIONS, AND HOSPITALITY: RECONNECTING CHRISTIAN BELIEFS AND PRACTICES

In this last part of this chapter, I want to suggest how the pneumatological theology of hospitality that I have sketched above can contribute to charting one way forward for fresh Christian thinking about theology of religions today. My basic thesis is that when Christian beliefs about the religions (theology of religions) is understood as connected with and even emergent from basic Christian interfaith practices,[17] then a pneumatological theology of hospitality can help us embrace exclusivist, inclusivist, and pluralist practices so that what emerges is a more flexible, dynamic, and integrated theology of religions more appropriate for the Christian encounter with the religions in the twenty-first century. I will briefly unpack the basic elements of this hypothesis by looking at, in order, exclusivism, inclusivism, and pluralism.[18]

What are the practices "behind" Christian theological exclusivism regarding the religions? First, we distinguish between exclusivism as a theological idea (accepting this) and some of the attitudes and even practices that have come to be associated with it, such as elitism, triumphalism, proselytism, and even the colonial enterprise (rejecting these). If we begin with the former theological understanding of exclusivism, it consists, I suggest, of three basic sets of ideas, introduced in the New Testament and reshaped in the history of Christian practices. First, exclusivism is deeply informed by the missionary impulse encapsulated in the Great Commission. If Christian salvation is tied in with the person and work of Jesus of Nazareth, then the commission to take the gospel to the ends of the earth revolves around bearing witness to the Christ. But secondly, exclusivism was also forged amid and through the hostilities experienced by the early church at the hands of persecutors. Early Christian sectarianism was, at least in part, a response of threatened Christian communities under pressure from other religious groups (the Second Temple Jewish leadership, for example[19]), sociocultural forces, and governmental dictates. Against this background, Christian identity was itself at stake, and the church's practices led to the formation of a distinctive Christian community. Finally, extended into the later history of Christian thought, the axiom "no salvation outside the church" (*extra ecclesia nulla salus*) itself emerged through intra-Christian disputes about ecclesial and episcopal authority, sacramental efficacy, and the nature of heresy. The question here was how to be the one body of Christ amid the disintegration of Christian practices, and it was only later that the formula itself was applied to those of other faiths "outside" the church.[20]

My proposal is that a pneumatological theology of hospitality allows us to retrieve and reappropriate some of these fundamental Christian practices for the interfaith encounter even as we reject as anti-Christian the elitist, triumphalist, and colonialist attitudes regarding the religions.

The central practices underlying exclusivism, it seems to me, are those related to Christian proclamation and those related to Christian identity. How is the Christian interfaith encounter empowered with regard to these central elements when set in a framework of hospitality? From the perspective of Christian hosting of people of other faiths, there is no denying both that hosts invite guests into the home "space" or "turf" (which requires hosts to be who they are rather than pretending to be something or someone else), and that hosts create a "safe" environment for their guests (which allows their guests to be who they are rather than having to be something or someone else). This means that there will be opportunities for bearing witness, but that such testimonies are sensitive to the power that is wielded by hosts and also respectful of the vulnerability of guests. From the perspective of being guests of people of other faiths (as missionaries often find themselves), the appropriate moments for Christian proclamation must be discerned. Guests must defer to hosts, and not needlessly antagonize or disrespect those who are providing for their needs. At the same time, as guests develop relationships with their hosts, they will be more attuned to the host culture so that any sharing of the gospel will be more appropriately "contextualized" (or "inculturated" or "accommodated") to host-perspectives. Central to Christian proclamation in the guest-host dynamic, then, is the discernment of the Spirit's leading. In some contexts, the gospel is declared up front, while in others, verbal articulation may have to be postponed (perhaps indefinitely, depending on how the future unfolds). Which is which depends on how Christian hosts and guests discern the work of the Spirit in their midst.

What about Christian inclusivism regarding the religions? Inclusivism as a theological idea, I suggest, has been honed out of two streams of development over the last century: that related to the Christian mission and that related to Christian participation in the academy. In the former case, the Christian missionary movement gradually was impacted by their observations that perhaps there was a sense in which God had been present and active among those being missionized long before the missionaries arrived. There was a growing recognition of the richness of the social, cultural, and even religious history of non-Christian peoples that could not be dismissed. At the same time, most of the missionaries were convinced that even if Christian salvation had been accessible all along, the basis of such salvation was the person and work of Jesus Christ.

Similarly, Christian involvement in especially the theological academy gradually brought about the realization that there were moral values, cultural aesthetics, and even religious and theological insights in the various non-Christian religious texts. Further, with the acknowledgment of the close tie between religious beliefs and practices (as argued, for example, by Lindbeck) came also the awareness that religious conversion was not just a matter of exchanging one set of beliefs for another, but involved a complicated and extended process of resocialization (or "enreligionisation" as Aloysius Pieris calls it).[21] This meant that Christian religious scholars and theologians could no longer just learn about the doctrines of other faiths, but also had to develop ways to appreciate other religious practices. Hence as Christians, such scholars reformulated the exclusivist doctrine in two directions: in order to account for the possibility that people of other faiths might well have access to the saving grace of God in Christ, even if not known by those names (Rahner's "anonymous Christian" hypothesis), and in order to provide theological justification for taking the Christian dialogue with other faiths more seriously. With the latter option, the goal is not to be more effective evangelists (even if such might be a by-product) but to learn from and perhaps even be transformed as Christians by the encounter with other religious traditions and their representatives.

At one level, I suggest, Christian inclusivism is a theological strategy that values the interfaith dialogue and encounter for its own sake or for the sake of what it meant for Christians themselves, rather than as being instrumental for other purposes (e.g., related to proselytization). Within the pneumatological theology of hospitality I am proposing, this fundamental thrust of Christian inclusivism is preserved and even brought to the fore. From the perspective of Christians as hosts to people of other faiths, for example, there is clearly the Levinasian and even Derridean sense that the host is "hostage" to the guest. This means not that the guest is free to destroy the host (remember that there is always protocol constraining the actions of guests in the presence of hosts), but rather that Christian hosts welcome guests not only for the sake of guests but also to be enriched by them. This enrichment is only possible, of course, if guests are received, to the degree such is possible, on their own cultural and religious terms rather than on the terms established by their Christian hosts. I suggest that such mutuality and reciprocity is precisely what is fostered in the pneumato-theological framework proposed here.[22] Christian hosts receive from their guests freely precisely because they have received freely from God and are in the position of being able to lavishly open up to guests out of the abundance of divine hospitality. The emphasis here is on Christians participating in the redemptive hospitality of God and being continuously transformed in the process, rather than on converting people of other faiths to Christianity. If the latter happens, of course, Christians rejoice—but only because they themselves have already been enriched through the interfaith encounter.

From the perspective of Christian guests being "entertained" by hosts belonging to other faith traditions, there needs to be sensitivity about the social and political framework structuring the encounter. Christian guests who are "professional" missionaries to other countries play by one set of rules, while Christian refugees, exiles, or im/migrants who are beneficiaries from cultures and peoples of other faiths play by another.[23] There are many other forms of Christian guests being hosted by those in other faiths. I would argue, however, that regardless of socioeconomic or political circumstances, the "Christian as guest" is actually a normative Christian posture. The Christian Testament talks about Christian existence in terms of being aliens and sojourners in strange lands. As such, there is always a deferral to our hosts, a recognition that we receive the gospel precisely through the "others"—the Good Samaritans, or the hungry, the poor, the naked, and those in prison (cf. Matt. 25:31–46)[24]—who have been given to us by God. Yet such deferral is deeply informed by a dynamic Christian identity that is seeking life in the city to come (Heb. 11). A pneumatological theology of hospitality accentuates this guest-mentality precisely by emphasizing how guests need to be discerning about their relationships with hosts, to act appropriately in the myriad circumstances that frame guest-host relations, and to be sensitive to the many tongues and practices that might be inspired by the Spirit for life in a pluralistic world.

Finally, what about a pluralistic understanding of the religions? I think the pluralistic option problematic in terms of its formal theological claim: that the various religions are but culturally and historically differentiated responses to the divine, each viable in its own way. The difficulties I have with this claim have been voiced by many others and concern its assumptions that the many religions of the world are all seeking Christian salvation, that pluralists have something like a "God's eye view" from the mountaintop (as it were) that allows them to see the various religious trails are actually converging as they make their way up the side of the mountain, and that the particular claims of the religious are reinterpreted according to Christian premises. But when we switch to the level of Christian practices, however, I affirm the following commitments of pluralist advocates: to insist on an epistemological humility that fosters rather than shuts down dialogue and the process of inquiry (Hick); to develop dynamic and flexible if not multiple religious forms of Christian identity in a pluralistic world (Panikkar); to lift up a liberationist criterion for assessing the capacity of the religions to enable human flourishing (Knitter); to be more intentional about the social and political dimensions and implications of Christian interfaith relations (Pieris), and so on. I suggest that for these pluralist interpretations, the practices underlying their theological claims are most important.

It is here that I think a pneumatological theology of hospitality can in fact preserve what is most important about pluralist convictions without having to embrace their theological speculations. To begin, the practice of Christian hospitality in the academy will encourage a hermeneutic of charity with regard to different, even opposing, views, without lapsing into epistemological, hermeneutical, or theological relativism; this virtue secures the concerns of those such as Hick without adopting his theory of the Real.[25] Further, the sustained practice of hospitality will transform both hosts and guests, and at this phenomenological level, the observations of those like Panikkar that there are many forms of Christian identity are on the mark. But guests and hosts remain distinct (although they may in fact change positions) rather than morphing into one, so that hospitality will always involve the give-and-take of differences rather than devolving into any (pejoratively construed) syncretism. The pneumatological theology of hospitality I am proposing provides theological warrant for both the hermeneutics of charity and the kind of dynamic and transformational processes advocated by pluralistic theologians without endorsing their theological hypotheses.

Finally, the liberationist and sociopolitical concerns of pluralists like Knitter and Pieris are essential for both Christian theology and practices. A pneumatological theology of hospitality based on the lives and ministries of Jesus and the earliest Christians, as recorded by Luke, would observe that the Spirit's empowerment to bear witness involves not only the proclamation of the gospel but also the release of captives and those on the underside of history and the formation of a new community that stands in stark social, economic, and political contrast to the dominant powers that be, whether of the first-century Roman Empire or the twenty-first-century empire of market capitalism. The tension for Christians today is how to be both socioeconomically and politically engaged without being merely sectarian. The interreligious arena provides one of the challenging test cases for such negotiation of Christian identity and practices, since many of the most important questions to be engaged on those fronts—like global warming, environmental waste, economic justice, and civil rights—cannot be addressed by isolated communities working on their own. Rather, these matters require Christians be inspired by the Spirit of hospitality to work together not only with non-Christians in general but also with people in other faiths more specifically. At this level, pluralist theologians like Knitter and Panikkar are right: the truth of Christian faith and of other religious traditions depends, at least in part, on how their devotees respond to the injustices that persist in the human condition. And from a pneumatological point of view, perhaps one way to understand the Spirit's outpouring on all flesh (Acts 2:17) is as God's means of galvanizing human beings to join hands across faith lines to act concertedly in ways that will make a difference in the world.

My goal in this chapter has been to retrieve and perhaps reappropriate traditional Christian discourse about the religions. Toward that end, I have suggested that exclusivism, inclusivism, and pluralism are indicative not only about what Christians believe about other religions, but that they perhaps encapsulate distinctive Christian interfaith postures and practices. I am convinced that we must inculcate and nurture the wide range of these practices even if we do not endorse their associated theological claims. To do so, I have proposed a pneumatological theology of hospitality to accomplish this task. On the one hand, the pneumatological aspect of my proposal, developed from out of the early church's, specifically Luke's, narratives of hospitality, insists that the many tongues of Pentecost can be understood not only to open up to the many practices of the earliest Christians but also to have been anticipated and paradigmatically enacted by the hospitable life of Jesus the Christ, the one anointed by the Spirit. On the other hand, the hospitality aspect of my thesis, developed in dialogue with Derrida, expands on the dynamic practices of early Christian hospitality toward what might be called a pneumatological theology of guests and hosts that enables mutual engagement and mutual transformation without negating their distinctive and particular witnesses. It is within this framework of a pneumatological theology of interreligious hospitality that I think we can invigorate the wide range of Christian practices that have been subsumed over time into exclusivist, inclusivist, or pluralist theologies, without having to take on the impossible assignment of blending these theological positions into a coherent whole. If the preceding ideas have any value, then the latter undertaking has itself now been transformed, I believe, by the Spirit of the hospitable God.

6
The Spirit Rests on the Son Paraphysically

Eugene F. Rogers Jr.

Mary's eyes   beholding Eve
   And looking down on Adam, were impelled to tears,
But she stays them   and hastens
     To conquer nature   she who para phusin gave birth to
     Christ her son.
                  Romanos the Melodist, Hymn XI[1]

The Spirit rests on the Son paraphysically: alongside, in excess of, and in addition to the physical. It rests on the Son paraphysically because the Son became physical, incarnate. It rests on the Son paraphysically as its *gift* to the Son, a gift of solidarity and company with the Son, the Spirit's own characteristic gift of witness and koinonia. It rests on the Son paraphysically as a gift to the *Son,* to the one who took on a body and a human nature, or *phusis.* The Son does not need the Spirit to obtain a body or remain divine: but, counting neither body nor divinity a thing to be grasped, the Son may choose to receive from the Spirit what he enjoys by right.[2]

The Spirit rests on the Son paraphysically because the Spirit gives itself—or in the Syriac tradition, herself—to *accompany* the physical for the Son's sake. The Spirit rests on the Son paraphysically because the Spirit *befriends* the physical for the Son's sake. The Spirit rests on the Son paraphysically because the Spirit *transcends* and *surpasses* the physical for the Son's sake. The Spirit rests on the Son paraphysically because it is the physical that the Spirit elevates, perfects, and glorifies; it is the

87

physical, rather than something else, that the Spirit goes on from; it is the physical, and not something else, that the Spirit transforms. (That means the Spirit transforms the soul, too: The soul is not nonphysical in the New Testament, and not divorced from the physical until Descartes; the soul is the form of the body, and part of the human nature, or *phusis*. Even faith comes "by hearing," and grace by water and the word.) The Spirit redeems *the body* because she rests on the Son paraphysically, wishes to give the Son the additional, superfluous gifts of other human bodies redeemed. The Spirit wishes to give the Son the gift of *other* human bodies redeemed because the Son has shown, in his incarnation and death, that he loves human bodies. The Spirit wishes to give the Son more of what he loves. The Spirit resurrects *the body* because she rests on the Son paraphysically, wishes to give the Son the additional, superfluous gift—to give it *para*, alongside, in addition to, in excess of— other human bodies resurrected. The Spirit wishes to give the Son the gift of other, additional human bodies, in excess of—*para*—his own, paraphysically, because the Son has shown that he loves human bodies, even when dead. As in the icon of the Anastasis, the Son takes the dead human body by the hand, holds it, lies in solidarity and company with it, lifts and loves and takes it with him. The Spirit comes to dwell paraphysically—as if physically, beyond physically—in these our mortal bodies, so that we too should be raised from the dead (Rom. 8:11). She does that because she loves, rests on, accompanies, is in addition to and excess of—*para*—the Son. The Spirit is the para-Son, another comforter, the para-advocate, the Paraclete.[3] Why another? Is not the Son enough? Yes, but that is the para-logic, the logic of excess, the economy of abundance. As the para-Son, the Spirit makes additional sons to the Son, brothers with him and fellow-heirs with Christ. As the para-Son she *adopts,* she performs *huiothesia,* the making of additional sons.[4] In ancient rhetoric, adopted sons received the *pneuma* of their adoptive fathers quasi-biologically, as natural sons received the *pneuma* of their natural fathers by sexual conception, so that adopted sons, by *krasis* or mixing, could inherit even physical characteristics from both fathers.[5] The Spirit does this, too. "Not of blood nor of the will of the flesh, or of the will of a man,"[6] but adoptively, para-naturally, and indeed once again by flesh and blood, if we mean by the flesh and the blood of the One she accompanies. She does this neither naturally nor unnaturally, but paraphysically, by adoption, where the water breaks from above in baptism.

The Father creates the body; the Son assumes the body; the Spirit deifies the body. Each appropriates in the economy what each does in the Trinity. The Father sources the Son and the Spirit. The Word expresses the Father. The Spirit perfects the community of the Three. So the Father sources also the body; so the Son expresses also the body; so the Spirit perfects also the body.

The Spirit divinizes, perfects already in the Trinity? The Spirit makes God the God that God is, the Trinity: The Spirit makes God perfectly the God that God is, completing the God triune. "The Spirit searches everything, even the depths of God."[7] If, as many patristic authors agree, the Spirit's appropriated activity in the economy is *teleopoiesis,* perfecting or completing, then that can only be by analogous activity among the Three. If the Spirit's appropriated activity in the economy gathers community, *koinonia,* then that can only occur by analogous activity among the Three. If the Spirit's appropriated activity in the economy is to divinize, that can only be by analogous activity among the Three. So Basil of Caesarea—trying to avoid the then-novel assertion "the Holy Spirit is God" and thereby offending the Pneumatomachians, lands in a much bolder assertion: that the Holy Spirit is "none other than the divine-and-blessed-Trinity-completing Spirit of God"; that the Holy Spirit makes the Trinity, too, a community, completes and perfects it, fills it out as the God that the Trinity is.[8] Because the Holy Spirit diversifies God in the Trinity, so it distinguishes human beings also in the economy. Because the Holy Spirit makes God the God that God is in the Trinity, so it divinizes human beings also in the economy. Because the Holy Spirit makes community in the Trinity, so it gathers human beings also in the economy. Because the Holy Spirit makes the Trinity blessed, so it blesses even human beings in the economy. We need not know what these words mean in the Trinity, to understand the logic that ascribes to the Trinity the appropriations in the economy.

But the works of the Trinity toward the outside are indivisible. So the Holy Spirit does not do what it does for human beings *by itself.* The Holy Spirit does what it does for human beings from the Father and alongside, *para,* the Son. And yet it does not merely repeat the work of the Son, but enlarges and expands it, giving it the divine character of infinity or unboundedness. Better, the Holy Spirit gives not a static character of unboundedness, but it performs, enacts, and unbinds infinity; it crosses boundaries, transgresses them. That is what it means, according to Gregory Nazianzen, to be divine.[9] Thus it falls to the Spirit, the Lord and Giver of life, to transgress the bound of the incarnation that is death and reunite Father and Son in the Resurrection. Thus it falls to the Spirit, the Spirit of adoption, to transgress the bound of the incarnation that is ethnic identity and make the Messiah of Israel also the Savior of Gentiles. So the Spirit also works *para,* beyond, in excess of the Son.

The Latin tradition hesitated before translating *para phusin* as *contra naturam.* Rufinus tried *extra naturam;* Tertullian *ultra naturae;* the Codex Boerneriani *secus naturam.*[10] The *Glossa Ordinaria* preserved the sense of excess so that Aquinas could class the *vitium contra naturam* under the rubric of *luxuria,* excess.[11] *Extra:* the Spirit adds to the Son. *Ultra:* the Spirit goes beyond the Son. *Secus:* the Spirit stays close or next to the Son, in his human as in his divine nature. These translations of *para* indicate no contrariety: The Spirit *parallels* the Son, accompanying and befriending also other human bodies for his sake, and including even Gentile bodies as an extra, additional, superfluous gift to him. The Spirit *emparables* the Son, redescribing, retelling, and renarrating other human lives for his sake, including even Gentile lives as an extra, additional, superfluous gift to him. The Spirit is a *Paraclete* for the Son, one who calls or cries out alongside, who advocates, for other human beings in sighs too deep for words, teaching even Gentiles to call the God of Israel "Father" as an extra, additional, superfluous gift to him. That is what it means for the Spirit to work alongside and in excess of the Son, but never against him.

The Son, as Athanasius says, logifies the body, or retells it, makes it once more into God's own argument. The Spirit inspires the body, divinizes and glorifies it, prepares it for koinonia with the Trinity. The Son begs the Father to receive a body from the Spirit,[12] that those with bodies may receive the Spirit for communion with the Father, to witness or see the Father.

This is so far, you might object, no argument. At most it is an elaboration, a conceit. It is not logical, but more of an unfolding, unrolling, unbraiding of the Spirit's pattern. That feature of the exposition is itself revealing. The Spirit does not follow a straightforward logic, you might say, but a logic of its own, a paralogic.[13] What would that mean? Something that accompanies logic, expands upon it, embroiders, elaborates, filigrees, celebrates it. Especially if "logic" means "having to do with the Logos." What is paraphysical in the economy, accompanying the human nature taken on by the Logos, is first paralogical in the Trinity, accompanying the Logos in itself, ready to expand upon its structure and story. As the Breath of God accompanies and amplifies God's Word, so the Paralogical—or the Paraclete—accompanies and amplifies the Logos. So the Paraclete paralogically cries also for us human beings in sighs and groans too deep for words.

Does this define the Spirit by the Son, the Paraclete by the Word, the Paralogical by the Logos? Does this make the Spirit the creature of the Son (as Barth attempts, and Gregory decries[14])? No, the Spirit herself is God. As God she chooses to make Trinity of the Father and the Son and so deify them, that is, make them together the God that they are, not just any god, but this God, the one, true God, Father, Son, and Spirit.

The Spirit is not only paralogical, amplifying the Word, but also parapaternal, extending the Father, because the Spirit is the Spirit of adoption (Rom. 8:15, 23; Gal. 4:5–6). She teaches other human beings—Gentiles—to call the God of Israel "Father." The Spirit is the Spirit of *huiothesia,* "son-making," responsible for the sonship too by which Israel is God's son, the son of the Father (Rom. 9:4; Exod. 4:22; Deut. 14:1). The Spirit is the Spirit of *huiothesia* also in the conception of Jesus, the Son of the Father *par excellence.* In all those ways the Spirit is parapaternal, enlarging the paternity of the Father.

Indeed, as Romanos the Melodist insists, the Spirit enlarges the paternity of the Father *para phusin,* expanding on nature, in the virgin birth. The author of the *Gospel of Philip*—for whom the Spirit is feminine—worries that the virgin birth is *para phusin* in another sense, if Mary and the Spirit are both female: "Some have said, 'Mary conceived of the Holy Spirit.' They are wrong . . . when did a woman ever conceive of a woman?"[15] The comment reveals more than anxiety. "Their women exchanged natural relations for [relations *para phusin*], and the men likewise gave up natural relations with women and were consumed with passion for one another" (Rom. 1:26–27 RSV). If Paul, with the rabbis, regards female sexuality like Gentile sexuality as excessive,[16] and thus thinks of women before men as examples of same-sex activity, then the Gentile excesses of Romans 1 and the female excess of the virgin birth cease to seem so obviously unrelated. Philip protests too much. Paul may not know the virgin birth, but he sees Gentile and female sexuality alike. The Spirit enlarges the paternity of the Father both in the virgin birth and in the coming in of the Gentiles. The Spirit, if not Paul, analogizes the virgin birth and the rebirth of the Gentiles. She, if not he, patterns them alike. She widens the womb and prolongs the Parousia. The Spirit dilates: she both magnifies and delays, *o felix dilatio!* And it is nature she dilates, expanding space and extending time for the Son, making room for the babe in the virgin, for the Gentiles among God's people. She makes room for God in human nature. The paralogic of the Spirit relates virgin birth and Gentile inclusion as incarnation and church.

The Spirit relates to the Son in the Trinity paralogically, and to the Father in the Trinity parapaternally. It is both those intra-Trinitarian relationships that give rise in the economy to the Spirit's paraphysicality. The Spirit's befriending of the body and of matter creates both more *koinonones*—participants, sharers[17]—in the identity of the Son, and more adoptive children for the Father. The Spirit extends both the logic—the identity, the story—of the Son, and the paternity of the Father. She extends both paraphysically, by creating human beings who cry "Father" with the Son. The paraphysicality of the Spirit in the economy has at least two roots in the Trinity—her parapaternity toward the Father, and her paralogic toward the Son.

Thus the Spirit manifests herself particularly at baptism, where she births children of the Father and tellers of Jesus' story. Baptism is at once a parapaternal rite of adoption, whereby the Spirit makes more children for the Father, and a paraphysical concretion of witnesses, whereby the Paraclete creates more witnesses of the Son and callers on the Father.

Thus the Spirit focuses on *Gentiles*, unlikely children of the Father, who is the God of *Israel:* the Spirit's mission exceeds the Son's to be Messiah of Israel. The Spirit focuses on *women,* unlikely sons (that is, inheritors) of the Father: the Spirit's embodiment in the church bends the Son's embodiment in a male. The Spirit focuses on *slaves,* unlikely recipients of freedom: the Spirit's freedom prolongs the Son's to liberate society. It is by the Spirit that in the Son and to the Father there is no male and female, no Jew or Gentile, no slave or free. And the Spirit focuses on *sinners,* unlikely witnesses to the Son: the Spirit exceeds the Father's election of the holy and righteous. The Spirit frees the Son to defer the completion of his mission by death, and frees the Father to elect also sinners.[18]

Paul exploits his sense that Gentiles are more physical, excessively physical. He fashions a trope of Gentiles to expose the physicality of the Spirit. He associates Gentiles with idol worship: Gentiles are so excessively physical, that they assume physical idols for God. And yet idol worshipers are not wrong, just hasty: God will choose to become physical, available. God is not trapped outside or counter to the physical, but may draw close, to indwell, accompany, and transcend the physical, may be *paraphysical.* This radicalizes God's transcendence: God so transcends the world as to come closer to it than it is to itself.

The Spirit takes Gentiles into the people of the God of Israel, idolatry into the icon, the body of Christ. Even the *dead* body brings salvation. In Romans 1 the problem with Gentiles is that they "exchanged the glory of the *immortal* God for images resembling a *mortal* human being or birds or four-footed animals or reptiles" (1:23) and for that reason "they deserve to die [out]" (1:32): that is, idol worshipers acquire death from their dead gods by not reproducing. But in Christ, they acquire life from their dead God—not by reproduction, but by baptism and by bread.

The Spirit likes Gentiles because they are paraphysical, *like it is* (Rom. 1). Romans 1 presents Gentiles as excessively physical, sexual, desirous. The Spirit too is desirous—desirous of them. The Spirit discovers in the Gentiles those who transgress boundaries, *as she does.* Paul describes both the Gentiles and the work of salvation as *para phusin* because they have something in common: a physicality so desirous, so extreme, as to seem excessive, as of someone so in love as to lay down his life for his friends, so sexual as to adopt Gentiles. Paul describes both the work of the Spirit and the salvation of Gentiles as *para phusin* because the Spirit and the Gentiles *share something.* In saving the Gentiles, the God of Israel takes on something of the Gentiles' characteristic of excessive sexuality: it's promiscuous, or bigamous, like grafting the wild onto the domestic. "You have been cut from what is by nature a wild olive tree and grafted, contrary to nature [*para phusin*], into a cultivated olive tree" (Rom. 11:24).

The *content* of the paraphysical is narrated, logified. It arises from the stories of Jesus and how he re-befriends the body in his incarnation, his healings, his friendships with people of strong desires, like ascetics, prostitutes, and tax collectors; his going to death rather than abandoning solidarity with mortals. Jesus is not one who denies his desire by going to his death: he is someone who expresses the greatness of his desire by going to his death. "The crucifixion of Jesus with its pneumatic sequel is the final liberation of desire into the divine union that all desire is groping toward."[19] He shows there how great is his desire for the embodied, for humanity. The paraphysical contains the protoerotic.[20] Yearning, desire passes easily beyond the physical without leaving it behind. That's why the Spirit can use desire; that's why the Spirit calls out to and evokes it; that's why she inflames and purifies it. The desire of the Son for humanity is paraphysical, to divinize the human phusis. The paraphysicality of the Spirit carries forward the incarnation by other means; it elaborates the work of the Son and amplifies the groans of the Word.

Desire is paraphysical also in God. Because God befriends the body
in the incarnation, God's desire for human beings becomes physical.
God's desire for human beings elevates by the body. So salvation
becomes paraphysical from God's side, turning God's desire for humans
into something that accompanies and befriends the physical. So the
paraphysicality of desire is not first of all a fact of anthropology, a fact
about human beings. It is first of all a fact about God's bringing human
beings to Godself, about the Trinity's work of inclusion, about the Trinitarian embrace. We appropriate to the Father the Trinity's creation of
beings whom God desires to bring to Godself *with bodies.* We appropriate to the Son the Trinity's redemption of those with bodies whom God
desires to bring to Godself *by means of an incarnation.* We appropriate
to the Spirit the Trinity's expanding the work of the Messiah beyond the
crucifixion *in the redemption of our bodies,* as well as the Trinity's expanding the work of the Messiah beyond the Jews to those Gentiles who, by
worshiping dead idols, represent physicality, nonprocreative sexuality,
and death.

The paraphysicality of the Spirit also allows a reversal of the fall.
Adam's grasping after the fruit represents a desire to be God before or
apart from God's gift (Gen. 3:5). Adam would take by force (Gen. 3:6,
LXX: *labousa . . . ephagen,* Eve taking, ate) what God would give in time.
Adam's sin has the form of grasping, whether pride, theft, impatience,
or rape: the refusal to wait upon the gift of another. After the fall, Adam
looks down at his body and feels shame. He hides his genitals. Why?
Because his body tells the *truth,* and gives Adam the lie: he is not divine,
but still a creature. Adam hates the truth that he is not (yet) god. He
regards his body with scorn. Christ begins by befriending the body that
Adam had scorned.[21] He counts equality with God "not a thing to be
grasped [*ouk harpargmon*] . . . taking [*labon*] the form of a servant, being
born in the likeness of human beings" (Phil. 2:6–7 RSV). The Spirit
ends by redeeming even Adam's seizure: the Spirit too seizes, enraptures
(*haparxo,* Acts 8:39, 2 Cor. 12:2, 4; Rev. 12:5), so that Adam's theft
becomes Paul's prize.

Moreover, Adam's theft becomes Christ's command: "Take, eat"
(*labete, phagete,* Matt. 26:26). Eden's curse, "In the sweat of thy face
shalt thou eat bread" (Gen. 3:19 KJV; LXX: *phagei ton arton*) becomes
Christ's promise (*labon ho Iesus arton,* Matt. 26:26), the bread of his
physical body, his paraphysical bread (*arton epiousion,* Matt. 6:11), the
bread of heaven. The bread of heaven transforms, because the saying is
true, that we are what we eat.[22] Under the Spirit, eating becomes no

longer fall but sacrament, taking no longer rape but rapture. And yet that does not happen—the sweat of Adam's brow does not become the blood of Christ, and the toil in the field does not become the bread of heaven—except paraphysically, by the resting of the Spirit on the Son, and for the Son's sake on matter. The Spirit rests on the Son paraphysically, so that she can gather the diverse, and diversify the corporate, to vary and manifest the body of the Son.

7

The Spirit Holy, Hip, and Free

Barbara A. Holmes

Studies of contemporary culture have come increasingly to recognize the importance of what has been termed "folk piety." Whereas formal religion is characterized by codified doctrines, ecclesiastical organizations and professional clergy, folk piety consists of relatively amorphous beliefs, is extra-ecclesiastical, and is located among the common people.[1]

Picture it! A weathered-looking man dressed from head to toe in black clothing enters one of the fanciest malls in Dallas, Texas. He has ashes on his forehead, white socks, and a long wooden staff in his hand. In a stammering and raspy voice, he cries out, "Jesus loves you and died for you; turn your life around. Tomorrow is not promised. Will you continue to buy what the moth will eat, or store up treasures in heaven?" He looks like Johnny Cash's great great granddaddy. He takes a guitar from a ratty case, and begins to weave his way past chic store windows. The song he is singing is no ordinary hymn: "God is God, God don't never change, God is God . . . always stays the same." The crowds part around him as he walks. Some observers are amused, others ridicule, few listen, and security is on the way.

FOLK PIETY AND MALL PROPHETS

The person I have just described is the spiritual leader of an independent holiness sect that is headquartered in Texas and related to a network of loosely associated small churches throughout the United States. The ministries are connected not by creeds but by their "in but not of the world" commitments. Every decision is filtered through a belief in the imminent coming of the Savior. Believers seldom think in terms of career, because all will pass away when Christ comes. Temporary and functional jobs are preferred because they provide basic support, but don't take time away from worship and service to the church. I encountered this ministry while I was practicing law in Texas. I found their community values to be as affirming as an embrace, but their beliefs, core narratives, and idiosyncratic biblical interpretations both intrigued and confused me.

For the purposes of this chapter, the mall prophet's name is not as important as the folk piety prevalent in this style of ministry. Although there are many "Spirit-filled" sects who share the same beliefs, most are grounded in a postmodern religious ethos. The mall prophet's sect seems to emerge from a time warp. The women are clad in long dresses, their ears are sans "earbobs," hair is not cut (because it is the woman's glory), and makeup is shunned. The men dress austerely and leadership is granted to the person with the most evident and powerful manifestations of spiritual gifts. No smoke and mirrors for these folks; all gifts must be verifiable.

If the gift is prophecy, the forecasts must come true; if the gift is healing, someone must "take up their bed and walk." The mall prophet passed this test. I have seen him lift his staff and speak about events that would occur in the next hour, and they did. In the middle of a sermon, he stops; his eyes glaze over, becoming opaque. When he speaks his voice is distant and unusual in timbre and tone. He says, "There is an accident coming right outside of this tent. Don't leave right now. . . . I can't stop it but we can pray for the souls that will be lost." Followers immediately obey, and all that can be heard is glossolalia and wailing. Within twenty minutes, tires screech, a truck careens, and bodies are strewn over a rural highway.

As dramatic as this incident was, the mall prophet was surprisingly unassuming about his "gifts." I expected some show business pizzazz from this man that they called "prophet." Instead, I encountered a scrawny Anglo man with a very raspy voice and shockingly blue eyes, who commanded the attention of everyone within earshot. The followers were from every station in life, from middle-class seekers to poverty-stricken farmers from varied ethnic groups. But the most surprising thing of all was that by evangelical television show standards, he could not preach. Because they called him "prophet," I expected passionate

and compelling homiletical skills, but his preaching was just the opposite. His sermons were rambling and disjointed and barely understand-
able even with a microphone. He seemed to be making biblical small
talk, killing time, waiting for something.

On some nights nothing happened. The rambling ended with prayer
and an entreaty to fast and prostrate themselves before the Lord. But on
other nights, as if lightning were striking a power plant, something
incredible occurred. His persona and voice took on a power that sent
chills running up your spine. I don't have words to describe those times,
as I was just as transfixed as everyone else. He used no notes, he preached
directly from the Bible, but the insights and power of his delivery
exceeded his eighth-grade education.

The mall prophet is one among many grassroots leaders of similar
description. They can be found throughout the United States. The ministries that they lead operate below the media radar screen, unless the
oddities of their practices (e.g., snake handling, cultic healing practices,
or other unorthodox beliefs and literalist views) come to public attention. The existence of holiness expressions of folk piety surfaced a few
years ago when Robert Duvall captured the personality of a typical
leader in the film *The Apostle*. Reviewer Aaron Gallegos said this about
Duvall's portrayal of grassroots spiritual leadership:

> I have a confession to make. After viewing Robert Duvall's *The Apos-
> tle*, I want to return—for the first time in nearly twenty years—to the
> Pentecostal church. I realized I missed preaching that overflows with
> gospel clichés and the strange howl of people overcome with the Holy
> Ghost. I miss the big hair, the big cars, and the big extravaganzas put
> on to "win back our city for Christ." . . . I miss feeling the completely
> other-worldly sensation of being a born-again Holy Ghost filled
> believer. Don't get me wrong, I'm still a believer. But while watching
> *The Apostle,* I longed to be once again part of a culture of Christians
> who aren't the least bit embarrassed that their neighbors think they're
> nuts for yelling at God all night long.[2]

Gallegos is longing for the raw, unmediated exchange that is currently
muted by polite liturgies and spiritual conformity. Folk piety makes
room for present-day prophets who holler in the middle of the night to
get God's attention. In *The Apostle,* the surprise of Spirit-led practices
and issues in the lives of ordinary people startled those of us accustomed
to mainline church practices.

It wasn't until I lived in Dallas, Texas, that I encountered deeply religious people who live their lives without denominational labels. Growing up in New England meant that organized religion was essential to our identity. We belonged in one camp or another, Episcopal, Baptist, Congregational . . . something. The members of this sect preferred to identify themselves as Spirit-led progeny of the characters described in the Bible. If asked, they can explain the parallels between their own lives and the lives of biblical personalities. They see the world differently. They live simply, baptize in the back of an old pickup truck, and hold services in barns and tents.

The tents are the malleable spaces, canvas wombs that hold the shouts, exorcisms, and healings. They hold hundreds of people and can be set up in the "hood" on a vacant lot, or in a pasture in a rural southern town. In each location fresh hay is spread on the ground and the folding chairs are lined up in a way that allows for wide aisles for running and tent pole climbing. The people that I speak of embrace an alternative reality. Proof of this is the fact that they are willing to walk into a mall if "led by the Spirit" to prophesy to shoppers. In doing so, they proclaim a reality that collides with dominant myths, and with careful liturgical language.

My encounter and brief sojourn with this group amplified my call to ministry and affirmed my spiritual preferences. Although I could not foresee seminary, graduate education, and now theological administration, I have been honed in the fires of eclectic grassroots and storefront Spirit-led ministries that influence everything that I do. The Spirit leads, the Spirit warns, the Spirit comforts and guides, but primarily the Spirit is a mystery that unfolds before us. In this chapter I consider manifestations of folk piety: in an independent holiness sect, in a fast-food restaurant in Memphis, Tennessee, and during the blessing of a gang member.

WHAT FOLKS, WHOSE PIETY?

A popular religion deals with how people eat, work, relate and deal with life altering events . . . like birth, and loss, like death and illness. It gives a very clear and detailed method of how to live. It is about social structure and maintenance of equilibrium.[3]

The fact that we separate the sacred and the secular in our rhetoric and in our theological analysis speaks to the Western modality of radical individualism. In most community-focused societies, the sacred is considered to be an integral aspect of human life and endeavor. The work of the Holy Spirit is not confined to formal religious settings, but is presumed to be a constant aspect of reality. Folk piety in the early church was a function of ordinary family practice and daily worship. "Apparently one of the most common ways that trouble began in the New Testament church was that one group would label the piety of another group as inferior, or set up its own piety as a 'higher way.'"[4]

While folk piety includes a diversity of contexts, practices, and beliefs, there are common theological themes and expectations rooted in shared understandings of the Holy Spirit. These common expectations may include mystical manifestations related to divine presence along with stories of personal encounter. There are also polarities that seem to emerge in folk piety, including ritual and relevance, sacred accessibility and boundaries, lay empowerment and spiritual hierarchy, needs-based ministries and asceticism, marginalization and belonging, historicism and the apocalyptic, prophetic public discourse and cultural critique.

Today in the United States, folk piety is often ensconced within the larger concept of popular religion. The phrase "popular religion" alludes to the syncretism of popular culture and faith practices, and to the individual proclivities of leaders such as the one described at the beginning of this paper. Although folk piety may be considered one type of popular religious expression, I want to focus on the Spirit-led aspect of the phenomenon so sedimented in our everyday lives that we seldom take notice. When the Spirit of God is evident, it is usually in the midst of very specific events that cannot be confined to either secular or religious settings.

The Holy Spirit leads in ways that proclaim. Sometimes, these Spirit-led expressions are quixotic, temporary, reflexive, or extra-ecclesiastical. When the Holy Spirit leads, power is often vested in the people, the poor and marginalized, the powerless and forgotten. Charles Long captures this aspect of the phenomenon when he refers to folk piety as "the religion of the masses," a "kind of civil religion or religion of the public."[5] The presumption is that God can address the needs of the world through women, the homeless, children, social misfits, and the iconic shamans that emerge from marginalized communities. Those cast off by society, the mentally ill, and the radically idiosyncratic may indeed be the ones who find themselves barefoot before the burning bush.

Popular religious movements tend to have permeable boundaries that allow freer access to the sacred and to leadership positions. This inversion

of societal values gives ordinary people power over their lives. In the sect
that I described at the beginning of the chapter, power was not ceded to
the prophet alone, but to anyone sitting on the folding chairs, as long
as they had "gifts" and were "possessed by the power of the Holy Spirit."
A preacher who misquoted Scripture or who made any statement contrary to prevailing biblical interpretation would be addressed immediately by a person imbued with the "Spirit."

That "Spirit-possessed" person would rise and speak directly to the
preacher or prophet. What would follow would be either chastisement
or prophecy, "for this is what the Lord has said . . ." and the humble
response of the preacher or teacher would be, "I receive that Word."
Receiving did not necessarily mean agreement; it simply was an
acknowledgment that the Holy Spirit could speak through anyone, and
that each and every person in the congregation could access the power
of God. The pulpit offered neither protection nor preference but invited
a colloquy that extended beyond the usual Amen.

I don't know too many mainline churches that would stand for this
model of shared governance. The unspoken presumption in mainline
churches is that hierarchy is part of God's divine plan. Inevitably the lay
priesthood of believers is displaced and the relevance of religious experience is diminished. Folk piety is at its best when it manifests as a constructive and lived religious inclination that epitomizes the customs and
values of the community. In its more tangible forms, folk piety can sustain families and communities with anecdotal wisdom stories, herbal
healing remedies, and generational theories of well-being. The fact that
popular religion in the form of eclectic and self-actualized religious
expressions is on the rise speaks to the alienation of current generations.
It also exposes the gap between available spiritual resources and unmet
human needs.

Popular religious activities seem to proliferate where there is a critical backlog of human need that cannot be addressed by the formal practices of religious institutions. Any religion worth its salt must be capable
of responding to the times and needs of the people. Yet in the face of
monumental human suffering and intractable needs, sometimes institutions are silent or worse, offering platitudes and pabulum when the
grit of the gospel is needed. Unable to address the simplest command
to "feed the sheep," organizations turn from the homeless or enter the
cycle of feeding and sheltering in ways that foster paternalism and
dependency. Food pantries are wonderful resources for emergency sup-

port, but hinder rather than help long-term needs for sustenance. Inevitably, the relationships of those who give and those who receive are affected by the power differential.

Lately religious institutions have focused their energies around political debates that create win-lose situations among seekers: gay marriage or not; ecclesial leadership and the authority of women; war and peace. As the problematic issues proliferate and the desire to avoid conflict increases, the silences deepen. Ultimately, formal religious institutions are left with only their traditional language and historical rituals to address the pressing issues of their congregations. In the face of violence, family dissolution, and changing moral priorities, silence from churches presumed to be representatives of a "Word" God is problematic.

Is it any wonder that there is an intergenerational "disconnect" between churchgoers and their children? In the twentieth century, many congregants held on to the mysteries of faith, the opportunity for community building, and a deep respect for pastoral leadership. Today, the mysteries of technology provide enough "thrills" and community building, and social support is just an Internet click away. In addition, the reputation of pastoral leaders has diminished significantly. When postmodernity shattered grand narratives, it also exposed clergy and the religious institutions that they serve as human and persistently fallible. Each scandal that erupted redefined religious leaders as broken vessels mired in the same temptation pit as everyone else. The inevitable result was that the impetus for popular religion and expressions of folk piety gained credence. If there is no special unction, anointing, ability to resist sin, then why be led by professional clergy—why not be led by the Spirit?

This is not a fallback position, but the fulfillment of a neglected aspect of Christianity. As priests in the lay priesthood of believers, adherents of folk piety assume explicit religious leadership responsibilities. Just as many of us abdicate to the schools the responsibility to teach our children, we much prefer to assign leadership of our spiritual lives to specialists. Although I make my living training seminary students to serve in those ecclesiastical positions that I now question, I am always hopeful that the training is for honing and not hierarchy, for spiritual formation and not for dominance and abuse. Popular religion lays the responsibility for leadership, community care, and spiritual formation in the hands of the seekers.

FOLLOWING WHERE THE SPIRIT LEADS

A pervasive spiritual impoverishment grows. The collapse of meaning in life—the eclipse of hope and absence of love of self and others, the breakdown of family and neighborhood bonds. We have
created rootless, dangling people with little link to the supportive
networks . . . that sustain some sense of purpose in life. . . . The result
is lives of what we might call "random nows," of fortuitous and fleet-
ing moments preoccupied with "getting over"—with acquiring
pleasure, property and power by any means necessary.[6]

Cornel West offers a bleak picture of the pervasive spiritual impoverishment of our time. What is missing from his analysis is the inherent
resiliency of spiritual sources of empowerment. While we may exhaust
patience, love of neighbor, and our rootedness in God's cosmology of
justice and mercy, the Spirit does not. In the midst of life's inevitable
chaos, the Spirit of God leads and invites us to follow. Our discomfort
with this amazing opportunity for restoration is that it does not corre-
spond with our ideas of hierarchy and control. Religious organizations
are often known as much for the rules imposed as they are for their theological preferences. The focus is on who can or cannot perform rituals,
and which responses to the spoken or sung word are allowed.

Each sacred system allows a limited range of responses to the divine.
Those limitations can be liturgical, sermonic, or structural, but the
intent seems to be the control of unpredictable mysteries that lurk
within any human/divine relationship. Folk religion reclaims direct
access to the mystery of God by peeling away presumptions about everyday life and its spiritual grounding. Most religions know that the truth
about God may seem solid and implacable, when in fact it is a social
construction, an interpretation with many layers. Cosmologists refer to
this multivalent approach to reality as dimensional. Dominant religious
systems tend to simplify the dimensional aspects of religion to provide
their constituents with consistency, the comfort of repetition, and access
to projections of divine consciousness that mirrors human expectations.

Often God becomes a construction of the human image and not the
other way around. The end result, intended or not, diminishes access to
the Godself identified at the end of the book of Job. In Job, the God of
the ages essentially tells us that we might as well approach the sacred in
the spirit of freedom, since our efforts to get a handle on God through
the limitations of human intellectual categories will always fail. Folk

piety interprets the taken-for-granted within the expectations and needs of the seeker and offers opportunities to amend language, create rituals, and allow divine presence to inhabit the relevancy of the present time.

Youth amendments of traditional worship services, the Episcopal rap mass, jazz vespers, contemporary services, and African Diasporan reclamations of indigenous religious practices during Christian services are excellent examples of folk piety. There is the unspoken acknowledgment that the beauty of our uniqueness as individually created and loved children of God requires portals of access to wisdom, mystery, and truth that are as diverse as we are. Those portals have opened up to me at the most unexpected times.

The surprise was always that the in-breaking of the Holy Spirit was not always orchestrated by praise leaders or shared in the midst of a crowd. I have been surprised that sometimes it happened under viaducts in Miami, serving communion to the homeless using fish snack crackers and grape Kool-Aid. On one occasion the presence of the Holy Spirit interrupted a conference that I attended. Participants included American Indian and Mexican traditional healers, Buddhists, a Brazilian Candomblé priestess, African American and Anglo pastors. Instead of the usual theoretical patter, we tuned in to the spiritual energy that converged in that place and offered blessings to one another. We sang and danced, prayed and wept, and strengthened one another for the journey.

Painful memories hidden away for years emerged within the safety of this intentional spiritual community. It was only a three-day gathering of Spirit-led people, but the sharing and active communal worship had a lasting impact on each one of us. We left that place knowing that we had been part of something that might not ever happen again, and that the Spirit was present in our midst. There was probably very little that we would have agreed upon if creeds, practices, and liturgy were the basis for our coming together. And yet, our willingness to let go of an agenda and welcome the Spirit opened us up to a powerful experience.

The question for this age is whether we can follow the leading of the Spirit when we are not certain of the outcomes, whether we can be obedient when our actions defy rationality. Walter Brueggemann delineates the benefits of spiritual presence with particular attention to human agency. We are not led by the Spirit as lemmings headed toward the sea. Instead,

The spirit causes human agents to act afresh, in ways they had not intended or envisioned.

The work of the human agent thus spirited is to transform reality toward justice.

The spirited human agent need not be attractive, but only faithful and capable of risk-taking.

The agent works for the sake of the whole community.

The spirit does the work of restoration, which the community cannot do for itself.

The spirit works in ways the world does not expect or even recognize. The spirit invites daring acts of imagination.[7]

It is in these daring acts of imagination that I see the potential for transformation. To be human hosts of the Holy Spirit is an invitation to be emissaries of a living God. Brueggemann opines that when the spirit is unleashed, it is "a force set loose in the world that none of the assumed givens can finally withstand."[8] It is a force that empowers migrant workers, gang members, homeless neighbors, and a weathered prophet in a Dallas mall to affirm the presence of the God who loves the world. Prophetic discourses that emerge from popular religion focus less on theological predispositions than on human issues and pragmatic enactments of justice in daily life. To do the unexpected work of restoration and forgiveness of unforgivable acts offers a clue as to the presence of the Spirit of God. Ultimately, we arrive at our spiritual destinations not because we know where we're going, but because we are led.

FOLK PIETY: WHEREVER THE VILLAGERS GATHER

Explicit expressions of the spirituality of the people can be found wherever people gather. In the early twenty-first century, those gathering places differed significantly from the gathering places of the previous century. Although telephone party lines have been replaced by cell phones and chat rooms, some things never change. In Africana culture, grooming, and the completion of daily rituals like hair braiding, and eating became opportunities for sustained expressions of folk piety. The Internet is one of the new sites of popular religion, but barbershops, beauty shops, kitchen tables, and front porches have always been the locus of grassroots spirituality.

Through the power of a technologically connected life space, family members separated by distance participate in funerals, births, and significant life achievements by Internet. On these occasions, the distance created by absence is sometimes transcended by the inherent spirituality that attaches to the ritual or event. These events invite the participation of the gathered community. There are no pews or captive listeners to one voice, but rather the many voices praising in cyberspace, mourning and seeking answers.

I began this chapter with a discussion of the mall prophet. What I want to emphasize is that he is not alone. I find these men and women wherever people gather in the new village squares, cyberspace, and fast-food restaurants.

DO YOU WANT FRIES WITH THAT?

On any given morning, but particularly on Sunday mornings, a gaudy fast-food hamburger joint becomes a place of worship and debate. Elders gather, both men and women, to connect the biblical stories that they have heard growing up with the common sense of their current lives. There is nothing sermonic about the discussions, if we consider the common understanding of the word "sermonic" as individualistic and performative. This is a return to the African village and its grassroots wisdom. Without missing a beat they consider the unfairness of divorce laws, give advice about protecting the rights of a father grieving the loss of access to his child, while quoting biblical texts about the absence of marriage in heaven. There are shouts, jokes, and quiet head nodding during the scriptural sections.

I sit nearby surrounded by folk who might not be comfortable in most congregations that I know of. A woman is pushing an oxygen tank, a locally known schizophrenic speaks quietly to himself, but sits close enough to hear as he nurses his cup of coffee. The stories that they tell give strength for the journey, and this is their only intent. A typical conversation would sound something like this:

Elder or Regular: How have you been?
Responder: I'm fine but my sister [cousin, fill in the blank] is catching it . . .
Regular: Yeah . . . [then the problem is spoken and offered to the group for consideration]

Everybody: No kiddin . . . [heads nod in recognition of the severity of the issue; on occasion loud guffaws and back slaps assure the speaker that what's going on is "just a thing that will pass." On those occasions the assurances are: "Man that ain't gonna last . . . let that stuff go . . . you can ride this one out . . ."]

When the stories are difficult and ethically complex, everyone offers advice. Some advice is tied to Scripture, received in relative silence, but pontificating is not allowed. If the mini-sermon goes on too long, someone will interject: "I see your point . . . yeah you can't argue with the Word . . . but let me tell you what happened to my Aunt Jiggy . . ." They are not captive to pews and ushers, they can come and go as they please and enter or refrain from the conversation as they are led. Sometimes voices are raised and points are emphasized by fists that pound on the table.

The power of dialogue and refutation is often grounded in an appeal to the authority of holy texts including Torah, New Testament, and the Koran. You name it and it will find its way into the conversation. But most often, those gathered speak openly of the Holy Spirit and the mystery of relationships, theodicy, and the struggles of daily life. Moral examples are drawn from current events in the newspaper. The interest is not in what the politicians are doing, but in how their partisan high jinks affect neighbors' lives.

The gatherings usually end anticlimactically just as they began, when someone says, "Well, guess I'll get going." They leave knowing that there will be another time, and they sense the power of mutual caring that does not require a designated building. And so, in a small southern town, the people gather in their designated worship spaces, and in fast-food restaurants. They talk about God where steeples pierce the open skies, where mosques shelter kneeling supplicants, and where neon signs blink on and off. They assemble themselves together around ornate communion tables and around laminated table tops where they can sip coffee and season their grits. The Spirit leads where it will.

Folk piety is the response of the people to their lives, to the presence of the Holy Spirit in the rubble of collapsed buildings, and in divorce courts. It is the equal opportunity access to a faith journey that can't be packaged in neat ecclesial liturgies. The spirit shows up at the mall and amid the shards of failed human relationships. The leaders are not appointed, they emerge when needed and are often rejected and weird, and that is the joy of the journey.

WHEN THE SPIRIT BAPTIZES

Our seminary is open to "whosoever will" but it is not often that a gang member walks in and asks for one of our professors. The young man was not yet twenty years old, but his eyes were the eyes of a witness. They had seen what they were never intended to see, and now they could not find their way back to innocence. Instead of teen discomfort, I saw the steady defiance of one willing to risk everything in a flash. When he asked to see one of my colleagues, he was ushered in, and found his way to her office. Within moments, I was receiving a call to come upstairs.

When I walked into her office, the music playing on the stereo was from Sweet Honey in the Rock's album *The Women Gather*. This *a cappela* singing group, founded by Dr. Bernice Johnson Reagon, gives voice to the resistance and solidarity of the boomer generation. Dr. Reagon says that singing was her conduit to the Spirit. She remarks, "It really connects you up with a force in the universe that makes you different. It makes you capable of moving with a different kind of access. You're connected to something else, other than what people think you're connected up to."[9]

I was open to those connections as I entered the office. The young man sat in the chair not looking at either of us. The professor said, "He says that he wants to be clean. His hands have spilled blood and destroyed lives. He wants to be clean." I looked at him for confirmation, and received none. This was certainly not the usual order of business during my day. He said nothing, but stretched out his hands. As I looked at the young man I was reminded of the simple tasks that the Spirit leads us toward. We search for the magnificent and the noble: the Spirit leads us toward an embrace and a morsel of food. How simple it all seemed as the professor held a bowl of warm water.

The young man slowly lowered his hands, as she held them and washed slowly, whispering that he was God's beloved, a child worthy of our care and God's blessings. While I stood behind him with my hands lightly touching his shoulders, she whispered that the community needed him. He flinched at my touch, but then relaxed. She told him that he mattered, that his loss would mean that there would be a jagged hole in our lives where his gifts should have been offered. We told him that we knew him because we were mothers, and mothers know their children whether they have given birth to them or not. He wept and we all felt the release.

There was so much pain locked behind a practiced grimace, so much desire stitched throughout the "I don't care" slouch. It was over in a moment. There was not a "churchy" thing about it. It looked like baptism but was not; it seemed to be absolution but was simply "We love you." He never said a word, just looked at us, face still wet with tears, and left. We never saw him again.

CONCLUSION

Most of the expressions of folk religion discussed in this chapter have an underlying antiestablishment feel to them. The mainstream approach is recognized but then tweaked or revised as an improvisation upon the central theme. The spirit of invention and the opportunity to follow the Spirit toward unimagined newness is the reward that folk piety offers. The downside includes transpositions that become so idiosyncratic that they no longer resemble recognizable religious beliefs. To explain this in a Christian context is to consider the improvisations that Jesus offered. He did not come up with a religion that defied the cultural wisdom of the day; instead he interpreted Judaism in a way that made space for Christian improvisations.

The traveling evangelists and storefront apostles, mall prophets and itinerant preachers are keeping the spirit of popular religion alive. Through eclectic mediations of the Spirit, they are exposing beliefs and practices that are less systematic than some of us would like. We left one example in a Dallas mall. You remember the gentleman with the guitar slung over his back who was prophesying in the mall when I began this chapter? Well, he is being escorted out of the mall, his hand-carved staff held aloft as he shouts, "Get out of the cities. God is going to destroy the cities. Learn to grow your own food, sow and reap, give back these plastic goods and go back to the land."

People are watching; they are quiet as the hypnotic sounds of mall music underscore his words. We've been trained to be uncomfortable with the messenger, but the words reach places in our spirits that are seldom touched. He has turned the mall into a reluctant congregation. He has poked us where we hurt, because this mall is our land. It is the place where teens meet and date, where the elderly take their exercise in the mornings, and where we have complete anonymity amid the crowds. As we turn back to the task of buying what we already have enough of, the challenge stays with us. What would it look like . . . a life of the Spirit connected to the land, led by a wisdom far greater than ours, challenged to live the lives that we talk about in our churches? Isn't it worth thinking about?

8

"The Dearest Freshness Deep Down Things"

Some Reflections on the Holy Spirit and Climate Change

Sallie McFague

God's Grandeur

The world is charged with the grandeur of God.
    It will flame out, like shining from shook foil;
    It gathers to a greatness, like the ooze of oil
Crushed. Why do men then now not reck his rod?
Generations have trod, have trod, have trod;
    And all is seared with trade; bleared, smeared with toil;
    And wears man's smudge and shares man's smell: the soil
Is bare now, nor can foot feel, being shod.

And for all this, nature is never spent;
    There lives the dearest freshness deep down things;
And though the last lights off the black West went
    Oh, morning, at the brown brink eastward, springs—
Because the Holy Ghost over the bent
    World broods with warm breast and with ah! bright wings.
                                        —Gerard Manley Hopkins

INTRODUCTION

Twenty-five years ago a conversation about the Holy Ghost rescued me from an embarrassing social event. I was sitting across from the wife of Italy's ambassador to England at a high table dinner at an

Oxford college. I was definitely out of my comfort zone and wondered how I could manage over the next several hours of elaborate cuisine, copious wine, and clever conversation that lay ahead. The ambassador's wife asked me what I "did." I hesitated, knowing that "being a theologian" was comparable to "being a nuclear physicist" to most people. But I mumbled what I "did." She smiled warmly and replied: "You know, when I was a child, I always prayed to the Holy Ghost because I figured he was less busy than the other two." The rest of the evening was a smashing success.

But within this story lies an interesting historical note: the Holy Ghost (Spirit) has been the neglected third party of the Trinity—at least until about fifty years ago. Even in my own early writing, I disparage the "spirit" metaphor as "amorphous, vague, and colorless," "ethereal, shapeless, and vacant," concluding that "Spirit is not a strong candidate for imaging God's sustaining activity."[1] But how wrong I was! I should have known better, since I have loved Hopkins's poem about the Holy Ghost since I was in college. However, it was only recently as I reread the poem in the light of climate change that it has taken on new depth and meaning for me.

"God's Grandeur," written in 1877, bemoans nature's fate at the hands of Western industrialism: the separation of human beings from nature via shoes and the desecration of nature from human activity ("seared with trade"). What should be a world "charged" with God's glory, so that every single scrap of creation tells of God in its own way, has become smudged, bleared, and smeared, camouflaging the particular reflection of God in all things. Hopkins's vision of God and the world in which each and every iota of creation shines with some aspect of divine glory has faded in the last lights of a black Western culture. But the hope for the "bent world" here does not lie in nature's own restorative powers; rather, it rests in the warm breast and bright wings of the Holy Ghost. God's power of motherly brooding that hovered over the chaotic waters at creation is with us still in the bright, rising wings of new life. In this poem we have an argument for, a confession of, hope. Hopkins could not envision the destruction of nature that we now know, and that is epitomized in global warming, but the witness of this poem is that *no matter how bad things get*, there is hope—not because of human beings or even of nature, but because the power of life and love that was at the beginning of creation is with us still as our source and our savior. "Nature is never spent" and "there lives the dearest freshness deep down things" *because* of the sustaining power and love of God's spirit. The sextet of the sonnet could not be stronger, more intimate, or more hopeful. We who can now imagine, given climate change, the end of civilization as we know it, brought about by carbon dioxide emissions, shiver at the ominous line, "the last lights off the black West went," but take a breath of hope with the final three lines. Here, the "bent" world, our world indeed, is nonetheless the place where divine love is incubating new life after the terrible destruction we have brought to our planet. Like a mother bird tucking the new life under her own body and anxiously protecting it, God sustains and renews us, *no matter what*. The final four words are more than we could ask or imagine: "with ah! bright wings." We do not deserve this; we could not have expected it; we can scarcely believe it, but it is the one thing necessary as we face up to climate change and the needed changes in our behavior.

Surely, this image of God is the one for our time. Nothing less can speak to the depth of our despair as we well-off humans contemplate what we are doing through our reckless, selfish, out-of-control consumerism to the poor of the planet and to the planet itself. We now know that climate change, which will affect every plant, animal, and person on earth, is the most serious crisis of the twenty-first century. If we ever thought ourselves in charge of the earth, capable of managing the planet, we now know that we have failed utterly. We must undergo the deepest of all conversions, the conversion from egocentricism to theocentrism, a conversion to whom we truly are: reflections of God, as is everything in creation. The only difference between us and the rest of creation is that the others reflect God, tell of God, simply by being, whereas we must *will* that it be so. We must desire to be what we truly are—made in the image of God, and thus able to live justly and sustainably on earth with all other creatures.

GOD AND THE WORLD: A SACRAMENTAL SENSIBILITY

Hopkins is hopeful because he believes the world lives within God. Hopkins has a sacramental religious sensibility: God and the world are not two separate realities that exist independently and must somehow find each other. Rather, the world is "charged" with God as if with electricity. "All things therefore are charged with love, are charged with God and if we know how to touch them give off sparks and take fire, yield drops and flow, ring and tell of him."[2] Hopkins's sacramental sensibility, in which each scrap of creation becomes *more itself* as it lives more completely within God, can most adequately be expressed with the metaphor of spirit. God is the empowering spirit that brings all things to fulfillment, or in a gloss on Irenaeus, "The glory of God is all things fully alive." This is not a view of the God-world relationship in which the more power the one has, the less the other has; rather, God is the "Wild air, world-mothering air" in which all things grow and flourish.[3] Hopkins agrees with the medieval mystic Mechthild of Magdeburg: "The day of my spiritual awakening was the day I saw—and knew I saw—all things in God and God in all things." He also agrees with Augustine, who wrote in his *Confessions*, "Therefore, my God, I would not exist at all, unless you were in me; or rather, I would not exist unless I were in you 'from whom and by whom all things exist.'"[4] We live within God; hence, metaphors such as water, breath, milieu, ocean, and air are our weak attempts to express the utter dependence *and* radical uniqueness that lies at the heart of an incarnational understanding of creation. This understanding says that we live within the body of God; that the world is, and is not the body of God; that all things exist within the one reality that is and that reality is on the side of life and its fulfillment. God as Spirit is the power of life and love within which all bodies exist. Most creatures live instinctively as the sacraments they were meant to be: they reflect God's glory, each it in its own illimitable way. We humans have a choice: to live in reality, in and for God, or to live in and for ourselves—nowhere—outside of reality. We have the choice *to live a lie*, to live what we were not meant to be—in and for ourselves.

This ontology—the world within God—is what I understand Peter Hodgson to be saying as well: "The appropriate Trinitarian formula is God-World-Spirit, or God as World-Spirit, or God-in-Christ-in-the-world-as Spirit."[5] God as World-Spirit "means that the *whole* world is animated by Spirit and that Spirit proceeds from the whole world as God's body. It means that the Spirit manifests itself in nature, that Spirit slumbers in nature and nature cries out to Spirit."[6] If we accept this ontology, then a picture of the God-world relationship emerges which is the ground of our hope. It gives a reason to hope at a time when our planet seems doomed to destruction. Let us look at some of the features of this picture of God and the world.

WHO IS GOD?

If the world exists within God, if in the lovely words of Julian of Norwich, God holds the world as one holds a hazelnut in one's hand, then God is everywhere. God is either everywhere or nowhere. God cannot be in one place and not another place; a being might do that, but not God. God is right under the surface in everything; God accompanies us when we travel to the ends of the earth—we may have to leave our loved ones behind, but not God; prayer is merely the acknowledgment that God is always there, always available. *We* may not be present; in fact, we are often absent, but God is always present. God the Spirit is ubiquitous, everywhere at the same time, always hovering with warm breast over every inch of the earth (universe). God is the liminal presence in all things. The divine presence announces itself in a breeze on leaves, in the sound of a bird's call, in the face of a starving child (or a happy one), in a clear-cut forest. God is in all things because all things are in God—in all shapes and shades, all conditions and crises, all joys and sorrows. God is in birth and death and everything in between. God is ubiquitous: God is wherever I am, wherever each and every iota of creation is.

But God is not a being, even the highest being: God is reality. This is another way of saying God is being itself, or the ground of all that is real, is actual, exists. The tradition can lead us astray when it suggests that God is a supernatural being who is the only reality. This paradigm suggests unilateral divine power, power that takes over and sucks everything into itself. Here God is both not great enough and too great: not the source of all life and love, but the highest being, the only power in the universe, choking off all other powers. But if God is reality, in whom we find our own distinctive realities, then trees can still be trees and mountains can be mountains and even I can and must be myself. God is the Spirit, the breath, the ether, the atmosphere in which each and every thing grows and flourishes. Here there is no competition for power: the world is charged with the grandeur of God and it is so by *being most fully itself.* God as the body of the world *is* that body by way of all the zillions of bodies that compose the universe. There is one reality: God visible (body) and invisible (spirit), but the latter is known *through* the former. Everything is suffused, infused, with God's breath and light and power. The world is alive with God—but indirectly, incarnationally.

Christian mysticism—seeing God in all things and all things in God—is incarnational. We live *in God through the world.* Everything exists within God's womb, within God as womb. This womb, the earth, is the body from which we derive breath, food, water, and habitat. There is not God *and* the world, but the world *as it exists and only exists in God.* We become aware of God *through the earth*: we develop double vision, the ability to see God *in* the world, in its beauty and its horror, and even in the most ordinary things on ordinary days. Mysticism is this double vision, seeing everything as it is *and* as in God, both at the same time. Mysticism is radical incarnationalism, seeing God in the flesh *everywhere*. Mysticism is delight in things and in God; it is seeing, hearing, tasting, smelling, touching God in everything and everywhere, but *only* in and through all these wonderful creatures. Who would want a disembodied mysticism? "The world is charged with the grandeur of God"—indeed, it is. God is in all things incarnationally: God tells us of life, love, truth, beauty, and goodness as each of these qualities is realized in the world. Thus, the exquisite beauty of an alpine forget-me-not is the way we experience God's beauty; the energy and joy of a young child is the way we experience God's vitality and life. Everything is God—God is reality, but *only* as everything is exquisitely, precisely, idiosyncratically itself. Taking a cue from Irenaeus, we can claim that the glory of God is every creature fully alive. God and the world are not in competition: an incarnational theology does not say, "the more God, the less world," or "the more world, the less God." Rather, it says the more God, the more world and vice versa. We, the world, flourish *in* God, *only* in God, and *fully* in God.

God is not a being, then, but reality: God is the stuff out of which everything comes and to which it will return. Life emanates from God and is more like God than like anything else. All creation was made in God's image, as a reflection of God, and this is what we humans must acknowledge and live into. There is not "God and the world," but God and "God in the form of the world" (the world as God's body, God's incarnation). The world (all matter) is a manifestation of God, for God is reality. If the world were outside God then there would be something greater than God, that is, "God and the world."

But the most astounding thing of all is that reality is good—God is love. God is in, with, and for everything. The "with" and "for" part is what Christians read about reality in the face of Jesus: in his ministry of love and healing and his death for the oppressed, Christians claim that reality (God) is on the side of life and its fulfillment. This is the direction of reality, something we could not figure out on our own; in fact, most evidence appears to be contrary. God is like Jesus: "For it is the God who said, 'Let light shine out of darkness,' who has shone in our hearts to give the light of the knowledge of the glory of God in the face of Jesus Christ" (2 Cor. 4:6). Thus, reality (God) is not a being, but is personal in that we can use words like "love" and "fulfillment" regarding reality's intention. This assertion about reality's intention is what faith, rock-bottom faith, is: trust that love and not indifference, neutrality, or malevolence is at the heart of things. It is not belief in God, but trust that things will be all right or, in Julian's words, "all things shall be well."

Another way to express this understanding of the God-world relationship is the Trinity—not the conundrum of three persons in one substance, but that God (reality) is a giving and a receiving. The Trinity suggests what reality is: a continual flow of giving and receiving, of sharing, of living in one another, of counting on one another. We see a form of this reality in ecology: the interrelationship and interdependence of all things. Nothing is itself alone—even God, or perhaps most eminently, God. In the beginning was relationship, so says the Trinity. There is no beginning or end to this process—no self ("God" or creature) that is itself by itself. We become through relationship—with God and with our billions of neighbors. The Trinity reminds us that God is not an isolated individual—nothing is. Thus, God is not a being outside of other things; rather, God is the reality of all things, or all things become real (exist and are fulfilled) by living in God. Trying to live anywhere else is false, a lie, hopeless. Things *are* themselves as and to the extent they acknowledge the source of their being. This is an extraordinary thought: life and grace are the same thing. Grace is the gift of acknowledging one's total dependence on God, who is life and gives life.

WHO ARE WE?

If God is reality, in whom we live and move and have our being, from whom we come and to whom we return, then our time on earth is also lived within God. We are not on our own; we belong to God.[7] Believing in God is not primarily asserting that God exists; rather, it is acknowledging that I know who I am. I am a contingent, unnecessary, transient creature who has been given the gift of life and love. I am aware of being totally and gratefully dependent on the earth and all its interlocking support systems, on others whom I love and who love me, and on whatever is in, through, with, and for life and love—what we call "God." I did not create myself; I cannot sustain myself; I cannot transform myself. I live within the womb that gives me birth, feeds and nurtures me, gives me delight and joy, strengthens me through loss and suffering, and will be my tomb when I die.

Remembering daily and in particular ways who I am and where I fit in the scheme of things is a central spiritual discipline. Coming to faith is not so much knowing who God is, but who I am. I am not the center of things; I do not live by my own merit or means; I am finite, mortal, and small. And yet, coming to faith as this dependent, vulnerable creature means that I trust (know) that I live in God: God is my reality. I am not on my own, I cannot account for my own existence, let alone its moments of flourishing, from myself. I belong to something outside of myself which is at the same time inside and all about me. I belong to the source of my breath, my delight, my need, my hope. And in pain, loss, sorrow, disappointment—and even destruction and death—I will still belong to God, though I often do not know how.

The acknowledgment of who we are (our faith) means a dual realization: of gratitude and of responsibility, of delight and duty. The primary religious emotion is wonder, amazement, and thankfulness. Simply to be alive, along with all the other fascinating, diverse, beautiful, and wonderful creatures, is a gift beyond imagining. Once one wakes up to the glory of planet earth in all its spectacular particularity and complexity, one is blown away. Once we see the world—and ourselves as part of it—with double vision, as grounded in God and resplendent with the individuality of each thing, from slugs to forget-me-nots, whales and big cedars, including fields of waving wheat and crouching tigers, we want to shout hallelujah! To see things, including human beings, becoming our illimitable selves *as* we live within and for God—this is a great joy. We realize that there is no either/or, but a both/and: it is not God versus us, our freedom and fulfillment, but rather God as the ground, source, breath, water, womb, bath, air, breast, and tomb within which we become who we truly are. Each scrap of creation, including us human beings, becomes the unique individual that in its own distinctive way tells of God's glory.

And our peculiar, distinguishing characteristic, the way that we tell of God, is by *choosing to do so*. We are the one creature that has to decide to reflect God. What is becoming increasingly clear is that the way we must reflect God is to accept responsibility for planetary well-being. Accepting this responsibility is an awesome task. Never before have human beings *known* that they were responsible for planetary health. Until the second half of the twentieth century, human beings could, with good conscience, still claim that our behavior might not be the cause of earth's increasing deterioration. But that is no longer the case. The first step in accepting responsibility as God's partner in sustaining creation's health is to admit that *we* are a major cause of the crisis facing the twenty-first century: global warming. Denial is no longer possible. This first step is finally occurring, even in Western governments and oil companies.

The second step is to become informed about climate change. This is not easy. It is an incredibly complex phenomenon; in fact, it involves the most complicated, profound, and important systems on earth. Global warming has no one cause; it has many feedback systems; it has some unknowns. It is not something we *want* to be responsible for—any more than the generation that fought the Second World War wanted to do so. But it is our fate, our calling, our destiny, and our duty. It is the planetary agenda that faces all people, all religions, all fields of expertise, all professions of our time. The consequences of global warming will reach into every corner of the earth, from the decline of biodiversity to the desertification of land, from the spread of tropical disease to the flooding of cities, from melting ice caps to wars over food and water and the retreat of the wealthy to fortified spaces as the poor cry at the gates. The prospects of the earth's future with uncontrolled global warming, according to a number of sober sources, are frightening, if not terrifying.[8] But do we have a choice? Once we see who we are in the scheme of things—the neediest of all creatures dependent on our planet's health for every breath we take, every cup of water we drink, and every piece of food we eat—we realize that we *must* take care of the earth that is taking care of us.

One of the central tasks for the world's religions, including Christianity, is to attend to the image of human beings that functions in our society. Anthropology, the study of human beings and their place in the scheme of things, is the business of religion. Religions are central in forming the most basic assumptions about God and the world, and especially of human beings, for the cultures in which they exist. It is for this reason that we have undertaken to present in these pages a Christian vision of God and the world that is both deep within the tradition and relevant to our time. *If* people were to see themselves at the deepest level as living within God along with and for all other creatures, might we not have a vision of humanity that would encourage both responsibility and hope? Would we not see that *we are not alone*; rather, we are part of a magnificent creation in which all creatures are interdependent and all radically dependent on the source of their life and well-being? Would we not take courage—along with the great responsibility we now feel—*because* "there lives the dearest freshness deep down things," the Spirit of God, whose warm breast and bright wings are the hope of planet earth?

WHAT IS OUR TASK? CARE AND HOPE

Surely, the most difficult task facing us as we finally acknowledge our responsibility for planetary health is summed up in one small word: hope. Is it possible to have any? The more one learns of climate change—the apocalyptic future that awaits us unless we make deep, speedy changes in our use of fossil fuels—the more despairing one becomes. Whether it is a 50 percent, 70 percent, or 90 percent reduction in carbon dioxide emissions worldwide that must be reached by 2050, it is a task that seems beyond our physical—and more importantly, our moral and emotional—capacity. It appears that we human beings do not have the *will* to live differently—justly and sustainably—to the degree necessary to save ourselves and our planet. The single most difficult obstacle to overcome is, then, our own lack of hope. This issue cannot be brushed aside. It is important to face the facts.

Increasingly, in popular media such as films and novels we see pictures of the dystopia that awaits us in a future of profound environmental degradation. It will not be a world simply of less water, more heat, and fewer species of plants and animals; rather, it will be one of violent class wars over resources, the breakdown of civilization at all levels, and the end of assumptions about ordinary life that we have come to expect—the opportunity to have meaningful work, to raise healthy children, to enjoy leisure activities. Life as we well-off North Americans know it—the life that we have come to expect as natural and as our right—will come to an end. The most ordinary activities that rely on access to basic resources will disappear: going to school, putting on parties, enjoying concerts, taking vacations, watering the flowers. The ordinary things that make up the fabric of our days and that we love are at stake. An environmental dystopia will not only be piles of garbage in the streets, violent gangs of thugs, new dangerous diseases, and constant fear for one's safety, it will also be the fraying of the most basic civilities between people, the undermining of solidarity and community, and in its place we can expect a raw, radical, and very sad form of individualism.

As we imagine this dystopia, as we begin to feel what daily life will be like, we are horrified. Most people do not allow themselves to imagine this possibility, claiming that it is an exaggeration, that human ingenuity can cope with the situation. But increasingly, this is difficult to do: denial and rationalization appear to have had their day. It is necessary to allow our imaginations to begin to live within the world that responsible science is telling us will be our fate unless drastic measures are made soon. We must do this so that we can acknowledge where our hope really resides—not with us, but in the power of love and renewal that lives within the universe, the Holy Spirit, the Spirit of God.

As we consider the basis for our hope, let us recall who God is. We must and can change our ways, live justly and sustainably on our planet, because of God, not because of ourselves. The hope we have lies in the radical transcendence of God, a transcendence that exceeds all our notions of transcendence. A supernatural transcendence—God as the highest being who controls the world—is a paltry view of transcendence compared with God as radically immanent to and with and for *everything that is*. God's transcendence—God's power of creative, redeeming, and sustaining love—is closer to us than we are to ourselves. God is the milieu, the source, of power and love in which our world, our fragile deteriorating world, exists. The world is not left to fend for itself, so to speak, nor is God "in addition" to anything or everything. Rather, God *is* the life, love, truth, goodness, and beauty that empowers the universe and shines out from it. God is the reality of everything that is; hence, without God, nothing would be. Therefore, God is always present, always here (and there); we simply have to open ourselves to become aware of and acknowledge God's presence. This is the basis of our hope: the world is created, loved, and kept by God.

Thus, "mysticism" is simply this awareness of God's presence in and through and with everything for its well-being. Mysticism is not—or need not be—a one-on-one relationship between a human individual and God; rather, it is acknowledging that everything lives and thrives and rejoices—and grieves and dies—*in* God. Mysticism is radical incarnationalism, seeing God in the flesh *everywhere* and in all conditions of embodied life. Mysticism is the recognition that we are never alone—nothing is—for God is ubiquitous.

Julian's lovely story of the hazelnut sums up our hope: hope for the world lies with God, its maker, lover, and keeper.

> At the same time, he [God] showed me something small, about the size of a hazelnut that seemed to lie in the palm of my hand as round as a tiny ball. I tried to understand the sight of it, wondering what it could possibly mean. The answer came: "This is all that is made." I felt it was so small that it could easily fade to nothing; but again I was told, "This lasts and it will go on lasting forever because God loves it. And so it is with every being that God loves." I saw three properties about this tiny object. First, God had made it; second,

God loves it; and third, God keeps it. And yet what this really means
to me, that he is the Maker, the Keeper, the Lover, I cannot begin
to tell.[9]

This is the religious sensibility that allows us to hope, a sensibility
that imagines the world as a hazelnut, held within divine love, trusting
not in its own powers to "last," but in the never-ending creative, redeeming, and sustaining love of God. Surely we feel about our sorry, belea-
guered planet as Julian did holding the hazelnut: "I felt it was so small
that it could easily fade to nothing," but she was told that it *will survive*
because God loves it. This is certainly an astounding statement of faith,
a statement of radical hope. Hope is trust, trust in God—not in things,
events, or people. To be trustworthy means able to be counted on,
counted on to hold one's life and all life in trust, in safekeeping. It means
that one can rest one's life—and the life of the whole planet—in God,
knowing that this trust will *somehow* be honored. Although, as Julian
acknowledges, what it means to say God makes, loves, and keeps the
world, we "cannot begin to tell."

This, then, is an odd kind of hope. It does not mean that things will
necessarily turn out as we hope, nor does it mean that we will be successful in our attempts to save the planet, but it does mean that God
will "make all things well," as Julian writes in her mysterious, enigmatic,
and profoundly hopeful words. "It was in this way that our Good Lord
answered all questions and doubts I might make, comforting me greatly
with these words: 'I may make all things well; I can make all things well,
and I will make all things well, and I shall make all things well; and you
shall see for yourself that all manner of things shall be well.'"[10] Faith in
God is the sense that since everything lives within God—that the reality we inhabit is love—things will be all right. But this sounds absurd,
if not morally repugnant. How can "things be well" if people and the
planet are dying from global warming? We do not know how. We
believe, however, that it is so, not because we will make it so, but because
of God. This is not a sentimental or romantic hope that things will turn
out okay, but rather the faith that *however they turn out*, the world and
all its creatures are held, kept, within God.

Since reality is oriented, however obscurely, mysteriously, and cir-
cuitously to the world's well-being, we *can* hope. We live toward this
future, because we already know something of it—if we did not, we
could not hope. The small glimmers we have of hope—the return of
flowers, the birth of a child, a compassionate deed—make us certain
that this is the way things were meant to be and will be, *because* these

reflections of God's love are shining forth in our world. Having hope is a sign that we are already on our way: we cannot know God apart from God, we cannot hope in God apart from the gifts of hope that God gives us in the most ordinary—and precious—moments of our lives. If one has hope, one has all things, for trusting in God means that nothing can separate us from the source of power and love in the universe.

Curiously, this faith, not in ourselves but in God, can free us to live lives of radical change. Perhaps it is the only thing that can. Rather than relying on such hope as a way to escape personal responsibility—"Let God do it"—it frees us from the pressure of outcomes, so that we can add our best efforts to the task at hand. It allows us to look to God's way of loving the world, a way expressed in the Christian doctrines of incarnation, cross, and resurrection: God loves the world totally and completely. God gives everything, goes the limit, to be on the side of life and its fulfillment. But God does this in a way suited to us embodied beings who live in our physical "house." The story of Jesus Christ is the story of God incarnate, facing the worst that the world (human beings) can offer in terms of oppression and destruction, and rising to new life—the cross and the resurrection. It is a story that goes *through* physical horror, physical death: it is inclusive of the worst dystopia we, in the twenty-first century, can imagine for our deteriorating planet—and yet, it is the story of "the dearest freshness deep down things," of the bright wings of the Holy Spirit. The two major days of the Christian calendar—Christmas and Easter—are about hope and renewal. They are about new life. Christmas is the celebration of birth, the incarnation of God in the world; Easter is the celebration of rebirth, the world's rebirth. The resurrection is a Yes to life against death, or perhaps more accurately, it is the recognition that death and life, life and death, are all parts of God, who is all Yes. Even death takes place within the great Yes (though what this means, we "cannot begin to tell").

So, on the one hand, it appears that it is impossible to despair, since we live (and even die) within God, within reality which is love. Whether we are joyful or despairing, healthy or sick, alive or dead, we live in love. Nothing can be totally negative or final or fearful (even despair and death), because everything happens *within* God's love. There is always hope that something else, something more, something good might happen (yes, even in death) because we live and die in God's world. In a sense, then, everything that happens, good or bad, happens to God also. There are no scraps, no leftovers, no tail ends of creation that do not rest in God; nothing is neglected or passed over.

But, on the other hand, what of the evil, perverse, murderous, greedy events that we humans are responsible for? Even here, God is—not as the power behind such events, but as the negative critique of them. God is incarnate as the Yes beneath all that is life and love and goodness and truth and beauty, and as the No in all that is cruel, perverse, false, greedy, and hateful. To practice the presence of God means to embrace what God embraces: life and love. But we must not shy from imagining the worst possible outcome from human behavior, a sickening hopeless dystopia, and then put even this picture of the world where it belongs—within God. Whatever happens to us and to our world, however horrendous, happens to God as well. We are cupped within the divine hands, warmed in the divine breast, held close through our greatest fears, comforted when things go wildly wrong. If this were not the case, then, we are indeed forsaken. When we need God the most, as we earthlings surely will in this precarious twenty-first century, we cannot *not* trust. Faith in God is faith that *no matter how bad things get*, somehow or other, it will be all right.

Julian's hazelnut story tells us that God made the earth, God loves it, and God keeps it—three phases of the ever-widening contemplation of the trustworthiness of things, of reality. The hazelnut story is a metaphor of rock-bottom trust that reality is good, that the direction of things is Yes. Everything is loved—the lamb *and* the tiger, the messiness and cost of evolution, all the contrary events (from any particular perspective), and all the darkness of life—and everything is "kept" by God (whether it lives or dies). These three moments are the ever-widening contemplation of the world as within God. Each moment is more difficult because more inclusive: it is hard to believe that everything is created by God, harder to claim that everything is loved by God, and harder still to trust that everything is kept—protected and cherished—by God. And yet, this hope is the one thing needful as we face planetary living in the twenty-first century. "Nature is never spent" and "there lives the dearest freshness deep down things" *because* of the sustaining power and love of God, within whom the earth, our bent world, lives.

ADDENDUM

The spring of 2000 was my last semester at Vanderbilt Divinity School after thirty years of teaching. I was selling my house, leaving my children and grandchildren, as well as my country and the job I loved, in order to join my partner in Vancouver, British Columbia. All of this was disorienting and difficult, but most difficult of all was the death of my wonderful ninety-five-year-old mother. Moreover, I was ill with a then undiagnosed immune disease that made me constantly tired and prone to respiratory infections. It was a challenging time for me personally and I had many dark days.

But in the backyard of my house in Nashville was a cherry tree, a thing of rare beauty. I wrote about it in my journal.

March 19, 2000

My cherry tree is in full bloom and it is raining—a good, solid, penetrating rain that all the wonderful new buds need. It is Sunday; I am alone, still under the influence of an awful cold, but happy to have a quiet day.

I look at that cherry tree and feel "touched by God." It is a glorious thing and tells of God's glory. Only a cherry tree, *this* cherry tree, can tell of the particular aspect of divine beauty that it alone embodies. It "incarnates" God (as each and every creature and thing does), but in its own special way. There is only one Jesus of Nazareth, but there is also only one cherry tree in the backyard at 3703 Meadowbrook Avenue, Nashville, Tennessee. We are all touched by God, stamped and sealed with some aspect of God. What a different and wonderful way to understand reality: everything is itself *as* it tells of God. The delicate, irregular limbs and blossoms of this cherry tree, swaying in the breeze, shimmering in the sun: a hymn to God's glory in every twig.

God is not the far off, but the near God, nearer to me than my own breath. God is in the cherry tree—oh, yes, especially in my cherry tree! Every time I look at that beautiful creature, I see it shouting out the glory of God. It would not be so beautiful, or so transparent to God, if it were not for the breeze. The filmy white blossoms on the irregular, fragile limbs move in the wind, in the breath of the Holy Spirit, calling me to deeper appreciation of its loveliness. It is saying: "See me speak of God, of a tiny bit of the divine glory, the bit that I can image." I *do* see and I thank you, my cherry tree, for telling me of God. I wish I might do the same. Can any of us be as fine an image of God as a cherry tree?

9

Resistance Spirit[1]

The Holy Spirit and Empire

Joerg Rieger

Awareness of the Holy Spirit, like of any other subject of theology, does not emerge in a vacuum. For this reason alone we need to seek to understand how our thinking about the Spirit is influenced by various factors that often suffuse our thinking unconsciously. In a recent book I have shown how many of the most important turning points of our understanding of Jesus Christ are located in the context of empire, and it appears that the understanding of the Spirit is never far behind. The hope with which we enter into these reflections is that, as I discovered in regard to Christology, the powers of empire can never completely and absolutely assimilate the reality of God; there are good reasons to expect that this holds true for the Holy Spirit as well. In this context, the ambivalence that postcolonial theorists like Homi Bhabha find at the heart of colonial situations is crucial also for our own situation and for the reflections on the Holy Spirit that follow. Ambivalence is disturbing to colonial discourse because it resists control and "poses an immanent threat to both 'normalized' knowledges and disciplinary powers."[2] A challenge to empire is posed by a "*double* vision, which in disclosing the ambivalence of colonial discourse also disrupts its authority."[3]

Understanding how our images of Christ and the Holy Spirit are being shaped by empire is, therefore, not a fatalistic move; the opposite is the case. The search is on for what I have called a "theological surplus,"[4] that is, for the divine reality that escapes the assimilating pressures and the repressions of empire, even if only under the conditions of ambivalence. This divine reality that resists assimilation can only be seen clearly if we understand which images of the divine have been assimilated by empire. In this chapter, I will launch an investigation of what we might call a pneumatological surplus. Perhaps we could talk about a spiritual surplus as well, but this notion carries the baggage of an understanding of spirituality that is otherworldly and a related misunderstanding that spirituality is dealing only with a limited aspect of life (that which is not political, economic, practical, etc.).

RESISTANCE SPIRIT: PAST

A brief definition of empire holds that empire is that which seeks to control all aspects of life and all of reality. Empire is a conglomerate of massive concentrations of power which permeate all aspects of life and which cannot be controlled by any one actor alone.[5] This is one of the basic marks of empire throughout history. Empire seeks to extend its control as far as possible; not only geographically, politically, and economically—these factors are more commonly recognized—but also intellectually, emotionally, psychologically, spiritually, culturally, and religiously. The problem with empire is, therefore, that no one can escape its force fields completely. Nevertheless, a sense of ambivalence remains and thus empire is never quite able to extend its control absolutely. Whatever the extent of its influence, no empire has managed yet to co-opt Christianity altogether.

In the early decades before and after the birth of Christ the Roman Empire evolved from a republic into an empire. Its military conquests were stunning, its control often violent, represented for instance in mass crucifixions of political rebels. But the more integral parts of the Roman Empire rarely required such violent acts; cultural and religious means provided effective and less visible control, including the emperor cult, which also contributed to the unity of the empire.[6] Literary production, art, and festivals all helped to solidify the control of the empire. Building projects such as temples and other public buildings, as well as roads that allowed for easier trade relationships (and military movements if necessary), would serve the same purpose. Economic structures such as the patronage system, through which wealthy benefactors maintained their influence on the lower classes and determined their world, also helped to pull together the various constituencies of the empire. Not surprisingly, money played a major role in the formation of empire; it is quite telling that even Jesus used coins that bore the imprint of the Roman emperor. In sum, the Roman Empire was present at all levels of life.

When the control mechanisms of empire are so deeply engrained, is there anything left but to acquiesce? Does not the Spirit's often emphasized role as "sustainer" imply that the Spirit unambivalently sustains the way things are and that, by extension, Christians too need to accommodate to the status quo? Can Christians under the influence of empire still imagine the work of the Spirit as sustaining and inspiring ambivalence and alternatives, resisting the powers that be? Is there anything in the work of the Holy Spirit that continues to inspire us in ways that go against the grain of empire? Can we conceive of the inspiration of the Holy Spirit as that which pushes beyond the system and opens new vistas?

In many biblical traditions, this is indeed how the Spirit is conceived—as that which inspires us in ways that cut against empire. If empire is that which seeks to control, the Holy Spirit by contrast is that which cannot be controlled; it is like the wind which "blows where it chooses" (Jesus' image in John 3:8). Moreover, not only can the Spirit not be controlled—"everyone who is born of the Spirit," says the Johannine Jesus, shares in this uncontrollable existence that "blows where it chooses." Why is this so? It is tempting to respond that this has to do with the immaterial nature of things spiritual. But that response, although deeply engrained in the logic of mainline churches and theologies, is not quite correct: wind, although it cannot be seen directly, is certainly not immaterial. We can perceive it in bodily ways and hear its sound (John 3:8) and its material impact can be tremendous, for good or for ill. This insight is also contained in the Old Testament notion of *ruach*, a term that can be translated as wind, breath, aspiration, respiration, but also as spirit: Spirit is not something that is immaterial in this way of thinking. There is no dichotomy of spiritual and material in this perspective.[7] The winds of the Spirit cannot be controlled, not because they are immaterial, but because they are the winds of the Spirit of Christ, and this Christ is clearly someone who cannot be controlled.

Obviously, there are many diverse images of the Spirit in both Testaments of the Bible and even in the Greco-Roman world itself.[8] Nevertheless, resistance to control may well be one of the most fundamental traits of Christ and the Spirit, a trait that finds expression in the communal memory of many otherwise different accounts. The efforts to control Christ and Christ's resistance are unmistakable. In the beginning of the Gospel of Mark (3:6), the Pharisees and the Herodians (the latter vassals of the Roman Empire) conspire to get rid of Jesus because of his uncontrollable act of healing on the Sabbath. In the Gospel of Luke, Jesus' own fellow citizens of Nazareth try to throw him off a cliff because he proclaims good news to the poor, release to the captives, recovery of sight to the blind, and that the oppressed will go free—explicitly noting his inspiration by the "Spirit of the Lord" (Luke 4:16–30). In the Gospel of John, Jesus once again turns out to be uncontrollable in his run-ins with establishment religion, enraging his powerful opponents to such a degree that they try to kill him (John 8:39–59). Jesus cannot even be controlled by the kinds of lures that hardly fail in the context of empire, both ancient and contemporary: led into the wilderness by none other than the Spirit, he demonstrates the Spirit of resistance when he rejects the devil's temptations of absolute power and control—the trademarks of empire (Matt. 4:1–11; Luke 4:1–13). When the Roman officials and the Jewish high priests (who collected the tribute to Rome and were selected by Herod[9]) finally manage to do him in for good and to crucify him, he rises up again—this time from the dead—breathing the Spirit of resistance (John 20:22). Only later, as dehistoricized and disembodied religious symbols, do Jesus and the Spirit become more controllable, although even those symbols never get rid of the sort of ambivalence that maintains a challenge (and not all religious symbols could be completely dehistoricized and disembodied). The resurrection serves as an indefatigable reminder that the risen Christ in the power of the Spirit continues to blow where he chooses, to the chagrin of the powers that be.

The Spirit who refuses to be controlled in the midst of the pressures of empire can be traced through the centuries, although such a historical-theological survey cannot be pursued in this limited space. A reference to Basil the Great may suffice. His insistence that the Holy Spirit is indeed part of the Godhead reminds us of the fact that the church does not own the Spirit and is therefore not in a position to control it. As free agent, the Spirit retains the ability to transform and challenge the church and the powers that be, rather than vice versa.[10] This is the resistance Spirit indeed.

RESISTANCE SPIRIT: PRESENT

Today we are witnessing a new emphasis on the Holy Spirit that has been described as "a profound sea-change in the course of the theological dialogue."[11] Whatever the state of theological reflection on the Holy

Spirit in the past, attention to the Holy Spirit has increased as the Pentecostal and Charismatic movements are stronger than any Spirit movement in history, and postmodern sentiments have produced a wealth of new interests in spirituality.[12] This is the context in which we need to wonder about whether and how the Spirit continues to sustain and inspire alternatives to the control of empire. In order to address this question, a brief reflection on empire in our own time is in order. After all, we live at a time when the prominent empires of the past have withered away, and with them their influence on Christianity. The Roman Empire, the empires of medieval Europe, and the empires of colonial Europe including the British Empire have all crumbled, and we are not even quite sure whether empire still exists. Is not the word on the street that we find ourselves in an era that is postcolonial?

Reflections on empire today might be focused by the paradoxical term "postcolonial empire."[13] This term acknowledges that the era of colonialism is mostly over but it also holds that empire has found new ways to manifest itself. In the contemporary United States, the administration of President George W. Bush is often perceived as seeking to build a new empire—a charge that is proudly embraced by some of its supporters. Yet even the politics of the Bush administration, characterized by unilateral assertions of power and aggressive use of military force, is sufficiently different from older colonialisms. Its ongoing war in Iraq, for instance, is not aimed at colonizing Iraq in the traditional sense; neither is it aimed at the expropriation of Iraqi property since even the vast oil resources, often named as one of the key interests behind the war, remain in the hands of the nation of Iraq. The interests of contemporary empire can rather be found in economic arrangements such as "production sharing agreements," according to which the oil remains in the possession of Iraq but the oil fields are operated by U.S. companies, a deal that is extremely lucrative for the companies. This takes care of an old concern raised by Adam Smith that owning and maintaining colonial properties was not cost effective.[14] Despite aggressive and open displays of power by the current U.S. government, in the long run the less visible manifestations of the postcolonial empire that are worked out in economic agreements and other multilateral deals are more significant. To be sure, this postcolonial empire began to put down its roots long before the Bush administration, and its thoroughly economic character serves as a reminder that empire today is not a phenomenon that can be identified by developments in the United States alone but is related to the influence of other powerful economic players located in the European Union and the other nations which make up the G8 (Canada, France, Germany, Italy, Japan, Russia, and the United Kingdom).

One of the most distinctive challenges of the postcolonial situation is that official colonialism and its more direct political forms of domination and control have been replaced by less visible forms of power. Moreover, those less visible forms of power are often more far-reaching, working through hidden economic dependencies as well as cultural processes that touch all areas of life, effectively transmitted through the mass media. This has created a paradoxical situation: the powers of empire are stronger than ever but are perpetuated through relationships that seem to be more egalitarian and equal on the surface. While in the colonial period other people were subdued by colonial governments and their operatives, in a mostly postcolonial world colonial governments are no longer needed to exercise the power of empire. In this context, the "hard power" of the Bush administration that has attracted so much (and often negative) attention both nationally and internationally appears to be less effective in shaping the world than the "soft power" promoted by earlier U.S. administrations. The display of hard power itself is only effective if it can be translated into soft power manifest, for example, in business relationships where the two parties meet in the spirit of a seemingly free market. In this model, buyers and sellers appear to enjoy a basic equality that, at least on the surface, shares little resemblance with hierarchical colonial structures. Little wonder that free-trade agreements are pursued so vehemently by the wealthy nations. With the end of unilateral colonialism the doors appear now open for multilateral and pluralistic relations.

In the postcolonial empire, the real powers have become more difficult to identify because they have extended their reach beyond the limits of direct political domination.[15] This lack of visibility of the flow of power in the postcolonial empire is paralleled by the lack of visibility of the flow of power between the classes in the contemporary United States, another flow of power that was much more visible in empires past. One of the most persistent misconceptions in the United States is that class differences do not matter anymore because most people are members of the middle class. Even where it is noted that there continue to be class differences—and that in fact the gap between the classes is steadily widening—there is little awareness of the differentials of power and of the fact that the wealthiest are living at the expense of all others (whose wages have either not seen significant increases over long periods of time or have even gone down if adjusted for inflation, as is true of the minimum wage).

As the direct exercise of power has given way to more subtly powerful and far-reaching forms of power, the forces of culture and religion have become more important, especially as they work in sync with economic expansion. As direct political power has given way to economic influences that move according to the seemingly universal, neutral laws of the free market, the realm of culture has also adjusted. Direct political control of education, for instance, and other intellectual endeavors has given way to the commercialization of education and the more subtle cultural influences of mass media such as television, the World Wide Web, and other mushrooming forms of communication. In the realm of religion, direct political control over the church, as practiced, for instance, by the various state churches in Europe, has given way to other, more subtle forms of marketing the sorts of religious expression that promise to keep people happy (that is to say, well-adjusted to the demands of the powers that be).

This new form of postcolonial empire is evolving through the expansion of many areas of contemporary life that are generally celebrated and welcomed. One of the key examples is the uncritical celebration of the broadening moves of a globalizing world that celebrates multilateral relationships and vibrant cultural exchange without realizing the underlying patterns of economic exploitation on which the tremendous and ever-growing power differentials of the contemporary empire are based.

In this context, how can the Holy Spirit continue to "blow where it chooses"? Are there not simply too many ways now in which the Spirit can be co-opted and controlled, including an ever more co-opted religion? I will examine this question in light of two major contemporary approaches to the Holy Spirit that seek to account for the liberating potential of the Spirit in one of the more powerful parts of the world that make up the web of postcolonial empire: Germany.[16]

THE SPIRIT OF PLURALISM

While empire is not the key category of the work of Michael Welker, there are numerous references to it.[17] One of the problems that challenge the doctrine of the Holy Spirit, he says, are "the dominant, mostly imperialistic forms for structuring experience, especially in Western cultures," manifest for instance in "technical-scientific rationality" which "compel conformity in the Western world."[18] In this context, our search for a pneumatological surplus can only affirm Welker's overall goal, namely to come to a new perception of God and God's power (Welker, ix).

Welker's perception of empire, however, is still that of a traditional colonial empire. Empire is identified with what he calls "imperialistic monocultures" (147), a notion developed in relation to Joel 2:28–32. Characteristic of such a monoculture is that it is determined from the top down. Like other German thinkers critical of empire, the empire on Welker's mind resembles the German Third Reich, a system of "political demonism and culpable collective callousness and brutality" (24). In this light, his critique of the "imperialistic subjugation of smaller, weaker peoples and cultures by powers that are superior militarily, economically, and in terms of communications and technology" (94) makes perfect sense. Along the same lines, there is a problem in the intellectual world with what Welker calls "the artificial light of an apparently unbroken reality and rationality continuum" and "an integral moral market."[19] Interestingly enough, however, Welker notes that today many people are aware of these problems and lament them: there seems to be some kind of resistance—and thus a pneumatological surplus—built into a postmodern mentality that rejects the structures of unilateral empire. Postmodern ambivalence appears to have some positive aspects.

Given this account of empire as a totalitarian monoculture and unilateral move of power, Welker assumes that empire is resisted as the Spirit somehow enables broader inspirations. The Joel text referenced above predicts the outpouring of the Spirit on "all flesh." This is clearly a broadening move that has potential, yet Welker interprets it in a way that ultimately corroborates the logic of the postcolonial empire when he takes this to mean merely that "the Spirit *also* descends on population groups that do *not yet* stand in full possession of spiritual, political, and economic powers" (150; emphasis mine). As the reach of the Spirit broadens, more people will come into fuller possession of the spiritual, political, and economic powers already at work while the powers of the status quo appear to be left intact. Even though Welker notes that "the 'rulers' as well are in need of deliverance by God" (150), the challenge to the powers of postcolonial empire is fairly superficial since the problem with these powers is mostly that they, too, are "frail and perishable" rather than wrongheaded and troublesome. Broadening the powerbase without significantly challenging the powers of the status quo (a move that resembles the development of contemporary free-trade agreements), Welker asserts, means that "a specific group of people, a specific stratum, a specific tradition, or a specific culture can no longer claim for itself alone God's presence, the reception of the Spirit, prophetic testimony, and true definitions of reality" (155). While this pushes beyond totalitarian monocultures, the emerging pluriform culture does not necessarily challenge the powerful if all it does is increase diversity and add a few more voices. In the contemporary United States, this would be like augmenting the well-known imperial slogan "God bless America" with the phrase "and the whole world": not only is America not challenged here, the assumption is that others should be blessed in a way that resembles our particular blessing.

Assuming that empire is manifest in unilateral and totalitarian structures, fostering pluralism and diversity seem to be the Spirit's ways of resisting empire: "The Spirit reveals the power of God in strong, upbuilding, pluralistic structures" (21), claims Welker. This pluralism does not negate unity but introduces unity in diversity.[20] The "unity of the Spirit," says Welker, "maintains and cultivates differences that do not contradict justice, mercy, and knowledge of God." Moreover, "the Spirit gives rise to a unity in which the prophetic witness of women is no less important than that of men, that of the young is no less significant than that of the old, that of the socially disadvantaged is no less relevant than that of the privileged" (22). In other words, the Spirit empowers everyone, and by doing so the Spirit provides unity. What is lacking here, however, is a sense that the Spirit's power might do more than augment the powers that already exist.

This lacuna is manifest most sorely when Welker discusses the diversity of the body of Christ, with reference to Paul's reflections in 1 Corinthians 12. In these passages, Welker finds "many hierarchical structures to exist side by side" which "alternate with each other" (23). Pneumatology manifests itself in terms of what Welker calls "*typical differences* that are bound together by the Spirit: old and young, rich and poor, socially privileged men and women of various religious, national, and cultural backgrounds" (23; emphasis in original). The image of the body, a mainstay of classical conservative thought, is thus justified once again, this time with reference to the Holy Spirit. The only difference is that while in antiquity the hierarchies were clearly established—feet were less powerful than heads, for instance—now the differences are declared interchangeable: sometimes eyes are particularly important, says Welker, sometimes ears or feet. This is what the idea of pluralism indeed suggests, and postcolonial empire builds on it; but is it really the case that pluralism erases differentials of power? The apostle Paul is not so naive. He refers to the conservative image of the body only in order to turn it upside down, stating for instance that "our less respectable members are treated with greater respect," and that "God has so arranged the body, giving the greater honor to the inferior member." Most importantly, Paul knows that "if one member suffers, all suffer together with it" (1 Cor. 12:23, 24, 26). As this Spirit pushes beyond the pluralistic sensitivities of a postcolonial empire, a pneumatological surplus once again manifests itself.

Welker's consistent emphasis on pluralism and diversity may be help-ful in resisting totalitarian structures of empire; yet in the context of postcolonial empire some serious problems are created. His generally valid concern for the Spirit connecting to a "broader public" (49) reveals the problem. The assumption is that by maintaining a neutral and uni-versal position somewhere in the middle, without "interest theology" (40)—what in the United States we might call "special interest theol-ogy"—the reach of the Spirit becomes broader. This may not be so sim-ple, however, under the conditions of postcolonial empire that wants us to believe that colonialism is a thing of the past and that relationships are now free to be constructed in pluralistic harmony, akin to how the system envisions relations between the buyers and sellers of Iraqi oil. Any broadening move will need to take a very close look at the flow of power that postcolonial empire does not want us to see.

In this context, Welker's idea of the "bearer of the Spirit" is espe-cially problematic. In reference to Isaiah 42, he introduces this "bearer of the Spirit" as a seemingly neutral character who rejects not only "political loyalty from above" but also "politics from below." As stated in Isaiah 42:2, applied to Jesus by Matthew 12:18–19, "He will not cry or lift up his voice, or make it heard in the street."[21] In a situation of severe yet hidden power differentials, it is not clear what is achieved by this "bearer of the Spirit" who, in Welker's interpretation, does not engage in "opposition politics" and "counter morality" (126). Not to engage in politics in a highly politicized situation does not necessarily mean that the political is avoided. Would not loyalty with those on the underside—to which the outpouring of the Spirit refers in Joel 2:29, which strangely enough includes female and male slaves—provide clearer forms of resistance to empire and ultimately more egalitarian relationships that include all? Here, paying attention to the suffering members of the body is not "special interest" politics or theology but the only thing that can truly keep the body together and the only move that can rebuild common interests, as the apostle Paul understood.[22] Moreover, here the Holy Spirit would take on a clearer and more scriptural shape. Under the conditions of postcolonial empire, any pluralism that does not address power differentials functions as a cover-up of the powers that be, which ultimately reinforces the status quo and assimilates the Spirit.

Despite his promotion of pluralism, at one point Welker realizes that not all differences should be reinforced and thus he suggests cultivating "creaturely differences" and removing "unrighteous differences," which can be economic, cultural, and social (25). But when it comes to these unrighteous differences, it is never quite clear what they are and where they come from. The "demons" of "addiction, drug problems, epidemic greed, repression of life and self-anesthetization of consumerist societies . . . , ecological exploitation and excessive debt politics" are all named by Welker, but the root causes are not clear. Nor does he encourage clarifying them, when he reminds us that in Jesus' pre-Easter activity the demons are not "removed with one blow"—"analogous to structural changes of a political, judicial, or moral sort"—but challenged "in and through varied, individual, irrepeatable concreteness" (202–3). Worse yet, everyone is implicated in the creation of unrighteous differences, as Jesus is said to have been crucified by "Jews and Romans, Gentiles and Jews, the pious and the impious, the political and the apolitical, rulers and ruled, the reflective and the frenzied" (209). But how did the disciples and the women, the common people contribute to Jesus' crucifixion? It is hard to imagine that all the "Jews" were likewise at fault, and such a claim makes no historical sense. Under the conditions of postcolonial empire, when power relations are hidden, these generalizations are especially problematic. An analysis of power is therefore more important than ever before and key to preventing yet another assimilation of the Holy Spirit to empire. Even though the powers of empire are perhaps clearest when it comes to unequal distribution of economic influence, Welker refuses to go deeper. His references to "greed" (303) and "consumerism" (308) barely scratch the surface of the forces that drive the economy; if greed and consumerism were at the very core, why would we need the advertising industry that encourages us to consume? Following the guidelines offered by Welker, could the Spirit of resistance stand any chance of identifying the core issues of the structures of postcolonial empire and challenge them?

THE EMBODIED SPIRIT

Jürgen Moltmann's theology of the Holy Spirit seeks to broaden Christian understandings of the Spirit which are limited by "the continuing Platonization of Christianity," which entails "hostility to the body," "remoteness from the world," and "preference for the inner experiences of the soul."[23] What gets lost, says Moltmann, is a concern for community and for nature. Worse yet, what gets lost is also a sense of the Spirit's relation to the political and economic aspects of reality, an issue that appears to be especially crucial under the conditions of postcolonial empire where these realities are powerfully and securely at work below the surface. Moltmann relates the rediscovery of these aspects to traditional Hebrew thought. The Old Testament notion of Spirit, *ruach*, as we have seen, does not allow for such spiritualization.[24] Moltmann interprets Joel 2:28–32 in a way that is distinctively different from Welker: as the Spirit is poured out on all people, limits are introduced: "traditional privileges come to an end—the privileges of men compared with women, of lords compared with servants, of adults compared with children" (Moltmann, 57). The power of the Spirit not only strengthens those with less power but also restricts powers that are harmful. In this context, the cries of the oppressed are not silent, as Welker would have it, but rise up to God and make a difference (77). Given the narrow interpretations of the Holy Spirit in many of the churches today, including large parts of the Pentecostal and Charismatic movements, Moltmann's approach reminds us of a pneumatological surplus that is mostly neglected at present.

As a result, "to experience the fellowship of the Spirit inevitably carries Christianity beyond itself into the greater fellowship of all God's creatures" (10). The Spirit is experienced here as the "Spirit of life," in ways that are both personal and communal and that include experiences at the brink of life and death (17). These kinds of experiences represent a theology of experience that does not fall into the traps of modernist, liberal, or pietistic theological emphases on experience that often operate with levels of experience that conform to the powers that be. Moltmann's own experience of near-death during World War II matches these deeper experiences that are so profound that the passing of time does not heal them and that there is no "merciful forgetting" (21). Moltmann's theology of experience promotes the voices of the laity, noting that empire has often been supported by church theology, which restricted the communication of the Spirit to the "spiritual pastors" and the "anointed apostolic majesties of the holy *imperium.*" In this context, "dangerous memories" of the Christ of the Spirit, the Sermon on the Mount, and his nonviolent passion were repressed.[25]

Moltmann introduces a broader understanding of the history of empire in Europe, noting that empire was often tied up with religious repression. While in some European liberation movements God and freedom were linked, this connection was rejected in many other cases, especially in the "clerical churches" in France and Italy, where the higher clergy were closely related to feudalism. The conservative counter-revolution was once again based on the relation and identification of God, king, and country (107). Theologically, God's authority is indeed easily identified with the authoritarian structures of feudalist European empires. In the United States, however, we need to remind ourselves that our history is different: here, freedom, economic liberalism, the authority of the (democratically elected) government, and national pride all tend to be seen as rooted in God. In this connection, a deeper analysis of the metamorphoses of empire is required of us so as not to accommodate the Spirit to empire in our own situation. Modern colonialism is, after all, not unrelated to Enlightenment ideals of freedom and progress. Moltmann's account does not realize that Germany, too, pursued colonial fantasies in the nineteenth century that were built on enlightened efforts to educate and civilize other nations—a manifestation of empire that is often forgotten today and that in Germany has been neglected in favor of a critique of the clearer structures of fascism and the Third Reich.[26] When Moltmann applauds Protestant contributions to the dignity of individual and to individual human rights, based on the insight that faith entails a personal relation to God (and others) (116), he sees this as the Holy Spirit at work in the resistance of empire. Nevertheless, discourses of individual dignity and individual human rights are not free from Eurocentric notions of the self, and thus the structures of empire can easily return through the back door, especially under the conditions of postcolonial empire.

Developing a sense of the Holy Spirit in human experience, Moltmann is aware of the problematic nature of human experience, including "collective experiences," which can both "serve the common life, but they can also be blind and criminal" (26). Examples include Auschwitz for Germans and Vietnam for Americans. It is only in times of danger and upheaval that people become aware of these problems. Consequently, seeing things from the perspective of the victims is crucial: Germans, states Moltmann, need to see themselves through the eyes of the victims of the Holocaust, and "northern industrial society" needs to see itself "through the eyes of the hungry children in the Third World." In sum, "the perpetrators are dependent on their victims' experience, if they wish to know themselves, for the memory of suffering does not end, whereas our remembrance of what we have done ourselves is short-lived" (26–27). Looking at experience and the Holy Spirit in this broader perspective reminds us that we live in a "pluralist, polycentric world of many dimensions" (34). These experiences are all potential experiences of the Holy Spirit, yet only when the view from the margins is explicitly affirmed does it become clearer how the Holy Spirit is at work in the expansion of human experience. Moltmann has a better sense than Welker that this "holistic view" of experience needs to be "critically related to the existing cleavages in human beings themselves, to the divisions between human beings, and to the disjunction between human beings and nature" (37–38). To be sure, these experiences in the midst of tension are mirrored in key experiences of the Holy Spirit in both Testaments of the Bible and in parts of the Christian tradition.[27]

Moltmann notes a change in the progression from industrial to postindustrial societies, a change that entails a transformation in the structures of empire. While in industrial societies the motto was "produce more—consume more," today we are beginning to realize the cost: faith in progress is crumbling in face of the progressive destruction of the environment. Moreover, "people feel dehumanized when they are seen only as producers, consumers and commuters," and they "are losing the subjectivity which was set free when industrial society began." These things may not be seen as clearly in the United States as in Europe, but Moltmann's observation that this leads to disease and depression applies in the United States as well: "the upwardly mobile classes in industrial and consumer society are becoming infertile—physically so, as well as psychologically"(171). In this context, the Holy Spirit as the sanctifying Spirit[28] creates another potential surplus: The destruction of the world is countered when we rediscover the "sanctity of life and the divine mystery of creation" (171). Practical steps include reducing technological violence against nature, reducing energy use, turning from "hard to soft technology"—parallel to "ending the violent regimentation of one's own body by the intellect." Another step is ceasing to live at the expense of others and learning to live together with them; even a challenge to the notion of property is noted briefly (172–73). No doubt, Moltmann's theology of the Holy Spirit recognizes some of the key issues, including the basic problem of empire that is still with us: "a world-wide economic order has grown up which makes the poor poorer and the rich richer" (138). The question is, however, how the Spirit will continue to guide us in these matters, especially where there are loose ends. Can we simply endorse "soft technology"? In a free market economy, how is soft technology fundamentally different from the rule of hard technology? What would it mean to liberate the body and what are the limitations? Most importantly, what about the "world-wide economic order," which is often seen as an achievement of the Christian Spirit, and the Spirit of Protestantism in particular (e.g., by Max Weber)?

That Moltmann as a Protestant theologian notes a lacuna in Protestant theology indicates one more place where we still need to take a closer look at the work of the Holy Spirit and its potential surplus: that "Protestant theology has not noticed the analogy between God's 'justifying' righteousness and his righteousness that 'creates justice'" (129) is more than just a surprising coincidence, as Moltmann seems to suggest, perhaps connected to some theological technicalities. We need to take a closer look at how empire controls even well-meaning theological efforts. Moltmann's rereadings of the notions of justice and of justification point the way: experiencing the Holy Spirit as the Spirit of Life, we need to heed God's own "preferential option for the poor," where God creates justice for the most vulnerable (129, 142). This does not mean that the nonpoor are excluded. Clearly, the perpetrators also need liberation, although they tend not to notice. Still, there is hope.[29]

In sum, the strength of Welker's and Moltmann's reflections on the Holy Spirit, particularly relevant in the contemporary United States, is that they are aware of the dangers of totalitarianism and fascism, due to traumatic experiences in Germany's recent past with fascism and the Holocaust. Both remind us of the ongoing need for watchfulness and self-critique, which may be more relevant in the contemporary United States than ever before. At the same time, however, one of the limits of both approaches is that they fail to work through earlier German colonial fantasies that shape up in a different context that is more enlightened and less totalitarian. After all, these earlier German colonial fantasies rejected the classical histories of the conquests and the more exploitative colonialisms of the other European nations.[30] Fantasizing about their own contributions to the colonies in the nineteenth century, Germans see themselves as mostly benevolent and concerned about the betterment of others. What is lacking here is a sense of the importance of power differentials and a deeper understanding of and respect for the difference of other people. It is this spirit that continues to be at work in many of the attitudes of postcolonial empire and thus we need to take a closer look yet at the work of the Spirit in the resistance of empire today.

WHERE TO GO FROM HERE

How do we know that the Spirit is free from the control of empire, especially when this control assumes less and less visible forms? Is not the Spirit the member of the Godhead that is most easily co-opted by the powers that be?

First of all, we should note that theological reflections that remain general and abstract pose the biggest problems. Both Welker and Moltmann provide some context for their reflections on the Holy Spirit, but many other approaches do not. In a recent book that establishes new grounds for thinking about the Holy Spirit in the United States, many of the essays develop general and abstract theological arguments discussing the Spirit in Trinitarian thought, philosophical and doctrinal developments, and so on.[31] Under the conditions of empire, that is to say in situations where severe power differentials are the rule, not addressing at least some of the tensions can easily amount to tacit endorsement.

Nevertheless, some of the contributions in the same book help me sum things up for our own situation of postcolonial empire and point out further manifestations of a pneumatological surplus. Like Welker and Moltmann, Anselm Kyongsuk Min notes the fragmentation of contemporary life, especially as far as the middle class is concerned. He also points out how "the clashes between classes, genders, ethnic groups, cultures, and religions have become more acute all over the world."[32] In this context, he argues that the personhood of the Spirit can be found in "being relational and creating relations," a stance which Min finds corroborated by many passages of the New Testament.[33] Min's approach deepens our investigation, however, where he notes that "no authentic dialogue is possible between oppressors and oppressed."[34] This insight reminds us of the tremendous difficulties faced by the Holy Spirit's work in the postcolonial empire; the conditions for a pneumatological surplus are not easily met. In this context, liberation requires new kinds of relationships as "the problem of liberation becomes the problem of collaboration and solidarity of Others in mutual liberation." No doubt, this includes a "preferential option for those who suffer more."[35] The biblical parallels for Min's argument should not be hard to produce, ranging from Jesus' frequent reminders that the last shall be the first to the Beatitudes of the Sermon on the Mount (Matt. 5:1–11; Luke 6:20–26). If this is correct, it should be clear that relationships need to be rebuilt from below, a process which gives us new vistas into the work of the Holy Spirit.

These considerations add some significant insights to our understanding of the Holy Spirit. Min observes that "the Holy Spirit is a self-effacing, selfless God whose selfhood or personhood seems to lie precisely in transcending herself to empower others likewise to transcend themselves in communion with others, to urge the Father to give himself to the Son and the Son to give himself to the Father and to the world for the sake of the Father, and to liberate humanity and creation from their self-isolation and empower them to transcend themselves toward one another and toward God in union and solidarity."[36] The Spirit thus embodies a new way of being a person. Clearly, there is a pneumatological surplus here to be mined, as the Spirit is active "wherever there is a moment of self-transcendence toward communion and solidarity at all levels."[37]

Nevertheless, Nancy Victorin-Vangerud, responding to Min's approach, pushes us to the next level when she points out what I would consider to be the key problem in any theology of the Holy Spirit that seeks to address relationship in a pluralistic, postmodern, and postcolonial context: "Part of the problem is that we assume a level dancing floor when we adopt the image of mutuality."[38] This appears to be due in part to the increasing invisibility of power in postcolonial times and thus it is not even necessary any more to explicitly assume such a level ground (neither Welker nor Moltmann do so); simply not questioning it is enough, as it seems to be the default assumption whenever we talk about relationship today. Paying attention to the differentials of power in the postcolonial empire teaches us that relationships are not always safe, especially for those on the underside. Here we run into a problem that affects even Min's approach, which is more sensitive to these issues: his emphasis on the self-effacement of the Spirit, while presenting a challenge to those in power, also "reifies a norm" that many women "know all too well," says Victorin-Vangerud.[39] While we need to hold fast to a search for new relationships that challenge the vast power differentials of the postcolonial empire, in our ongoing search for a pneumatological surplus we need to keep in mind her notion of a "poisonous pneumatology," as there are indeed serious flaws in a relational pneu-matology when it fails to question the flow of power in patriarchal fam-ilies that fosters conformity, blind trust, and repression of efforts for personal differentiation.[40] This insight must be applied to postcolonial empire and the hidden flows of money and power as well: failing to question the hidden power structures of the postcolonial empire—less visible yet than that of patriarchal families and no less insidious—can lead to substantial distortions of our understanding of the Holy Spirit with the troubling result that we might miss the Spirit's work in sus-taining and inspiring another and perhaps more real world.

Nevertheless, in the midst of all of these pressures the hope with which we began this exploration of the Holy Spirit and empire has also been confirmed. Becoming more aware of the structures of empire in our own time, we realize that the powers of empire can never completely assimilate the reality of the Spirit, and that the Spirit that continues to "blow where it chooses" may yet be key to our hope for a new world.

10

The Holy Spirit and the Present Age

John B. Cobb Jr.

THE SPIRIT IN THE BIBLE

What do we mean by "the Holy Spirit"? The simple and accurate answer is "God." God is spirit, and God is distinguished from other spirits by being, in an unqualified sense, holy. God is "the Holy One," and that One is Spirit. Accordingly, "Holy Spirit" is a name for God.

Of course, there are other names for God. Muslims have a hundred. Christians could list a good many, but a limited number are especially favored. God is known as Creator, as Word (*Logos*), as Wisdom (*Sophia*), as Lord (*Kyrios*), as Christ. The language of Father and Son has been especially prominent in speaking of God because Jesus addressed God as Father (*Abba*), and is often spoken of as *a* or *the* Son of God. The term "Son," then, is also applied to the risen Jesus and to that in God which was incarnate in the human Jesus—the Word or the Wisdom of God. The baptismal formula identifies God as Father, Son, and Holy Spirit, and the long, complex, and confusing history of Trinitarian doctrine deals with the relation among these three.

Although one and the same God is named thus in many ways, the terms that are used *do* make a difference. In the early church some took from the story of the baptism the idea that the deity in Jesus was the Spirit that descended upon him. If that language had come to dominate the discussion, we would probably be dealing with a Binity instead of a Trinity. Or, if we had followed Paul in focusing on the Wisdom of God, instead of following the prologue of John's Gospel in speaking of God's Word, the views of God throughout Christian history might have been less patriarchal.

In the course of the actual discussion there was a move from trying to distinguish the "persons" of the Trinity in terms of their operations in the world to recognizing that all three "persons" are involved in every act of God. For example, the Son and the Spirit can both be called Creator. Nevertheless, the term usually calls forth the image of the Father. Similarly, if we try to distinguish the risen Christ too sharply from the Holy Spirit, we are checked by the encounter with Paul's assertion that the Lord (meaning Christ) *is* the Spirit (2 Cor. 3:17). When we want to emphasize God's immanence in the world, we can speak of any member of the Trinity. Nevertheless, it is especially as Holy Spirit that we speak of God's presence to us and, in particular, in us.

I have emphasized this point so that we will never get into arguments about whether it is right to attribute this or that divine action to one divine person or another. The Bible is not terminologically consistent in this respect. As long as we understand that these are human terms about God, this is not a problem. When the church has reified the persons in such a way as to imply their separate existence, great damage has been done. Muhammad might well have become a Christian had not the Trinitarian teaching he encountered sounded polytheistic to him. The official basis for the split of Christendom between Western Catholicism and Eastern Orthodoxy was over the question of whether the Spirit proceeds from the Son as well as from the Father. Too often people are told that their spiritual condition depends upon affirming paradoxical statements about God as Three and God as One.

Accordingly, we should recognize that everything God does is done by the Holy Spirit. Nevertheless, the topic of the Holy Spirit leads us, quite properly, to focus on some aspects of God's work in the world rather than others. For example, when we think of God as the ultimate source of order in the world, although it would not be theoretically wrong to attribute this to the Holy Spirit, it would run against the rhetorical grain.

The term "spirit," *pneuma* (Hebrew: *ruach*), is associated with wind and especially with breath. Breath is vital for the life of animals including human beings. In the second Genesis creation story, the human being receives life when God breathes into the human body that God had made out of "the dust of the ground" (Gen. 2:7). This breath of God is also Spirit, that which makes alive. It is profoundly immanent.

Our breath is within us. These notions of enlivening and immanence belong with the idea of God as Spirit throughout the Bible and church history. Accordingly, in this chapter, I will continue this tradition and emphasize God's enlivening presence to us and within us.

Of course, this presence does more than make us biologically alive. "Life" has a much richer meaning both in the Bible and in current usage. We could say that the Holy Spirit makes us "spiritually" alive. It inspires and strengthens us. It gives us aspirations. It opens us to new truth and enables us to integrate this into our minds and lives. God's presence also assures us of divine acceptance and companionship. It guides and directs. It binds us to one another. It calls us into God's purposes for us and urges us to fulfill them. But the Spirit does not compel us.

The emphasis on God's presence comes out clearly in the invocation "Come, Holy Spirit." Of course, this does not mean that we think God is located at some distance and that we are asking God to change locations. It expresses, instead, our hope that the universal presence of God will become more real to us subjectively. We want to know God's presence not only intellectually but also existentially. We want God to open us to the presence of the Spirit, so that we may be transformed. We believe that this openness to God's transforming presence will make us more truly alive.

Paul is our greatest theologian, and Romans is his most theological book. One main theme of that book is the contrast of orientation by and to the Spirit and orientation by and to the flesh. The first half of the eighth chapter is devoted to this contrast. I will quote just two verses: "For those who live according to the flesh set their minds on the things of the flesh, but those who live according to the Spirit set their minds on the things of the Spirit. To set the mind on the flesh is death, but to set the mind on the Spirit is life and peace" (Rom. 8:5–6).

It is this dual possibility to which this essay is addressed. What does it mean today to live according to the Spirit rather than according to the flesh? To answer this responsibly, we first need to consider more carefully what it meant to Paul.

It is important to be clear what it does not mean. In the course of time, the distinction between flesh and Spirit came to be identified all too often with that between body and mind. The body and its desires came to be viewed as the enemy of the human mind or spirit. Ascetic practices were adopted to subordinate the body to the spirit. The special difficulty of controlling sexual desires led to preoccupation with genital sexuality as evil and "dirty." For many Christians, the primary meaning of "flesh," and therefore also of "sin," has been connected with sexual thoughts and acts. For centuries Christian teaching held that celibacy is the spiritually preferred lifestyle. Protestants rejected this, but they retained the idea of sexual feelings as being in marked opposition to the spiritual. Roman Catholics long continued to favor celibacy.

This focus on sexuality as the primary center of opposition to the Spirit is not biblical. Paul does favor celibacy for his followers, but not because sex in general is sinful. He believed that a person who was celibate was able to give more undivided attention to the work of the Christian community and its extension. But if a single person became preoccupied with sex, it would be better to marry (1 Cor. 7:9). These are matters to be decided on a case-by-case basis according to the needs and capacities of the people involved.

Paul is often thought to have himself been preoccupied with sexual matters. This view derives from the widespread emphasis on two verses in the first chapter of Romans. When describing how idolatry leads to social distortion, he devotes two verses to what he saw as the disruption of normal sexuality. He apparently thought that the prevalence of same-sex desires and actions resulted from the misdirection of social order by worshiping what is less than God. Few of us would make that analysis today. In any case, there is no indication that he regarded what he thought of as normal sexuality as a social or spiritual problem, and he understood what he thought of as abnormal sexuality as a symptom of social disorder rather than the evil as such. The evil is idolatry. In verses 29–31, where he spells out the vices that are the final results of the prevalence of idolatry, sexual matters are conspicuous by their absence.

This is not to say that Paul never mentions sexual sins. In some of his letters they are included in rather conventional lists of vices. Also, in Romans 7 and 8, there are indications that even when the followers of Jesus succeed in orienting their *minds* to the Spirit, their *bodies* remain resistant. The full redemption of these bodies awaits the eschaton. In this life this process is not complete. Indeed, only with the body's redemption will the full glory of God be manifest. Clearly, the body as such is not evil or inferior.

Paul interrupts his discussion of flesh and Spirit in Romans 8 with a three-chapter excursus on Israel and Gentile Christians. When he returns to the general topic of chapter 8 in chapter 12, the language is a little different. Since I find the new formulation especially fruitful for our purposes, I quote the first two verses of this chapter: "I appeal to you therefore, brothers and sisters, by the mercies of God, to present your bodies as a living sacrifice, holy and acceptable to God, which is your spiritual worship. Do not be conformed to this world, but be transformed by the renewing of your minds, so that you may discern what is the will of God—what is good and acceptable and perfect."

Here the contrast is between being conformed to this world and being transformed by the renewing of our minds. I assume an equivalence between conformation to this world and setting our minds on the things of the flesh. I assume also an equivalence between being transformed by the renewing of our minds and setting our minds on the things of the Spirit. Indeed, I find the terminological shift from "flesh" to "world" helpful in understanding Paul's meaning. But it would not be helpful if one understood "world" to mean the planet Earth or the physical universe or the biosphere. Actually, the Greek makes very clear that this is not Paul's intention. The Greek word is not *cosmos* but *eon*. It is this "age" to which we are not to be conformed, the "age" that has been shaped by idolatry as described in chapter 1. There is no opposition to what we today would call the natural world or to creaturely existence as such, any more than to the body and its sexuality.

His reference to "this age" may also have a still sharper focus. He lived in the age of the Roman Empire. It was within that social order that he was discussing what God wants. To be conformed to "this age" would be to internalize the values of that imperial society, values that are not unlike those that have dominated other empires before and since. Clearly, he was contrasting conformation to the ways of life and thought of the Roman Empire with that to which the Spirit of God called followers of Jesus.

Paul's extensive discussion of the experience of these followers makes it clear that he did not expect complete transformation until the eschaton. Nevertheless, he celebrated the profound difference between the lives of those who participated in the communities he established and the lives characteristic of the society of that day. Transformation by the Spirit was far more manifest in the former. Entering a community in which such transformation was occurring certainly facilitated its happening in individual lives as well.

THE SPIRIT TODAY

What then about today? Is conformation to our age less problematic for the Christian than conformation to the Roman Empire was in the first century CE? Surely in some respects the answer is yes. Our age has been influenced by Christian faith. The idea that those who rule should be "public servants" has some effect in our society, as does the idea that every individual has value simply as being human. Legal slavery has largely disappeared. In American society today women have far more status than they did in Roman society. American society includes a democratic spirit that checks hierarchy. Many influential groups in our society are free to challenge government actions, and, in general, our society is far more diverse. We can conform to one segment of the society instead of another. Accordingly the contrast between conformity to the age and transformation by the Spirit may not always be as clear for us as it was for Paul.

The picture is further clouded when people identify living according to the Spirit with following the teaching of one or another branch of Christianity. We have already noted that this sometimes leads to a focus on rules of sexual conduct. This is often part of a larger pattern of legalism. Paul regarded all legalism as belonging to the sphere of the flesh— that from which the Spirit frees us. He would be appalled to find that today, among those who often appeal to his writings, the legalism is typically greater than in the secular society around them.

How appropriate to us is his letter to the Galatians in which he exclaimed: "You foolish Galatians: Who has bewitched you? . . . Did you receive the Spirit by doing the works of the law or by believing what you heard? Are you so foolish? Having started with the Spirit, are you now ending with the flesh?" (Gal. 3:1–3).

Why have so many of our churches in fact followed the Galatians rather than Paul? There seems to be a deep human need for rules of conduct. There is a great fear that if we do not have and enforce such rules we will behave badly. But just that attitude is part of the life according to the flesh against which Paul warns us. The freedom from the law provided by the Spirit is the freedom to love God and neighbor, from which love follow actions that fulfill the intention of the law without binding either the doer or the one who is loved. In order to realize this life of true freedom in the Spirit, we need communities of mutual support and love, and fortunately some congregations are that, even when they are not completely free from the legalism against which Paul inveighed.

Our age is characterized by religion both within and outside the church. Most of that religion, both within and without the churches, is legalistic. In Paul's day, there was much religion in the Roman Empire. Paul saw that it was idolatrous. Sadly, the same is true of much religion inside and outside the church today. The Spirit is directed against all forms of idolatry, even those, perhaps especially those, that claim to be Christian.

Today some people reject religion, and with it especially all forms of Christianity, in order to escape legalism and idolatry. They suppose that a fully secular existence is free from both. Sometimes the move away from the church is indeed one of which Paul would approve. There are those who stand outside all religious institutions who embody the Spirit more fully than many who are within.

Unfortunately, this does not characterize the secular aspect of our age in general. Indeed, no age has been more antithetical to the Spirit than ours. In this chapter I focus on those values of our age that express the secularization of Western culture rather than the distortions to which the churches are most prone. Sometimes resistance to the cultural values of this age is stronger in congregations that are also legalistic and idolatrous in their own ways than in those that are relatively free from these distortions. We all live in glass houses. We all need to free ourselves from the logs in our own eyes.

In the more legalistic churches, the feature of the age that strikes members most directly is likely to be the sexual one. Our society is drenched in sexual images and sexual talk. The secular world has reacted against the long repression of sexuality during the dominance of the Christian church by claiming freedom, much of which is healthy. But this healthiness is often invisible to those who approach sexuality legalistically because it is so closely connected with a preoccupation with sex that is tinged with idolatry. In significant parts of the culture, the whole of life seems to be ordered to sexual enjoyment, instead of sexual activity being ordered to the genuine well-being of both the partners and the wider society. Those who are celibate, it is often assumed, cannot have a rich and meaningful life. Adolescent society often pressures youth into sexual activity before they are ready. The legalism of forbidding is replaced with a legalism promoting sexual activity. People are often encouraged to expect more of sex than in fact it provides.

To be conformed to this age and to live according to the flesh, therefore, is likely to mean giving too large a place to the quest for sexual gratification with too little concern for its wider consequences for the partners and for the community. In his own day, Paul was accused of opening the door to all kinds of immorality by rejecting the laws that forbade them. Today we can see that the rejection of restrictive sexual rules, a rejection of which Paul would approve, has indeed led to all kinds of immorality in secular society. It has contributed to the breakdown of many marriages, often with destructive consequences for children. All this leads to intensified legalism on sexual matters in many churches.

Paul's rejection of law moves in a quite different direction. To be transformed so as to live according to the Spirit does not entail belittling of sexual enjoyment or a legalistic approach to controlling it. Nor does it mean regarding sexuality as "unclean." But living according to the Spirit *will* entail placing sexual activity in the context of what God calls us to do with our lives. We will act sexually only in ways that promote God's purposes in the world.

THE SPIRIT AND THE MARKET

Equally important, living according to the Spirit ends the preoccupation with sexual matters so characteristic of our culture and our churches. It enables us to identify what are truly the most important features of our society. Today these are shaped by capitalism both as ideology and as structural reality. Even sexuality has been commodified and brought into the service of capitalism. Some of the features of our society that I noted above as showing the influence of Christianity are in retreat before this capitalism, for example, the ideal of political leadership as service, the democratic spirit, and human rights.

Those who are conformed to this age understand that success in the market is the primary goal of life. In our age, whether the way one succeeds benefits or harms society is a question that is definitely a secondary consideration, if it is asked at all. Even questions of legality are couched chiefly in terms of the penalties that follow if one is caught.

How can any Christian fail to recognize that ordering our lives around success in the marketplace is part of that conformation to the age from which the Spirit frees us? Nothing could be clearer than Jesus' statement that we cannot serve both God and wealth (Matt. 6:24). Yet no previous society has ever been so fully organized in the service of wealth. Sadly, the opposition of the churches to this feature of our age has been far less clear and emphatic than the opposition of many churches to changes in sexual mores, about which Jesus had little or nothing to say.

The transformation of our minds by the Spirit does not lead to condemnation of markets any more than it leads to condemnation of sexual desires and acts. Condemnation of an "eon" obsessed with wealth does not mean that economic activity through which people make a profit is rejected. What is condemned is the ordering of society and of individual life to making money. In Jesus' words, we are to seek first the commonwealth of God.

A few of us may be able to work directly for the church or for causes that we understand to be directly related to realizing God's purposes in the world. We depend on the gifts of others. Most will need to work in economically productive ways to supply real needs of people, and to support themselves, their families, and the causes to which they are committed. But this need does not justify placing the activity of moneymaking first in their lives.

The other role that is made important by the capitalist system is that of consumer. The goods produced by a capitalist society must be consumed in ever-increasing quantity. Acquiring them has become the most enjoyable activity for many people. The shopping mall has become the gathering place for many youth. Many study the advertisements in the newspaper more carefully than the news. Changing styles and improving technology make our present possessions inadequate and direct us toward new purchases. More and more of our purchases are disposable after one or a few uses. We call this a consumer society and its collective values are often called "consumerism."

Consumerism does, indeed, function as the real religion of many people. That is, the acquisition of goods becomes the organizing principle of their lives. The "good life" is the one that consumes a great deal. To conform to our age is to participate in this way of life, all too often called "the American way of life." Our leaders declare this to be nonnegotiable, even when its continuation threatens the health of the biosphere and the well-being of future generations.

Nevertheless, I prefer to describe the now-global religion as "economism." As recently as the first half of the twentieth century, American society was radically pluralistic. Money played a large role in all spheres, but each sphere still had a sense of its own distinct functions and norms. The economy was of immense importance, but it remained one sphere among several.

Consider what has happened to education. Whereas in the first half of the twentieth century we thought of higher education as preparing people for service and leadership in society, today the goal is overwhelmingly improved economic status. Indeed, the state now funds much of education explicitly to prepare people to be good workers rather than good citizens or good persons. High school graduates often have too little knowledge of the world and its history to understand current events. Concern for enriching personal life that is expressed in the teaching of literature and music has been marginalized. Schooling is thought to be successful if graduates are able to satisfy the needs of employers.

As late as the first half of the twentieth century, the political and legal spheres were understood to be distinct from each other and also from the economic sphere. Government now functions largely to support our corporations in their global reach. The courts have been heavily politicized, and today that means brought into the capitalist system, and market principles are being applied to legal decisions.

In the first half of the century we understood that the field of medicine belonged to the medical profession. Doctors were in charge and, despite many failures, the public trusted them to make their decisions according to their professional judgments. Now we speak more of the medical industry. Doctors are employees.

In the earlier period we assumed that science was basically the disinterested quest for truth. Scientists also had their professional standards, and the public trusted their pronouncements to be guided by their standards. In the second half of the century we have come to assume that scientific research has a practical purpose. Chiefly it serves business. Some of it does so indirectly through serving the military. Even research related to human health is heavily affected by the prospects of profits for the pharmaceutical industry. Too often we expect to hear from scientists what their employers want them to say.

Journalism was also an independent profession with its ideals of accuracy and fairness. Today journalists are employees of large media organizations operated by large corporations controlled by persons of great wealth. If journalists want to keep their jobs they must avoid offending their bosses. In general that means that they must work in the service of the capitalist system.

Sports and entertainment were once primarily local and amateur. For example, students from different colleges competed with each other in football. This was part of an athletic program designed to teach sportsmanship and to be good exercise. Now sports are dominated by professional teams that are part of big business operations. Even college sports have been largely oriented to profit. Players are admitted to colleges more as players than as students, and their financial support is often indistinguishable from employment. Much the same change has occurred in the field of entertainment. It has become an important part of the capitalist system.

Religious institutions are the institutions most resistant to incorporation into the capitalist system. However even in the field of religion, capitalist principles have made considerable headway. Religious broadcasting is certainly a big business. But even ordinary congregations are likely to think in terms of their product and their market. Some people go church shopping, trying to find the church that will meet the family needs best at the least cost.

No doubt I have exaggerated the change that has taken place as the economic order has been accepted as dominant over all the others. The other spheres have always been somewhat distorted by the influence of wealth; they were never completely independent from the economy. And they have not been completely swallowed up. Schools at all levels still have some teaching that is not focused on preparing students for economic success. Politicians listen to other voices than those of economists and the rich. We can still get judgments in the law courts that challenge the power of the economic elite on grounds of justice. The medical industry still gives large scope to the professional judgments of doctors. Most scientists, even those who are paid by corporations, have a strong commitment to the methods of responsible science. High school sports are still played largely for the sake of athletics and recreation. Many community theaters and church choirs give expression to amateur talent. Some journalists take risks in order to get real news to the public. But the shift from many relatively autonomous spheres to domination by the global market is real and extensive.

Since society has given primacy to the economic sphere, it has called upon economists to play the leading role in advising governments and shaping policies. For this reason, the theoretical justification for much of the way the world is now organized is taught in departments of economics. Included in this teaching is the importance of ever-increasing consumption. This certainly supports consumerism. However, the social organization that encourages this consumption is itself in the service of those who profit from production. Although no one is forced to subscribe to the religion of consumerism, its deepening hold on life in wealthy countries and its spread around the world are results of decisions made, not by consumers, but by those who control the economy. Consumerism is more a by-product of the commitment to increasing wealth for the few than an independent product of its ordinary followers.

Accordingly, a major task of Christians is to detach themselves, their thinking, and their actions, from the control of economistic theory and practice. To be conformed to this eon is to accept the view that life and society should be organized around the quest for wealth. The Spirit seeks so to transform us that our minds will be made new and we will work for a society in which the quest for wealth is subordinated to the quest for the commonwealth of God.

Given the importance of economic theory in forming our national and global societies, those who are not simply conformed to this age have the responsibility of examining its assumptions and basic principles. We have already noted that the theory is based on the assumption that the increase of wealth is the one proper goal of the economic activity that is to dominate society. If those who call themselves Christians in fact take Jesus seriously, they cannot accept this idea. As we study the additional assumptions and the further implications, the reasons for this rejection become even clearer.

It was once assumed that political theory dealt with justice and that governments would give at least equal consideration to political theory along with economic theory. Therefore, the absence of any role for justice in economic theory did not seem to be of crucial importance. But now that society has given the supreme place to economic theory, the consequences of this indifference become clear. The efforts to achieve some measure of justice for workers and the poor and some security for the middle class jointly constituted the New Deal. Since 1980 the dominance of economistic thinking has led to the gradual dismantling of these programs. The gap between rich and poor has grown, with virtually all economic growth going to the richest segment of society, domestically and globally. In the United States, the ratio of CEO pay to that of the average worker increased from 24 to 1 in 1967 to 300 to 1 in 2000. On a global scale, the annual income of the richest 1 percent in the world is equal to that of the poorest 57 percent. There are more children living in poverty today than was the case thirty years ago. It is clear that wealth begets wealth, and that when society takes no actions to counter the concentration of wealth in fewer hands, that concentration takes place. An economistic society sees nothing wrong with this outcome. If our minds are made new by the Spirit, we will reject this indifference.

Some of the social sciences have emphasized the importance of human community. People need human relationships with other human beings in order to thrive. Economists developed their view of human beings and their needs by observing market transactions. The early economists, such as Adam Smith, recognized that the community context of the markets played an important role, but in the systematization of economic theory, community disappeared. It is not surprising that theories developed on a purely individualistic basis have supported individualism in practice.

The actual results have led to the widespread destruction of human communities. The rural landscape was once dotted with villages that have now disappeared. The communities that once developed around factories have also been wiped out in large numbers. Economists, thinking according to the principles of their own discipline, see no losses. If fewer people are now producing more goods, then for them, this is all gain. One who has been transformed by the Spirit cannot view the situation in that way.

Especially since 1970 we have been learning to take our natural environment seriously. Resources are exhaustible; the ability of the environment to absorb our wastes is limited. Endless expansion of the human economy is destroying the habitats of thousands of species of creatures that are rapidly becoming extinct. The ocean's capacity to produce food for human consumption is rapidly declining. Even global weather is being adversely affected. It seems evident that we should take these matters into consideration in planning our economic activity.

However, economic theory was developed at a time when natural resources were vast in relation to industrial use. Conserving such resources did not enter into economic theory. That theory is now so entrenched that it seems virtually impervious to being reconstructed to take account of the needs of the natural world. Efforts to protect nature from overuse and destruction are viewed more as obstacles than as desirable complements to economic activity. Hence, the overwhelming hegemony of economism contributes to the rapid degradation of the earth. Those who are no longer conformed in their thinking to this age will resist these degrading practices and propose others.

For millennia one main function of education was to communicate values and to help people to learn to distinguish what is truly of value from the objects of desire that may actually, in the long run, be harmful. Mainstream economic theory stands in opposition to this effort. For it, whatever is desired is of value. Indeed, the value of anything is what people will pay for it. Crack cocaine is far more valuable than water, because it is so much scarcer in relation to demand. That the world would probably be better off if there were no crack cocaine and that water is essential to life on the planet do not affect their relative value in this standard economic theory. To be conformed to this eon is to abandon notions of value that are not simply reflections of what people want or are taught to want by advertising. Christians cannot allow themselves to be so conformed.

It is hard to think of a set of teachings and practices more in need of transformation by the Spirit! Yet, sad to say, the churches are just beginning to voice serious concerns. The Spirit may be at work as much outside as within the churches in countering the pressures of this age. Since many of those outside the churches have suffered more directly from the practical outcome of economic theories, resistance has grown more rapidly in some circles outside the church than within it.

For years the world's elite have met at Davos, Switzerland, in the World Economic Forum, to congratulate themselves on their victories in promoting a global situation that subordinates all other considerations to the economic growth from which they have gained wealth and power. However, there is now also a World Social Forum, associated especially with Porto Allegre in Brazil. The difference in names points to the latter's desire to subordinate market activity to the needs of real human beings. Few of the rich and powerful attend these meetings. But this forum reflects a new global consciousness of the horrors of the victorious globalization in the service of wealth alone. Should those concerned for the primacy of human well-being succeed, there would be an enormous transformation, one which all Christians should celebrate. Meanwhile, many Christian groups are working for this outcome, and an increasing number of international church bodies have spoken strongly against the worship of wealth and its consequences. As individuals, we can seek to open ourselves personally to being freed from our subservience in thought and act to this age.

THE SPIRIT AND EMPIRE

Another feature of our age is now even more apparent and immediately dangerous. We Americans have typically thought, erroneously, that we were, in our deeds as well as in our rhetoric, opposed to imperialism. After all, we fought against it for our own freedom as a nation.

We see now that we have long acted imperially in relation to the indigenous people of our land and to the Latin Americans. Today we find that among our political leaders there are many who idealize the *pax Romana* of Paul's time and who want to impose on the world a *pax Americana*. The Roman peace of which they speak was enforced by the armies of the Roman Empire, and it is clear that the current aim is to impose peace on today's world by a similar monopoly of military power by the United States. Our officially announced policy is to have such strength that no other country will even consider challenging our hegemony.

Sadly, we now recognize that this is not a sharp break with past policies of the United States; it is a highly visible and public expression on a grandiose scale of what had previously been both less visible and less grandiose. In any case, it adds to the importance of Paul for our time. We now, like Paul then, find ourselves living inside the unique imperial power. Our age, like his, is shaped by the values of a global empire.

These values, now as in Paul's day, override those of peace and justice and nonviolence. They justify preemptive strikes and the use of torture to extract the information we need to implement our imperial goals. They justify taking away the rights of those who oppose the imperial power or refuse to give it the primacy it requires.

Paul lived in an empire that was well established in all of these ways. The Jewish revolts only served to demonstrate the futility and self-destructiveness of overt resistance. Its citizens could not directly oppose even its values. For Paul, the only solution was to create communities in which very different values were internalized. Still the empire rightly recognized even this as an important form of opposition. Paul was executed, and many other believers followed him in martyrdom.

We live in a time when the situation is far more fluid. Opposition to the adoption of the policies and practices expressive of imperial values is still possible. To whatever extent we are transformed by the Spirit into adopting the values of Jesus and Paul, we can participate in public opposition to the threatening teachings and forces. But more than before, we also need the support of communities that are open to the Spirit's transforming work and provide us with mutual support as we try to discern the calling of God's Spirit.

If we cannot stem the tide of imperialism and yet we ourselves refuse to conform to this age, we may learn that the days of Christian martyrdom are not past. The Spirit leads us into life, but it is a life in the Spirit that may also lead us to physical death. Both in life and in physical death, the Spirit will be with us.

Notes

Chapter 1: Discerning the Spirit

1. The language for Holy Spirit in Christian traditions is infinitely rich. Images from nature and human biology saturate the biblical and theological corpus: wind, fire, dove, breath. Though this chapter eschews any one image for Spirit, I have chosen to employ the pronoun "she," as it has deep resonance with much of that heritage. I do not mean to compensate for the patriarchal baggage of that tradition, but rather to indicate that there are fractures within traditional language. My hope is that the church will awaken to the depths and richness of its language for the Triune God and cease to be held captive to one language or image alone.

2. Michael Welker, *God the Spirit*, trans. John F. Hoffmeyer (Minneapolis: Fortress Press, 1994), 52.

3. I do not mean to imply that Luke wrote this narrative in a Trinitarian fashion. Rather, the pericope offers one of the few instances in the New Testament where we can glimpse the interaction between God's love, the Son's submission, and the Spirit's procession. This narrative (as well as the resurrection, annunciation, and transfiguration) has proven richly suggestive in Christian iconography, offering one portrait of Triune life given for the world. See Eugene Rogers, *After the Spirit: A Constructive Pneumatology from Resources outside the Modern West* (Grand Rapids: Eerdmans, 2005), 75–199.

4. Irenaeus often uses the terms "Spirit of God" or "Spirit of the Father" when referring to the Holy Spirit.

5. Irenaeus, *Against Heresies,* in *Ante-Nicene Fathers*, ed. Alexander Roberts and James Donaldson (Peabody, MA: Hendrickson, 2004),1:534.

6. Ibid., 535.

7. Ibid., 538.

8. "It is manifest that the souls of His disciples also . . . receiving their bodies, and rising in their entirety, that is bodily, just as the Lord arose . . . shall come thus in to the presence of God." Ibid., 560.

9. Ibid., 445.

10. His vision of the resurrection also includes animals. Ibid., 563.

11. Origen, *De Principiis,* in Roberts and Donaldson, *Ante-Nicene Fathers*, 4:242.

12. Ibid., 253.

13. Ibid., 254.

14. Ibid., 380.

15. Ibid., 285.

16. Origen, *On First Principles,* in *Readings in Christian Theology,* ed. Peter C. Hodgson and Robert H. King (Minneapolis: Fortress Press, 1985), 34.

17. Gregory of Nazianzus, "The Theological Orations," in *Christology of the Later Fathers,* ed. Edward R. Hardy (Philadelphia: Westminster Press, 1954), 199.

18. Ibid., 201.

19. Ibid., 209.

20. See *On the Spirit and the Letter,* in *Nicene and Post-Nicene Fathers,* First Series, ed. Philip Schaff (Peabody, MA: Hendrickson, 2004), 5:80–114.

21. Augustine, *The Trinity,* trans. Edmund Hill (Hyde Park, NY: New City Press, 1991), 197.

22. "Man's love, proceeding from knowledge and joining memory and understanding together . . . has in this image some likeness, though a vastly unequal one, to the Holy Spirit." Ibid., 428.

23. The narrative of Mary and Martha (Luke 10:38–42) provided many monastics with a proof text of the superiority of the contemplative vis-à-vis the active life. While the labor of Martha was necessary to show hospitality, the attentiveness of Mary evoked the response of Jesus, "Mary has chosen the better part, which will not be taken away from her" (v. 42). Many monastics read themselves in the person of Mary, while Martha represented those outside the cloister walls. See James Walsh, ed., *Cloud of Unknowing* (Mahwah, NJ: Paulist Press, 1981), 156–58.

24. "For the love of God, or the love that is God, the Holy Spirit, infusing itself into man's love and spirit, attracts him to itself; then God loves himself in man and makes him, his spirit and his love, one with himself." William of St. Thierry, *The Golden Epistle,* trans. Theodore Berkeley (Kalamazoo, MI: Cistercian Publications, 1971), 67.

25. For a brief, albeit more recent, example of biblical commentary suffused with erotic imagery, see Saint John of the Cross, "From The Spiritual Canticle: Songs Between the Soul and the Bridegroom," in *Theology and Sexuality: Classic and Contemporary Readings,* ed. Eugene F. Rogers (Malden, MA: Blackwell, 2002), 107–13.

26. William, *Golden Epistle,* 96.

27. See ibid., 92, where William describes the spiritual life as sweetness, exultation, and jubilation.

28. Thomas Müntzer, "A Manifest Exposé of False Faith," in *The Collected Works of Thomas Müntzer,* ed. Peter Matheson (Edinburgh: T. & T. Clark, 1988), 322.

29. Ibid., 274.

30. Ibid., 304.

31. "Interpretation of the Second Chapter of Daniel," in Matheson, ed., *Müntzer,* 247–51.

32. John Calvin, *Institutes of the Christian Religion* (1559), 1.9.2; ed. John T. McNeill, trans. Ford Lewis Battles, LCC (Philadelphia: Westminster Press).

33. John Wesley, "The Use of Money," in *John Wesley's Sermons: An Anthology,* ed. Albert C. Outler and Richard P. Heitzenrater (Nashville: Abingdon Press, 1991), 348–57.

34. For a contemporary Wesleyan theological economics, see M. Douglas Meeks, *God the Economist* (Minneapolis: Fortress Press, 1989).

35. See Peter C. Hodgson, *G. W. F. Hegel: Theologian of the Spirit* (Minneapolis: Fortress Press, 1997).

36. Peter C. Hodgson, ed., *Hegel: Lectures on the Philosophy of Religion*, One Volume Ed., Lectures of 1827 (Berkeley: University of California Press, 1988), 391.

37. Sister Kelly, "Proud of that 'Ole Time' Religion," in *Afro-American Religious History: A Documentary Witness,* ed. Milton C. Sernett (Durham, NC: Duke University Press, 1985), 72.

38. James H. Evans Jr., *We Have Been Believers* (Minneapolis: Fortress Press, 1992), 35.

39. Jarena Lee, "A Female Preacher among the African Methodists," in Sernett, *Afro-American Religious History*, 178.

40. Frank Bartleman, quoted in Amos Yong, *The Spirit Poured Out on All Flesh: Pentecostalism and the Possibility of Global Theology* (Grand Rapids: Baker Academic, 2005), 72.

41. Karl Barth, *Church Dogmatics* IV/1 (Edinburgh: T. & T. Clark, 1960), 643.

42. Ibid., 646.

43. Barth, *The Holy Spirit and the Christian Life: The Theological Basis of Ethics*, trans. R. Birch Hoyle (Louisville, KY: Westminster John Knox Press, 1993), 3.

44. Ibid., 66.

45. Elizabeth Johnson, *She Who Is: The Mystery of God in Feminist Theological Discourse* (New York: Crossroad, 1992), 83.

46. Ibid., 127.

47. Ibid., 135.

48. Ibid., 146.

49. Peter C. Hodgson, *Winds of the Spirit: A Constructive Christian Theology* (Louisville, KY: Westminster John Knox Press, 1994), 276.

50. Peter C. Hodgson, *Christian Faith: A Brief Introduction* (Louisville, KY: Westminster John Knox Press, 2001), 136.

51. Hodgson, *Winds*, 282.

52. Hodgson, *Christian Faith*, 140.

Chapter 2: The Holy Spirit and Scripture

1. For the purposes of this essay, the noun "Scripture" will refer to the text of the Christian Bible. Its plural, lower-case form, "scriptures," will refer to the sacred texts of all religious communities, including the Christian community.

2. Frederick Douglass, *Life and Times of Frederick Douglass: Written by Himself* (New York: Collier Books, Macmillan Publishing Co., [1892] 1962), 90. See "A

Douglass-Garnet Debate, 1849," in *A Documentary History of the Negro People in the United States*, ed. Herbert Aptheker, 2 vols. (New York: Citadel Press, 1st Carol Publishing Group ed., 1990), 1:278–87.

3. Frederick Douglass, *My Bondage and My Freedom*, Part 2, Life as a Freeman, (p. 159), http://docsouth.unc.edu/neh/douglass55/douglass55.html, accessed Feb. 23, 2007.

4. Vincent L. Wimbush, *The Bible and African Americans: A Brief History* (Minneapolis: Fortress Press, 2003), 24.

5. Allen Dwight Callahan, *The Talking Book: African Americans and the Bible* (New Haven, CT: Yale University Press, 2006), 25.

6. John Calvin, *Institutes of the Christian Religion* 3.2.33; ed. John T. McNeill, trans. Ford Lewis Battles, LCC (Philadelphia: Westminster Press, 1960).

7. William Stringfellow, *An Ethic for Christians and Other Aliens in a Strange Land* (Waco, TX: Word Books, 1973; 3rd paperback ed., 1979), 78. I am indebted to the analysis of Charles L. Campbell, *The Word before the Powers: An Ethic of Preaching* (Louisville, KY: Westminster John Knox Press, 2002).

8. Howard Thurman, *Deep River and the Negro Spiritual Speaks of Life and Death* (Richmond, IN: Friends United Press, 1975), 16–17.

9. Frank Macchia and Yohan Hyun, *Spirit's Gifts—God's Reign* (Louisville, KY: PC(USA) Occasional Paper, No. 11, 1999), 4–5.

10. Rowan Williams, "Historical Criticism and Sacred Text," in *Reading Texts, Seeking Wisdom: Scripture and Theology*, ed. David F. Ford and Graham Stanton (Grand Rapids: Eerdmans, 2004), 224.

11. Thomas S. Kepler, ed., *The Table Talk of Martin Luther* (Mineola, NY: Dover, 2005), 197.

12. Augustine, *De Doctrina Christiana*, trans. R. P. H. Green (Oxford: Clarendon Press, 1995), 7, 9.

13. Since Scripture is a text in conversation with itself, an intricate tapestry of revisions, retellings, and reappropriations, we should also affirm the Spirit's work in binding together the writers of Scripture.

14. Calvin, *Institutes* 4.3.1.

15. David H. Kelsey, *The Uses of Scripture in Recent Theology* (Minneapolis: Fortress Press, 1975), 105 (emphasis in the original).

16. Ellen F. Davis and Richard B. Hays, eds., *The Art of Reading Scripture* (Grand Rapids: Eerdmans, 2003), 9.

17. Wayne Meeks, "A Hermeneutics of Social Embodiment," *Harvard Theological Review* 79 (1986): 184.

18. James Alison, "'But the Bible says . . .'? A Catholic Reading of Romans 1," http://www.jamesalison.co.uk/texts/eng15.html, accessed on Feb. 21, 2007.

19. Fiona Bowie and Oliver Davies, eds., *Hildegard of Bingen: An Anthology* (London: SPCK, 1990), 118.

20. Andrew F. Walls, *The Cross-Cultural Process in Christian History: Studies in the Transmission and Appropriation of Faith* (Maryknoll, NY: Orbis Books, 2002), 29–30.

21. Karl Barth, *Church Dogmatics* I/2 (Edinburgh: T. & T. Clark, 1956), 728–29.

22. Rowan Williams, *On Christian Theology* (Oxford: Blackwell, 2000), 147, quoting Paul Ricoeur.

23. Albert Barnes, *The Church and Slavery* (New York: Negro Universities Press, 1969), 168.

24. Martin Luther King uses this metaphor in his famous "Letter from a Birmingham Jail."

25. Kwame Bediako, "A Half Century of African Christian Thought," *Journal of African Christian Thought* (June 2000): 11.

26. Stanley J. Samartha, "Scripture and Scriptures," in *Voices from the Margin: Interpreting the Bible in the Third World,* ed. R. S. Sugirtharajah (Maryknoll, NY: Orbis Books, 1995), 22, 32.

27. David F. Ford, "Faith in the Third Millennium: Reading Scriptures Together," address at the inauguration of Dr. Iain Torrance as President of Princeton Theological Seminary and Professor of Patristics, March 10, 2005. This address and other writings on Scriptural Reasoning are available at http://etext.lib.virginia.edu/journals/jsrforum/writings.html.

28. Samartha, "Scripture and Scriptures," 32.

29. Mar Gregorios, "Hermeneutics in India Today," *Indian Journal of Theology* 31 (1982): 155.

30. "Theologian Takes On Establishment," *Joongang Daily,* June 24, 2004. Quoted in Philip Jenkins, *New Faces of Christianity: Believing the Bible in the Global South* (Oxford: Oxford University Press, 2006), 159.

31. Kevin J. Vanhoozer, *The Drama of Doctrine: A Canonical-Linguistic Approach to Christian Theology* (Louisville, KY: Westminster John Knox Press, 2005), 137.

32. Ibid., 294–95 (emphasis in the original).

33. Vanhoozer does not draw these particular implications from his *atlas* image.

34. Elsa Tamez, "The Bible and 500 Years of Conquest," in *God's Economy: Biblical Studies from Latin America,* ed. Ross Kinsler and Gloria Kinsler (Maryknoll, NY: Orbis Books, 2005), 8.

35. Davis and Hays, *Art of Reading Scripture,* 16.

Chapter 3: Breathing, Bearing, Beseeching, and Building

1. Hans Küng suggested that it was more important to believe the church than to believe *in* the church, a fallible human community. He writes: "It is striking that in general the creeds speak of believing *in* God and *in* the Holy Spirit but of believing *the* church," *The Church* (New York: Sheed & Ward, 1967), 30. So it is with Scripture; believing the Bible matters more than believing *in* it.

2. See Hans W. Frei, *The Eclipse of Biblical Narrative: A Study in Eighteenth and Nineteenth Century Hermeneutics* (New Haven, CT: Yale University Press, 1974), for an extensive exploration of the conformity of biblical hermeneutics to positivistic historical and scientific methods, thus distorting the narrative character of Scripture.

3. John Webster, *Holy Scripture: A Dogmatic Sketch* (Cambridge: Cambridge University Press, 2003), 27.

4. Ibid., 6.

5. Telford Work, *Living and Active: Scripture in the Economy of Salvation* (Grand Rapids: Eerdmans, 2002), offers the most comprehensive articulation of a Trinitarian doctrine of Scripture.

6. Jürgen Moltmann, *The Spirit of Life: A Universal Affirmation* (Minneapolis: Fortress Press, 2002), 41.

7. Basil, *Against Eunomius* 3.4; *On the Holy Spirit* 16.38; 18.46; 19.49, cited in Denis Edwards, *Breath of Life: A Theology of the Creator Spirit* (Maryknoll, NY: Orbis Books, 2004), 26.

8. I have offered an extended reflection in my pneumatology, *Joining the Dance: A Theology of the Spirit* (Valley Forge, PA: Judson Press, 2003), 20–26, on the multivalent use of *ruach*. Also helpful is Denis Edwards, *Breath of Life: A Theology of the Creator Spirit* (Maryknoll, NY: Orbis Books, 2004).

9. Moltmann, *Spirit of Life*, 42.

10. Webster, *Holy Scripture*, 9.

11. Sigmund Mowinckel, in *The Spirit and the Word: Prophecy and Tradition in Ancient Israel*, ed. K. C. Hanson, Fortress Classics in Biblical Studies (Minneapolis: Fortress Press, 2002), 85, notes that "whereas the older reforming prophets and several of the later prophets say nothing whatsoever about a personal relation to Yahweh's spirit, the consciousness of this relation reappears in Ezekiel and several of the later—chiefly literary—post-exilic prophets."

12. See Alan J. Torrance, *Persons in Communion: Trinitarian Description and Human Participation* (Edinburgh: T. & T. Clark, 1996), for a fine critique of Barth's hesitance to use language of persons in Trinitarian construction.

13. Thomas Hoffman, "Inspiration, Normativeness, Canonicity, and the Unique Sacred Character of the Bible," *Catholic Biblical Quarterly* 44 (1982): 457.

14. Kilian McDonnell, *The Other Hand of God: The Holy Spirit as the Universal Touch and Goal* (Collegeville, MN: Liturgical Press, 2003), 3.

15. C. F. D. Moule, *The Holy Spirit* (Grand Rapids: Eerdmans, 1978), 69.

16. Webster, *Holy Scripture*, 27.

17. Ibid., 29.

18. Eugene F. Rogers Jr. uses the terminology of the Spirit "resting upon the body." He offers a wonderful articulation of where the Spirit rests in his *After the Spirit: A Constructive Pneumatology from Resources outside the Modern West*, Radical Traditions: Theology in a Postcritical Key, ed. Stanley M. Hauerwas and Peter Ochs (Grand Rapids: Eerdmans, 2005).

19. Pheme Perkins, *First and Second Peter, James, and Jude*, Interpretation: A Bible Commentary for Teaching and Preaching (Louisville, KY: John Knox Press, 1995), 173.

20. Webster, *Holy Scripture*, 38–39.

21. Reading the systematic theology of Hendrikus Berkhof first introduced me

to the notion that "condescendence" could be an act of humility rather than domination and dismissive superiority. See his thinking on transcendence and condescendence in *Christian Faith: An Introduction to the Study of the Faith,* rev. ed. (Grand Rapids: Eerdmans, 1986), 126–34. Of course, he is following the pattern of his theological forebear, John Calvin, who wrote about God bending down to us to speak, and thereby "provides for our weakness in that he prefers to address us in human fashion through interpreters in order to draw us to himself, rather than to thunder at us and drive us away." See John Calvin, *Institutes of the Christian Religion* 3.2.36, ed. John T. McNeill, trans. Ford Lewis Battles, LCC (Philadelphia: Westminster Press, 1960).

22. Cynthia M. Campbell, "We Believe in the Holy Spirit, Who Has Spoken through the Prophets," in *Fire and Wind: The Holy Spirit in the Church Today,* ed. Joseph D. Small (Louisville, KY: Geneva Press, 2002), 42.

23. Stephen E. Fowl, *Engaging Scripture: A Model for Theological Interpretation,* Challenges in Contemporary Theology (Oxford: Blackwell, 1998), 114. Also see his edited work, *Theological Interpretation of Scripture: Classical and Contemporary Readings* (Oxford: Blackwell, 1997).

24. No doubt, part of the resonance of the text was that the seminary hymn, *Soldiers of Christ in Truth Arrayed,* by Basil Manly Jr., one of the four founders of the seminary (1859), was based, in part, on Psalm 126.

25. "Letter to Marcellinius" 12, in *Life of Anthony,* 111, cited in Roberta C. Bondi, *To Pray and to Love: Conversations on Prayer with the Early Church* (Minneapolis: Fortress Press, 1991), 62.

26. Ibid.

27. Ellen F. Davis and Richard B. Hays, eds., *The Art of Reading Scripture* (Grand Rapids: Eerdmans, 2003).

28. Ibid., 3.

29. Robert W. Jenson, "Scripture's Authority in the Church," in Davis and Hays, *Art of Reading Scripture,* 30, insists "our common life is located *inside* the story Scripture tells."

30. Webster, *Holy Scriptures,* 6, describes Scripture as "the self-presentation of the triune God, of which the text is a servant and by which readers are accosted, as by a word of supreme dignity, legitimacy and effectiveness." See also Jürgen Moltmann, *The Trinity and the Kingdom: The Doctrine of God* (San Francisco: Harper & Row, 1981), for a clear articulation of Scripture's role in narrating God's own Trinitarian history with creation.

31. See my article, "Plowing the Soil of the Heart: The Psalter and Spirituality," *American Baptist Quarterly* 21, no. 4 (December 2002): 499–509.

32. Davis and Hays, *Art of Reading Scripture,* 4.

33. Work, *Living and Active,* 220.

34. The seminal work was *A Theology for the Social Gospel* (New York: Macmillan, 1917).

35. Ibid., 134.

36. Walter Rauschenbusch, *Dare We Be Christians?* (Cleveland: Pilgrim Press, 1914), 3.

37. Martin Luther King Jr., *Stride toward Freedom: The Montgomery Story* (New York: Harper, 1958), 66. See James Wm. McClendon Jr., *Biography as Theology: How Life Stories Can Remake Today's Theology* (Philadelphia: Trinity Press, 1974), for an analysis of how the religion of the black church shaped the whole of King's vision and practice.

38. L. Gregory Jones, "Embodying Scripture in the Community of Faith," in Davis and Hays, *Art of Reading Scripture,* 144.

39. Ibid., 148.

40. Davis and Hays, *Art of Reading Scripture*, 4.

41. As a Christian interpreter of Scripture, I am committed to a Trinitarian understanding of Scripture in the economy of salvation. This does not mean that I believe the Spirit is not at work through other texts and other messengers; however, how a rabbi reads the Hebrew Scriptures or an imam reads the Koran entails a different hermeneutical process. Thus, the form of Christian Scriptures as Old and New Testaments determines the mode of reading. I am influenced in this perception by Hans Urs von Balthasar, *The Glory of the Lord,* vol. 1, *Seeing the Form,* trans. Erasmo Leiva-Merikakis (San Francisco: Ignatius Press, 1983), 151.

42. This is a key metaphor for John V. Taylor, *The Go-Between God* (New York: Oxford University Press, 1972).

43. Davis and Hays, *Art of Reading Scripture,* 5.

44. McDonnell, *Other Hand of God*, 216.

45. See pages 123–27 in my *Joining the Dance.*

46. Frank Rogers Jr., "Discernment," in *Practicing Our Faith: A Way of Life for a Searching People*, ed. Dorothy C. Bass (San Francisco: Jossey-Bass, 1997), 113.

47. Christopher Morse, *Not Every Spirit: A Dogmatics of Christian Disbelief* (Valley Forge, PA: Trinity Press International, 1991), 181.

48. Edwards, *Breath of Life*, 159.

49. Luke Timothy Johnson, *Scripture and Discernment: Decision Making in the Church* (Nashville: Abingdon Press, 1996), 109.

50. Ignatius of Loyola, *The Spiritual Exercises of St. Ignatius* (New York: Doubleday, 1964).

51. Michael L. Birkel, *Silence and Witness: The Quaker Tradition,* Traditions of Christian Spirituality, (Maryknoll, NY: Orbis Books, 2004).

52. Johnson, *Scripture and Discernment*, 43.

53. From his study of how the authority of the New Testament functions in the church, Johnson concludes two things: "identity is more important than ritual consistency"; "the New Testament actually legitimates a healthy pluralism of practice within the same basic identity." Ibid., 42.

54. See Sue Annis Hammond, *Thin Book of Appreciative Inquiry*, 2nd ed. (Plano, TX: Thin Book Publishing Company, 1996).

55. Charles M. Olsen, *Transforming Church Boards into Communities of Spiritual Leaders* (Bethesda, MD: Alban Institute, 1995).

NOTES 171

56. Webster, *Holy Scripture*, 87.

57. Ibid., 87–88.

58. James A. Harnish, *You Only Have to Die: Leading Your Congregation to New Life* (Nashville: Abingdon Press, 2004), describes his congregation's resurrection to this kind of generative life.

59. Richard B. Hays, "Reading Scripture in Light of the Resurrection," in Davis and Hays, *Art of Reading Scripture*, 235–36.

60. See Kenneth Grayston, *Dying, We Live: A New Enquiry into the Death of Christ in the New Testament* (New York: Oxford University Press, 1990).

61. See Paul Ricoeur, *Interpretation Theory: Discourse and the Surplus of Meaning* (Fort Worth: Texas Christian University Press, 1976).

62. James D. G. Dunn, *Jesus and the Spirit: A Study of the Religious and Charismatic Experience of Jesus and the First Christians as Reflected in the New Testament* (Philadelphia: Westminster Press, 1975), 352.

63. I am indebted to Greg Jones for this pairing. See his "Embodying Scripture in the Community of Faith," in Davis and Hays, *Art of Reading Scripture*, 147.

Chapter 4: Holy Spirit and the Religions

1. Edward Schillebeeckx, *Church: The Human Story of God* (New York: Crossroad, 1990), 165.

2. Frederic E. Crowe, "Son of God, Holy Spirit, and World Religions," in *Appropriating the Lonergan Idea*, ed. Michael Vertin (Washington, DC: Catholic University of America Press, 1989), 324–43. Crowe's is not the only possible interpretation of Lonergan on this question.

3. Ibid., 325–26.

4. Ibid., 335.

5. Jacques Dupuis, *Christianity and the Religions: From Confrontation to Dialogue* (Maryknoll, NY: Orbis Books; London: Darton, Longman & Todd, 2002), 159. "We see therefore how the universal salvific value of the historical event of Jesus Christ leaves space for an illuminating and salvific action of the Word as such, both before the incarnation and after the resurrection of Jesus Christ." Ibid.

6. Ibid., 178.

7. Gavin D'Costa, "Christ, Trinity, and Religious Plurality," in *Christian Uniqueness Reconsidered*, ed. John Hick and Paul Knitter (Maryknoll, NY: Orbis Books, 1990), 16–29; *The Meeting of Religions and the Trinity* (Maryknoll, NY: Orbis Books, 2000).

8. D'Costa, "Christ, Trinity, and Religious Plurality," 19.

9. D'Costa, *Meeting*, 115.

10. Michael Amaladoss, "The Pluralism of Religions and the Significance of Christ," in *Asian Faces of Jesus*, ed. R. S. Sugirtharajah (Maryknoll, NY: Orbis Books, 1993), 88.

11. Ibid., 91.

12. Michael Amaladoss, "The Mystery of Christ and Other Religions: An

Indian Perspective," *Vidyajyoti: Journal of Theological Reflection* 63 (1999): 332 and 333 respectively.

13. Amaladoss, "Pluralism of Religions," 100.

14. As represented in the following essay: Peter C. Hodgson, "The Spirit and Religious Pluralism," in *The Myth of Religious Superiority: A Multifaith Exploration,* ed. Paul F. Knitter (Maryknoll, NY: Orbis Books, 2005), 135–50.

15. Ibid., 139.

16. Ibid., 141.

17. Ibid.

18. For example, Thomas writes that "the creative power of God is common to the whole trinity; and hence it belongs to the unity of the essence [of God], and not to the distinction of persons." *Summa theologiae* 1, 32, 1, in *Basic Writings of Saint Thomas Aquinas,* ed. Anton C. Pegis (New York: Random House, 1945), 315–18. See also *ST* 1, 39, 7 ad 1 and 2 at 375–76.

19. One can, of course, also account for Jesus' divinity using the symbol and language of God as Word in the manner of Amaladoss.

20. Friedrich Schleiermacher, *The Christian Faith,* ed. H. R. Mackintosh and J. S. Stewart (New York: Harper Torchbooks, 1963), nos. 123–24, 569–78.

21. Elizabeth A. Johnson divides salvation theories into three kinds that are premodern, modern, and postmodern in "Jesus and Salvation," *Proceedings of the Catholic Theological Society of America* 49 (1994): 1–18. These roughly correlate with the three scenarios presented here.

Chapter 5: Guests, Hosts, and the Holy Ghost

1. While I have never met Professor Hodgson, I have long been stimulated by his constructive theological project in dialogue with Hegel. To the extent I have understood Hegel and have legitimately appropriated him for my own theological purposes, to that same degree I would count myself as a fellow pneumatological theologian who has been enriched by the gifts of the Spirit bequeathed through theologians of the stature of Peter C. Hodgson.

2. Here I follow Perry Schmidt-Leukel, "Exclusivism, Inclusivism, Pluralism: The Tripolar Typology—Clarified and Reaffirmed," in *The Myth of Religious Superiority: Multifaith Explorations of Religious Pluralism,* ed. Paul F. Knitter (Maryknoll, NY: Orbis Books, 2005), 13–27, who argues, convincingly, in my opinion, that exclusivism, inclusivism, and pluralism remain the three logical options with regard to the question about the relationship between Christian salvation and the world's religious traditions.

3. Those interested in the details of this thesis can consult my *Hospitality and the Other: Pentecost, Christian Practices, and the Neighbor* (Maryknoll, NY: Orbis Books, 2008), where the full argument is presented.

4. For an overview of the scholarship supporting such an assessment, see François Bovon, *Luke the Theologian: Fifty-Five Years of Research (1950–2005),* 2nd rev. ed. (Waco, TX: Baylor University Press, 2005), chap. 4.

5. This theme of hospitality has already been observed by other Lukan inter-preters—e.g., Andrew E. Arterbury, *Entertaining Angels: Early Christian Hospital-ity in Its Mediterranean Setting*, New Testament Monographs 8 (Sheffield: Sheffield Phoenix, 2005), and Brendan Byrne, *The Hospitality of God: A Reading of Luke's Gospel* (Collegeville, MN: Liturgical Press, 2000).

6. John Paul Heil, *The Meal Scenes in Luke-Acts: An Audience-oriented Approach*, SBL Monograph Series 52 (Atlanta: Scholars Press, 1999), 312.

7. I expand on this inclusive theology of hospitality toward a theology of dis-ability in my *Theology and Down Syndrome: Reimagining Disability in Late Moder-nity* (Waco, TX: Baylor University Press, 2007).

8. I elsewhere probe these questions at greater length; see Yong, *The Spirit Poured Out on All Flesh: Pentecostalism and the Possibility of Global Theology* (Grand Rapids: Baker Academic, 2005), 241–44.

9. Carisse Mickey Berryhill, "From Dreaded Guest to Welcoming Host: Hospi-tality and Paul in Acts," in *Restoring the First-Century Church in the Twenty-First Cen-tury: Essays on the Stone-Campbell Restoration Movement*, ed. Warren Lewis and Hans Rollmann (Eugene, OR: Wipf & Stock, 2005), 71–86, quotation from p. 85.

10. Karl Barth, *Church Dogmatics*, IV/1 (London and New York: T. & T. Clark, 1956), §59.1.

11. Here I am expanding on an argument first sketched in my "'As the Spirit Gives Utterance . . .': Pentecost, Intra-Christian Ecumenism, and the Wider *Oekumene*," *International Review of Mission* 92, no. 366 (July 2003): 299–314.

12. For an overview, see James K. A. Smith, *Jacques Derrida: Live Theory* (New York and London: Continuum, 2005), chap. 3.

13. Richard Kearney and Mark Dooley, eds., *Questioning Ethics: Contemporary Debates in Philosophy* (London: Routledge, 1999), 70 (italics orig.).

14. Jacques Derrida, *Acts of Religion*, ed. Gil Anidjar (New York and London: Routledge, 2002), 364.

15. Jacques Derrida and Anne Dufourmantelle, *Of Hospitality*, trans. Rachel Bowlby (Stanford, CA: Stanford University Press, 2000), 123 (italics orig.).

16. See Stephen H. Webb, *The Gifting God: A Trinitarian Ethics of Excess* (New York: Oxford University Press, 1996).

17. It might be surprising to note that the approach to theology of religions through Christian practices is only now beginning to be explored, one of the first to suggest something along these lines being George R. Sumner, *The First and the Last: The Claim of Jesus Christ and the Claims of Other Religious Traditions* (Grand Rapids: Eerdmans, 2004), esp. 53–60.

18. Again, I remind my readers that what follows is sketchy in the extreme; for a more rigorous argument about the Christian practices that correlate with the exclusivist, inclusivist, and pluralist theologies of religions, see my *Hospitality and the Other*, chap. 3.

19. I argue this point in my "'The Light Shines in the Darkness': Johannine Dualism and Christian Theology of Religions Today," *Journal of Religion* (under review).

20. This development is demonstrated by Francis A. Sullivan, SJ, *Salvation Outside the Church? Tracing the History of the Catholic Response* (New York and Mahwah, NJ: Paulist Press, 1992).

21. See Aloysius Pieris, *Love Meets Wisdom: A Christian Experience of Buddhism* (Maryknoll, NY: Orbis Books, 1988).

22. Barth himself argued this point from out of the parable of the Good Samaritan; see his *Church Dogmatics*, I/2 (Edinburgh: T. & T. Clark, 1956), 417–50.

23. By "im/migrant" (with the slash), I am pointing to the difference between those who have voluntarily chosen to move from one country to another (immigrants), and those who are vocational or seasonal workers who follow the crops, sometimes across international lines (migrants).

24. See Hendrikus Boers, *Theology out of the Ghetto: A New Testament Exegetical Study concerning Religious Exclusiveness* (Leiden: E. J. Brill, 1971), chap. 3.

25. Hick prefers the language of "the Real" rather than "God" since the latter excludes nontheistic religious traditions; see John Hick, *An Interpretation of Religion: Human Responses to the Transcendent* (New Haven, CT, and London: Yale University Press, 1989), chaps. 15–16.

Chapter 6: The Spirit Rests on the Son Paraphysically

1. Romanos the Melodist, Hymn XI (Nativity II), strophe 4, in *Hymns II,* ed. José Grosdidier de Matons, Sources Chrétiennes 110 (Paris: Cerf, 1965). Translation by Margaret Alexiou in *After Antiquity: Greek Language, Myth, and Metaphor* (Ithaca, NY: Cornell University Press, 2002), 422–23. For a compatible reading of this material in the context of the Annunciation, see Eugene F. Rogers Jr., *After the Spirit: A Constructive Pneumatology from Resources outside the Modern West* (Grand Rapids: Eerdmans, 2005, and London: SCM Press, 2006), 98–104. The present essay works a theological conceit. A more historical account including more reflections on Jews and Gentiles will appear in "Against/Alongside the Nature of Gentiles: *Para Phusin* in Paul's Epistle to the Romans," in *Jewish/Christian/Queer: Crossroads and Identities,* Queer Inventions Series, ed. F. S. Roden (Aldershot, Hampshire: Ashgate, 2009). For more on *para phusin,* see Dale Martin, "Heterosexism and the Interpretation of Romans 1:18–32," in *Sex and the Single Savior: Gender and Sexuality in Biblical Interpretation* (Louisville, KY: Westminster John Knox Press, 2006), 51–64.

2. Dumitru Staniloae, *Theology and the Church,* trans. Robert Barringer (Crestwood, NY: St. Vladimir's Seminary Press, 1980), 21, and Athanasius, *Contra Arianos,* 330, 435.

3. John 14:16.

4. Rom. 8:15, 23; 9:4; Gal. 4:5–6.

5. Stanley Stowers, "What Is Pauline Participation in Christ?" in *New Views of Jewish and Christian Self-Definition: Essays in Honor of E. P. Sanders* (Notre Dame, IN: University of Notre Dame Press, forthcoming).

6. John 1:13, author's translation, NRSV modified.

7. First Cor. 2:10.

8. This is Colin Gunton's maximal interpretation of a line in Basil's *Hexameron,*
Basile de Césarée, *Homélies sur l'Hexaéméron,* 2:6, ed. and trans. Stanislas Giet
(Paris: Éditions du Cerf, 1949), 168: "meden allo Pneuma Theou, e to agion to tes
Theias kai makarias Triadas sumplerotikon."

9. Fifth Theological Oration.

10. John Boswell, *Christianity, Social Tolerance, and Homosexuality* (Chicago:
University of Chicago Press, 1980), 112, n. 69.

11. "Luxuria est quaelibet superfluitas," *Summa theologiae* 2-2.153.1, quoting
the *Glossa.* Aquinas elsewhere distinguishes senses of *praeter* and *contra naturam,*
ST 1.105.6 ad 1, which Paul conflates.

12. *On the Incarnation of the Word,* chap. 54; *Orations against the Arians,* book 3,
chap. 29.

13. Others have invented the term "paralogic" independently. My use differs
from Lyotard's, and any overlaps are accidental. Unlike his, mine seeks to restate
Trinitarian practices of discourse. Against critics of logocentrism, this paralogic is
not logocentric, but precisely logo-*ec*centric.

14. See Eugene F. Rogers Jr., *After the Spirit: A Constructive Pneumatology from
Resources outside the Modern West* (Grand Rapids: Eerdmans, 2005, and London:
SCM Press, 2006), 19–23.

15. *Gospel of Philip,* chap. 17, in J. M. Robinson, *The Nag Hammadi Library*
(Leiden: E. J. Brill, 1977), 134. For context, see Sebastian Brock, *The Holy Spirit
in the Syrian Baptismal Tradition,* 2nd ed. (Poona, India: Anita Printers, 1998),
16–26; here, 16.

16. See Michael Satlow, *Tasting the Dish: Rabbinic Rhetorics of Sexuality* (Atlanta:
Scholars Press, 1995), and "'Try to Be a Man': The Rabbinic Construction of Mas-
culinity," *Harvard Theological Review* 89 (1996): 19–41.

17. Second Pet. 1:4.

18. For "frees" as a verb of the Spirit, see Robert W. Jenson, *Triune Identity*
(Philadelphia: Fortress Press, 1982).

19. Sebastian Moore, *Jesus the Liberator of Desire* (New York: Crossroad, 1989),
89, chap. reprinted in Eugene F. Rogers Jr., *Theology and Sexuality* (Oxford: Blackwell, 2002), 157–69.

20. I owe the word "protoerotic," applied to the Spirit, to Sarah Coakley.

21. Sebastian Moore, in Rogers, *Theology and Sexuality,* 162–63. See also
Ephrem the Syrian, *Commentary on Genesis,* in *Selected Prose Works,* ed. Kathleen
McVey and trans. Edward Mathews and Joseph Amar, Fathers of the Church series
(Washington, DC: Catholic University of America Press, 1994), on Gen. 3:26, and
Bernard of Clairvaux, who writes that "God indeed gave the human being an
upright stance of body . . . that the body of clay might rebuke the deformity of the
mind," *Cistercian Fathers* 7.46, in John R. Sommerfeldt, *The Spiritual Teachings of
Bernard of Clairvaux* (Kalamazoo, MI: Cistercian, 1991), 24.

22. This theme runs through twentieth-century Russian Orthodox thought, e.g.,

Sergei Bulgakov, *Philosophy of Economy: The World as Household,* trans. Catherine Evtuhov (New Haven, CT: Yale University Press, 2000; Russian, 1912), 75, 103–5; Alexander Schmemann, *For the Life of the World,* 2nd ed. (Crestwood, NY: St. Vladimir's Seminary Press, 1998; first ed., 1964), 11, 14–15. See Rogers, *After the Spirit,* 41–44, for more references.

Chapter 7: The Spirit Holy, Hip, and Free

1. Robert Wuthnow, *Meaning and Moral Order: Explorations in Cultural Analysis* (Berkeley, CA: University of California Press, 1987), 187, citing *Official and Popular Religion: Analysis of a Theme for Religious Studies,* ed. Peter H. Vrijhof and Jacques Waardenburg (The Hague: Mouton, 1979).

2. "Give Me That Ol' Time Religion: Robert Duvall's The Apostle," *Sojourners* 27, no. 3 (May–June 1998): 63–64.

3. Damayanthi Niles, "How the Study of Popular Religions Can Help Us in Our Theological Task," *International Review of Mission* 93, no. 369 (April 2004): 210–218.

4. Ibid., 119.

5. *The Encyclopedia of Religion,* ed. Mircea Eliade et al. (New York: Macmillan), s.v. "Popular Religion."

6. Cornel West, *Race Matters* (Boston: Beacon Press, 1994), 9.

7. Walter Brueggemann, *Gathering the Church in the Spirit: Reflections on Exile and the Inscrutable Wind of God* (Decatur, GA: CTS Press, 1995), 27.

8. Ibid.

9. *Bernice Johnson Reagon: The Singing Warrior,* video/DVD and study guide, (Denver: Veterans of Hope Project, 2000).

Chapter 8: "The Dearest Freshness Deep Down Things"

1. Sallie McFague, *Models of God: Theology for an Ecological, Nuclear Age* (Minneapolis: Fortress Press, 1987), 169–71. However, in my next book, *The Body of God,* I realize the importance of the model: see 141ff. (Minneapolis: Fortress Press, 1993).

2. *The Sermons and Devotional Writings of Gerard Manley Hopkins,* ed. Christopher Devlin (Oxford: Oxford University Press, 1959), 195.

3. "The Blessed Virgin compared to the Air we breathe" (1883), in *A Hopkins Reader,* ed. John Pick (New York: Oxford University Press, 1953).

4. *The Confessions of Saint Augustine,* Bks. 1–10, trans. F. J. Sheed (New York: Sheed & Ward, 1942), 1.2.

5. Peter C. Hodgson, *Christian Faith: A Brief Introduction* (Louisville, KY: Westminster John Knox Press, 2001), 140.

6. Ibid., 141.

7. This recognition echoes John Calvin, who writes in his *Institutes,* "We are not our own. . . . We are God's" (3.7.1).

8. The UN Intergovernmental Panel on Climate Change states in its fourth assessment report with "very high confidence" that human activities are contributing to global warming. See also George Monbiot, *Heat: How to Stop the Planet from Burning* (New York: Doubleday, 2006); Al Gore, *An Inconvenient Truth: The Planetary Emergency of Global Warming and What We Can Do about It* (Emmaus, PA: Rodale Press, 2006); Tim Flannery, *The Weather Makers: How We Are Changing the Climate and What It Means for Life on Earth* (New York: Harper/Collins, 2005).

9. Julian of Norwich, *Revelation of Love*, ed. and trans. John Skinner (New York: Doubeday Image Books, 1997), 10–11.

10. Ibid., 60.

Chapter 9: Resistance Spirit

1. The late Frederick Herzog had planned to write a book titled *Resistance Spirit* but was prevented from doing so by his untimely death. His approach to the subject would have been different from mine, but the resistance Spirit that ties us together is still at work.

2. For the notion of ambivalence, see Homi Bhabha, *The Location of Culture* (London: Routledge, 1994), 86. Bhabha connects this term with his more famous notion of "mimicry": "the discourse of mimicry is constructed around an *ambivalence*" (emphasis in original). By repeating colonial images with a slight difference, rather than representing them accurately, mimicry establishes a challenge to the colonial narcissism and fiction of self-identity (ibid., 88).

3. Ibid., 88.

4. See Joerg Rieger, *Christ and Empire: From Paul to Postcolonial Times* (Minneapolis: Fortress Press, 2007).

5. This definition is further developed in the introduction of Rieger, *Christ and Empire*.

6. The emperor cult was far more vital and significant than has commonly been recognized. See Rieger, *Christ and Empire*, chap. 1, for a more detailed account of these various influences.

7. See Werner H. Schmidt, "Geist/Heiliger Geist/Geistesgaben: Altes Testament," in *Theologische Realenzyklopädie*, ed. Gerhard Krause and Gerhard Müller, vol. 12 (Berlin: Walter de Gruyter, 1984), 170.

8. See John R. Levison, "The Pluriform Foundation of Christian Pneumatology," in *Advents of the Spirit: An Introduction to the Current Study of Pneumatology*, ed. Bradford E. Hinze and D. Lyle Dabney (Milwaukee: Marquette University Press, 2001), 66–85.

9. The Roman governors also could appoint their own nominees to the office of the high priest. See Richard Horsley, *Jesus and Empire: The Kingdom of God and the New World Disorder* (Minneapolis: Fortress Press, 2002), 32–33.

10. Wolf-Dieter Hauschild, "Geist/Heiliger Geist/Geistesgaben: Dogmengeschichtlich," in *Theologische Realenzyklopädie*, ed. Gerhard Krause and Gerhard

Müller, vol. 12 (Berlin: Walter de Gruyter, 1984), 200–201. See also Basil the Great, *On the Holy Spirit* (Crestwood, NY: St. Vladimir's Seminary Press, 1980).

11. Bradford E. Hinze and D. Lyle Dabney, Introduction, in Hinze and Dabney, *Advents of the Spirit*, 11.

12. Ibid., 17, report that these movements are approaching 500 million; only Roman Catholicism with 950 million adherents is larger. They also note the postmodern opening to the Spirit, related to increasing doubts about universal human rationality and the blessings of technological society, ibid., 21.

13. I introduce this term in chap. 7 of *Christ and Empire*; for more background on the following reflections, see *Christ and Empire*, introduction and chap. 7.

14. Revenue is first used to pay the company—sometimes at inflated cost—and then split 60/40, 60 percent for the state, 40 percent for the company. The contracts last for twenty-five to forty years, which is the life expectancy of an oil field; Iraq has the third-largest oil reserves in the world, after Saudi Arabia and Canada (*People's Weekly World* [January 7–13, 2006], 13). See also Robert J. C. Young, *Postcolonialism: An Historical Introduction* (Oxford: Blackwell, 2001), 82ff.

15. At the same time, this new distribution of power in the postcolonial empire does not mean that other powers, including the political powers of the nation-state, are fading away. The expansion of economic power needs stable and predictable social arrangements, and thus politics has an important role to play. See Ellen Meiksins Wood, *The Empire of Capital* (New York: Verso Books, 2003), 17.

16. Germany is a place to which I continue to be connected myself, although I have transitioned to the United States years ago.

17. Michael Welker, *God the Spirit*, trans. John F. Hoffmeyer (Minneapolis: Fortress Press, 1994), 15, notes that he seeks to develop his reflections on the Holy Spirit in a "sober" and "realistic" way; the project is spelled out on 46–47. "Realistic" theology takes seriously the differing biblical traditions; differences between past, present, and future experiences; and the "primary testimonies" of the biblical traditions and the "secondary testimonies" in our cultures. The page references in this section refer to this book.

18. Ibid., 13. The Charismatic movement is said to resist these moves by promoting "emotional intelligence," ibid., 14.

19. Ibid., 39–40. Welker rejects methods that proceed according to "part-hole patterns as well as uniform or unidirectional, hierarchical conceptions of unity"— this would be "old European metaphysics." He also rejects starting with the "I-Thou relation" because it implies a simplification of more complex relations. Neither does a "moral market" or "social moralism" work in which there is a constant "pressure to change." Ibid., 41–45.

20. Welker is aware of the dangers of pluralistic fragmentation due to "functional differentiation," a process that somehow isolates all aspects of life, such as economy, law, religion, education, and family, ibid., 29–31. Drawing on the work of Niklas Luhmann, Welker assumes that economy, law, religion, science, politics, etc. are all just subsystems. Ibid., 32.

21. Reference in Welker, *God the Spirit*, 125.

22. For an extended argument see Joerg Rieger, "Developing a Common Interest Theology from the Underside," in *Liberating the Future: God, Mammon, and Theology*, ed. Joerg Rieger (Minneapolis: Fortress Press, 1998).

23. Jürgen Moltmann, *The Spirit of Life: A Universal Affirmation*, trans. Margaret Kohl (Minneapolis: Fortress Press, 1992), 8. Moltmann notes that all the Greek and Latin Fathers had to wrestle with this attitude and that most of them gave in to it, ibid., 90. It is also of interest to note that Platonism is the position of the cultured and that the related ideas of Gnosticism can be found in the perspectives of the common people, ibid., 94. The page references in this section refer to this book.

24. "God is a tempest, a storm, a force in body and soul, humanity and nature," which is present even in suffering, ibid., 40. Moltmann also refers to the Hebrew notion of the "Shekinah," God's presence and indwelling of space and time. This presence of God also goes into the depth of suffering with us, ibid., 47–49.

25. Ibid., 59, 17. At the same time, Moltmann notes that "it is only in the narrow concepts of modern philosophy that 'revelation' and 'experience' are antitheses," ibid., 6.

26. This problem is also noted in the introduction of *The Imperialist Imagination: German Colonialism and Its Legacy*, ed. Sara Friedrichsmeyer, Sara Lennox, and Susanne Zantop (Ann Arbor: University of Michigan Press, 1998). For the notion "colonial fantasy" and an exploration of it in the context of German colonial history, see Susanne Zantop, *Colonial Fantasies: Conquest, Family, and Nation in Precolonial Germany, 1770–1870* (Durham, NC: Duke University Press, 1997). To be sure, Moltmann does not fail to critique the middle-class liberalism that succeeded feudalism in Western Europe, but his charge is that the middle class continued to pursue the model of the feudal lord with the result that "everyone sees everyone else as a competitor in the struggle for power and possessions," 118. Nevertheless, the problem is not return to feudalism; modernity has its own problems and the nature of domination takes on a different character.

27. Moltmann identifies an understanding of unity in difference also in the Christian tradition, especially in the classical doctrine of the Trinity. He sees problems with a Trinitarian concept of fellowship if it is seen from a unitarian perspective: starting from "the one, undifferentiated divine essence," as Schleiermacher does, for instance, leads to a conception of a unitarian community "which threatens to abolish the differences between the persons," ibid., 223. Schleiermacher's emphasis can be understood, says Moltmann, in the context of "bourgeois industrial society," which individualizes people as workers and destroys social connections, ibid., 224; yet he considers this sort of community to be merely the opposite of individualism.

28. This role of the Holy Spirit in the process of sanctification is rooted in the theology of John Wesley, as Moltmann notes, ibid., 163–75. In the German language, in which Moltmann's text is written, the parallel between the Holy Spirit (*Heiliger Geist*) and the sanctifying Spirit (*Heiligender Geist*) is more obvious.

29. According to Moltmann, God takes away the guilt of the perpetrators, which leads to self-destruction, ibid., 133–34.

30. For a more in-depth description of these fantasies and how they are manifest in the work of nineteenth-century theology, see Rieger, *Christ and Empire*, chap. 5.

31. See Hinze and Dabney, *Advents of the Spirit*.

32. Anselm Kyongsuk Min, "Solidarity of Others in the Power of the Holy Spirit: Pneumatology in a Divided World," in Hinze and Dabney, *Advents of the Spirit*, 417.

33. Ibid., 417. His conclusion after examining many passages in both parts of the Bible is that "the Holy Spirit is a self-effacing, selfless God whose selfhood or personhood seems to lie precisely in transcending herself to empower others likewise to transcend themselves in communion with others," ibid., 426.

34. Ibid., 421. I applaud the fact that he notes this as an issue also in interreligious dialogue, since what brings together the various religions today is the "global economic process," ibid., 420. Similar challenges for interreligious dialogue are addressed in David Brockman, *Turning to Religious Others: Visions and Blindspots in Modern Christian Reflection about Non-Christians*, PhD dissertation, Southern Methodist University, 2006.

35. Min, "Solidarity of Others," 422.

36. Ibid., 426.

37. Ibid., 435.

38. Nancy M. Victorin-Vangerud, "Response to Min and Wallace," in Hinze and Dabney, *Advents of the Spirit*, 468.

39. Ibid., 471.

40. See Nancy M. Victorin-Vangerud, *The Raging Hearth: Spirit in the Household of God* (St. Louis: Chalice Press, 2000), 117.

Index of Names

Abraham, 50
Adam, 94–95
Alison, James, 166n18
Amaladoss, Michael, 60–61, 172n19
Arterbury, Andrew, 173n5
Athanasius, 46–47, 90
Augustine, 11–12, 29, 116, 164n22

Balthasar, Hans Urs von, 170n41
Barnes, Albert, 33
Barth, Karl, 19–20, 32, 75, 91, 168n12, 174n22
Bartleman, Frank, 165n40
Basil the Great, 42, 89, 132, 178n10
Bediako, Kwame, 34
Berkhof, Hendrikus, 168–69n21
Bernard of Clairvaux, 175n21
Berryhill, Carisse Mickey, 173n9
Bhabha, Homi, 129
Birkel, Michael, 170n51
Boers, Hendrikus, 174n24
Boswell, John, 175n10
Bovon, François, 172n4
Brock, Sebastian, 175n15
Brockman, David, 180n34
Brueggemann, Walter, 105–6
Bulgakov, Sergei, 176n22
Bush, George W., 133–34
Byrne, Brendan, 173n5

Callahan, Allen Dwight, 26
Campbell, Cynthia, 45
Calvin, John, 15–16, 30, 169n21, 176n7
Coakley, Sarah, 175n20
Cobb, John, xvi
Crowe, Frederick, 57, 64, 68

Dabney, D. Lyle, 178nn11–12; 180n31
Davis, Ellen, 30, 38, 47–51
D'Costa, Gavin, 59
Derrida, Jacques, 76–79, 82, 85
Descartes, René, 88
Dooley, Mark, 173n13
Douglass, Frederick, 25–27
Dunn, James, 171n62
Dupuis, Jacques, 59, 171n4
Duvall, Robert, 99

Edwards, Denis, 51, 168n8
Eliot, George, xvii
Ephrem the Syrian, 175n21
Evans, James, 165n38

Flannery, Tim, 177n8
Ford, David, 34–35
Fowl, Stephen, 45
Frei, Hans, 167n2
Friedrichsmeyer, Sara, 179n26

Gallegos, Aaron, 99
Garnet, Henry Highland, 25–26
Gore, Al, 177n8
Grayston, Kenneth, 171n60
Gregorios, Mar, 35
Gregory of Nazianzus, 11, 89, 91
Gunton, Colin, 175n8

Haight, Roger, xv
Hammond, Sue Annis, 170n54
Harnish, 171n58
Hauschild, Wolf-Dieter, 177n10
Hays, Richard, 47–51
Hegel, G. W. F., xvii, 17–18, 172n1
Heil, John Paul, 173n6

Index of Subjects

Abrahamic traditions, 34–35, 50
abundance, 17, 82–83
academy, 81, 84
adoption, 88, 90, 92
African theology, 34
Africana culture, 106–7
agency, human, 106
American Indians, 37–38, 105, 160
apocalypticism, 15
The Apostle, 99
aseity, 22
Azusa Street, 19

baptism, 92, 109–10
Baptist tradition, 48–49, 53
beauty, 127
Bible. *See* Scripture
birth, 124–25
black theology, xvii, 18–19, 49
body, xiv, 1–2, 5–6, 8–9, 12, 14, 18, 20,
    23, 44, 87–92, 94, 137–38, 140,
    143, 149–51, 175n21
Bush administration, 133

canon, 37, 52
capitalism, 16–17, 154–56
castration, 10
celibacy, 150, 153
cherry tree, 127
children of God, 20
Christology, xv, 56
    New Testament, 64
    Spirit Christology, 59, 61–65
church, xiv, 20, 30, 47–50, 64–65, 80,
    111, 152–54, 157, 160, 167n1
climate change, 114–26, 159
communion, 145, 180n33
conquest, 4
consolation, 46
consumerism, xiii–xiv, 16–17, 110, 139,
    142, 155, 157

consummate religion, 17–18
contingency, 119
conversion, 115
creation, 3, 5, 8, 22, 31, 35, 42–43, 58,
    60–61, 64, 66–68, 114–15,
    117–18, 120
cultural context, 33–34

death, 4, 6, 9
debt and indebtedness, 77
denominations, 100
dependence, 121
desire, 93–94
dialogue, 59, 69, 82–84, 107–8, 144,
    180n34
discernment, 27, 30, 36–39, 41, 51–53
disease, 127
disembodiment, 1–2, 10, 22, 118
diversity, 137–38
divinization, 88–90, 93
doctrine, xiv
dualism, 17, 20–21
dystopia, 122, 125–26

ecology, 3, 119
economics, 4–5, 16–17, 133–34,
    158–60
economism, 155–60
economy of exchange, 77–79
economy of salvation, 89, 170n41
education, 155–57, 159
embodiment. *See* body
empire, xvi, 4, 12, 84, 129–46, 160–61
    postcolonial, 133–36, 138–40,
    144–45
    Roman, 5, 12, 130, 151, 160–61
environmental crisis, xiii–xiv, xvi, 22,
    35, 114–27, 159
epistemology, 84
eroticism, 14, 93
eschatological banquet, 75

185